365 Easy Pasta Recipes

Delicious, Versatile Recipes for Easy Meals

Cookbook Resources LLC
Highland Village, Texas

365 Easy Pasta Recipes
Delicious, Versatile Recipes for Easy Meals

1st Printing - March 2008
2nd Printing - August 2008
3rd Printing - December 2008

International Standard Book Number: 978-1-59769-031-7

Library of Congress Number: 2008008979

Library of Congress Cataloging-in-Publication Data

    365 easy pasta recipes : delicious, versatile recipes for easy meals.
      p. cm.
    Includes index.
    ISBN 978-1-59769-031-7
    1. Cookery (Pasta) 2. Quick and easy cookery. I. Cookbook Resources, LLC. II. Title: Three hundred sixty-five easy pasta recipes.
    TX809.M17A158 2008
    641.8'22--dc22
                    2008008979

Cover by Nancy Bohanan

Edited, Designed and Published in the United States of America by
Cookbook Resources, LLC
541 Doubletree Drive
Highland Village, Texas 75077

Toll free 866-229-2665

www.cookbookresources.com

Bringing Family and Friends to the Table

365 Easy
Pasta Recipes

365 Easy Pasta Recipes is all about one of the easiest, no-fail foods available – pasta. Pasta is a classic family favorite and these 365 recipes feature it in every size and interesting shape. Pasta is quickly prepared, making it easy and everyday even on a weeknight.

Increasingly, we have come to realize just how important mealtime together is to a family. Bonds are built and relationships are strengthened as healthy values and habits are instilled.

365 Easy Pasta Recipes makes it easy to plan, to cook and to serve delicious dishes to family and friends. All the ingredients are readily available in your own pantry, refrigerator or the familiar shelves in your local grocery.

Add a "bag salad" or a purchased dessert and consider everyone's favorite, garlic bread, as an accompaniment.

Do your part to enrich the lives of people around you. Serve a homecooked meal today!

Contents

Appetizers & Soups 7

Delicious starters for any meal, many are meals in themselves. Soups and stews are always warm gifts from the heart.

Scrumptious Salads 35

Veggie salads and meat salads that can be a complete meal are filling, tasty and easy.

Pasta with Beef 75

Appetizing and hearty recipes with beef at the center make pasta a family favorite.

Pasta with Chicken 121

Chicken is so versatile and when you add pasta, it's great for everyday meals – and entertaining.

Contents

Dedication

With a mission of helping you bring family and friends to the table, Cookbook Resources strives to make family meals and entertaining friends simple, easy and delicious.

We recognize the importance of a meal together as a means of building family bonds with memories and traditions that will be treasured for a lifetime. It is an opportunity to sit down with each other and share more than food.

This cookbook is dedicated with gratitude and respect for all those who show their love with homecooked meals, bringing family and friends to the table.

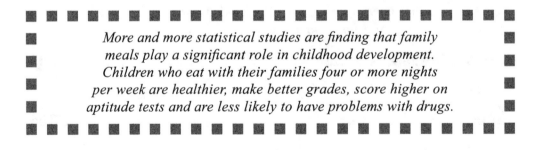

More and more statistical studies are finding that family meals play a significant role in childhood development. Children who eat with their families four or more nights per week are healthier, make better grades, score higher on aptitude tests and are less likely to have problems with drugs.

Appetizers & Soups

Delicious starters for any meal, many are meals in themselves. Soups and stews are always warm gifts from the heart.

Appetizers & Soups Contents

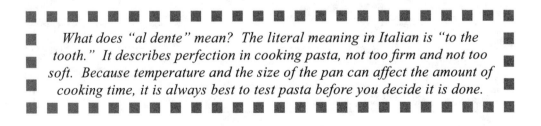

What does "al dente" mean? The literal meaning in Italian is "to the tooth." It describes perfection in cooking pasta, not too firm and not too soft. Because temperature and the size of the pan can affect the amount of cooking time, it is always best to test pasta before you decide it is done.

Appetizing Tortellinis

⅓ cup red wine vinegar	75 ml
¾ cup olive oil	175 ml
1 tablespoon dijon-style mustard	15 ml
1 teaspoon minced garlic	5 ml
1 teaspoon sugar	5 ml
1 (20 ounce) package refrigerated herb-chicken tortellini pasta	570 g
1 cup whole, pitted ripe olives	130 g
1 (8 ounce) package cubed mozzarella cheese	230 g
1 red bell pepper, seeded, julienned	
1 (7 ounce) jar baby corn, drained	200 g
2 tablespoons chopped fresh parsley	10 g

- To make marinade, combine vinegar, olive oil, mustard, garlic, sugar and a little salt and pepper in large bowl.

- Cook tortellini in saucepan according to package directions; drain and rinse in cold water. Place tortellini in large bowl and add olives, cheese, bell pepper and baby corn.

- Pour marinade over tortellini mixture and refrigerate for at least 1 or 2 hours. When ready to serve, sprinkle with chopped parsley and serve with toothpicks. Serves 12.

Seafood in the Shell

1 (12 ounce) box
  lumache (large
  shells) pasta   340 g
2 (8 ounce) package
  cream cheese,
  softened   2 (230 g)
⅓ cup mayonnaise   75 g
1 tablespoon lemon
  juice   15 ml
2 tablespoons sugar   25 g
1 teaspoon seasoned
  salt   5 ml
1 (16 ounce) package
  imitation crabmeat,
  finely flaked   455 g
1 (6 ounce) can tuna,
  drained, flaked   170 g
1 rib celery, finely diced

- Cook 36 jumbo pasta shells in saucepan according to package directions. Drain and place on large sheet of wax paper.

- Beat cream cheese, mayonnaise, lemon juice, sugar, seasoned salt and ½ teaspoon black pepper in mixing bowl until creamy and smooth. Fold in crabmeat, tuna and celery; mix until they blend well.

- Stuff cream cheese-tuna mixture into jumbo pasta shells, cover and refrigerate for at least 2 hours before serving. Serves 6.

TIP: *These shells can be served as a side dish or as appetizers.*

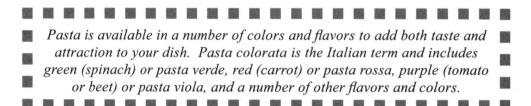

Pasta is available in a number of colors and flavors to add both taste and attraction to your dish. Pasta colorata is the Italian term and includes green (spinach) or pasta verde, red (carrot) or pasta rossa, purple (tomato or beet) or pasta viola, and a number of other flavors and colors.

Appetizer Bites

1 (8 ounce) package gnocchi (small shells) pasta	230 g
1 (12 ounce) can tuna, drained, flaked	340 g
1 rib celery, finely diced	
2 tablespoons diced green bell pepper	20 g
1 (4 ounce) jar chopped pimento, drained	115 g
¼ cup finely chopped pecans	30 g
¾ - 1 cup mayonnaise	170 - 225 g

- Cook pasta in saucepan according to package directions. Drain and rinse in cold water; drain again. Combine tuna, celery, bell pepper, pimento and pecans with a little salt and pepper in medium bowl. Stir in ¾ (170 g) cup mayonnaise and add additional ¼ cup (55 g) mayonnaise if mixture needs to be creamer for stuffing.

- Carefully stuff the shell macaroni and serve as appetizers. Serves 6 to 12.

Mexican-Style Minestrone Soup

1 (16 ounce) package frozen garlic-seasoned pasta and vegetables	455 g
1 (16 ounce) jar thick-and-chunky salsa	455 g
1 (15 ounce) can pinto beans with liquid	425 g
1 teaspoon chili powder	5 ml
1 teaspoon ground cumin	5 ml
1 (8 ounce) package shredded Mexican-style 4-cheese blend	230 g

- Combine all ingredients in large saucepan except cheese with 1 cup (250 ml) water. Bring to a boil, reduce heat and simmer for 8 minutes. Stir often and top each serving with cheese. Serves 6.

Garbanzo Bean Soup

2 tablespoons olive oil	30 ml
1 (16 ounce) package frozen chopped onions and peppers	455 g
2 teaspoons minced garlic	10 ml
½ teaspoon dried sage	2 ml
1 (15 ounce) can stewed tomatoes	425 g
2 (14 ounce) cans vegetable broth	2 (400 g)
1 (15 ounce) can garbanzo beans, (chickpeas) drained	425 g
½ cup elbow macaroni (tube) pasta	55 g
1 teaspoon Italian seasoning	5 ml
1 (5 ounce) package grated parmesan cheese	145 g

- Combine olive oil, onions and peppers, and garlic in soup pot and cook, stirring often on medium heat for 5 minutes or until onions are translucent. Stir in sage, tomatoes, vegetable broth, garbanzo beans and a little salt and pepper and cook for 10 minutes.

- Stir in macaroni and Italian seasoning and cook for about 15 minutes or until macaroni is al dente (tender, but not overdone). Place about 1 heaping tablespoon (15 ml) parmesan cheese over each serving. Serves 4 to 6 .

Italian Minestrone

1 (16 ounce) package frozen onions and bell peppers	455 g
3 ribs celery, chopped	
2 teaspoons minced garlic	10 ml
¼ cup (½ stick) butter	60 g
2 (15 ounce) cans diced tomatoes	2 (425 g)
1 teaspoon dried oregano	5 ml
1 teaspoon dried basil	5 ml
2 (14 ounce) cans beef broth	2 (400 g)
2 (15 ounce) cans kidney beans, drained	2 (425 g)
2 medium zucchini, cut in half lengthwise, sliced	
1 cup elbow macaroni (tube) pasta	105 g

- Saute onions and bell peppers, celery and garlic in butter for about 2 minutes in soup pot. Add tomatoes, oregano, basil and a little salt and pepper. Boil, reduce heat and simmer for 15 minutes, stirring occasionally.

- Stir in beef broth, beans, zucchini and macaroni and boil. Reduce heat and simmer for additional 15 minutes or until macaroni is tender. Serves 8.

Gomito maccheroni is the Italian for elbow macaroni.

Main Dish Minestrone Soup

1 tablespoon olive oil	15 ml
1 onion, chopped	
2 teaspoons minced garlic	10 ml
2 (15 ounce) cans Italian stewed tomatoes	2 (425 g)
1 (10 ounce) package frozen chopped spinach, thawed, drained	280 g
1 (8 ounce) can sliced carrots, drained	230 g
1 cup coarsely chopped zucchini	125 g
1 small potato, peeled, cubed	
2 ribs celery, sliced	
1 (10 ounce) can beef broth	280 g
1 teaspoon dried basil	5 ml
1 teaspoon dried oregano	5 ml
½ cup conchiglie or maruzze (shell) pasta	40 g
1 (15 ounce) can cannelloni beans, drained	425 g

- Heat oil in soup pot and cook onion and garlic for 3 minutes. Add tomatoes, spinach, carrots, zucchini, potato, celery, broth, basil, oregano and 7 cups (1.6 L) water.

- Bring to a boil and simmer for 15 minutes.

- Add pasta shells and beans to soup mixture and cook over medium heat for 10 to 12 minutes or until pasta is tender. Serves 6 to 8.

Pasta-Veggie Soup

2 yellow squash, peeled, chopped

2 zucchini, sliced

1 (10 ounce) package frozen whole kernel corn, thawed | 280 g

1 red bell pepper, chopped

1 (15 ounce) can stewed tomatoes | 425 g

1 teaspoon Italian seasoning | 5 ml

2 teaspoons dried oregano | 10 ml

2 (14 ounce) cans beef broth | 2 (400 g)

¾ cup gnocchi (small shells) pasta | 180 ml

Shredded mozzarella cheese

- Combine squash, zucchini, corn, bell pepper, tomatoes, Italian seasoning, oregano, beef broth and 2 cups (500 ml) water in 6-quart (6 L) slow cooker.

- Cover and cook on LOW for 6 to 7 hours.

- Add pasta shells and cook for additional 30 to 45 minutes or until pasta is tender.

- Garnish with a sprinkle of shredded mozzarella cheese on each bowl of soup. Serves 4 to 5.

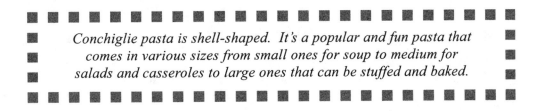

Conchiglie pasta is shell-shaped. It's a popular and fun pasta that comes in various sizes from small ones for soup to medium for salads and casseroles to large ones that can be stuffed and baked.

Veggie and Tortellini Soup

2 tablespoons butter	30 g
2 ribs celery, sliced	
1 carrot, peeled, sliced	
1 onion, chopped	
1 cup chopped green bell pepper	150 g
1 teaspoon minced garlic	5 ml
2 (14 ounce) cans chicken broth	2 (400 g)
1 (12 ounce) package dried cheese-filled tortellini pasta	340 g
1 tablespoon chopped fresh parsley	15 ml
½ cup grated parmesan cheese	50 g

- Melt butter in large soup pot over medium heat. Cook celery, carrot, onion, bell pepper, garlic and broth for about 6 minutes or until vegetables are tender-crisp.

- Stir in tortellini and parsley, cover and cook for about 20 minutes, stirring occasionally or until tortellini is tender. Sprinkle a little parmesan cheese over each serving. Serves 6.

TIP: *This soup is good without adding any meat, but if you like you could add chicken or ham to make a heavier soup.*

Pasta rigate refers to the pasta with ridges. The little grooves and ribs help sauce cling to these pastas.

Pizza Soup

3 (10 ounce) cans tomato bisque soup	3 (280 g)
1 (10 ounce) can French onion soup	280 g
2 teaspoons Italian seasoning	10 ml
¾ cup gnocchi (small shells) pasta	80 g
1½ cups shredded mozzarella cheese	175 g

- Place tomato bisque soup, French onion soup, Italian seasoning and 1½ soup cans water in 4 to 5-quart (4 to 5 L) slow cooker. Turn heat setting to HIGH and cook 1 hour or until mixture is hot.

- Add pasta shells and cook for 1 hour 30 minutes to 2 hours or until pasta is done. Stir several times to keep pasta from sticking to bottom of slow cooker. Turn heat off, add mozzarella cheese and stir until cheese melts. Serves 4.

TIP: *For a special way to serve this soup, sprinkle some french-fried onions over top of each serving.*

Warm-Your-Soul Soup

3 (14 ounce) cans chicken broth	3 (400 g)
1 (10 ounce) can Italian stewed tomatoes with liquid	280 g
½ cup chopped onion	80 g
¾ cup chopped celery	75 g
½ (12 ounce) box fettuccini (medium egg noodles) pasta	½ (340 g)

- Combine chicken broth, tomatoes, onion and celery in large soup pot. Boil and simmer until onion and celery are almost done.

- Add pasta and cook al dente (firm but tender). Season with a little salt and pepper. Serves 4.

Beef and Noodle Soup

1½ pounds lean ground beef	680 g
1 onion, chopped	
2 (15 ounce) cans mixed vegetables, drained	2 (425 g)
2 (15 ounce) cans Italian stewed tomatoes	2 (425 g)
2 (14 ounce) cans beef broth	2 (400 g)
1 teaspoon dried oregano	5 ml
1 cup fettuccini (medium egg noodles) pasta	105 g

- Brown and cook ground beef in skillet until no longer pink and transfer to slow cooker.

- Add onion, mixed vegetables, stewed tomatoes, beef broth and oregano.

- Cover and cook on LOW for 4 to 5 hours.

- Cook noodles in saucepan according to package direction.

- Add noodles to slow cooker and cook for 30 minutes. Serves 4 to 6.

Beef-Noodle Soup

1 pound lean ground beef	455 g
1 (46 ounce) can cocktail vegetable juice	1.4 L
1 (1 ounce) packet onion soup mix	30 g
1 (3 ounce) package beef-flavored ramen noodles	85 g
1 (16 ounce) package frozen mixed vegetables	455 g

- Cook beef in large saucepan over medium heat until no longer pink and drain. Stir in vegetable juice, soup mix, noodle seasoning and mixed vegetables and bring to a boil.

- Reduce heat and simmer, for 6 minutes or until vegetables are tender. Return to boil and stir in noodles.

- Cook for 3 minutes or until noodles are tender and serve hot. Serves 8.

Beefy Vegetable Soup

1 pound lean ground beef	455 g
1 (46 ounce) can cocktail vegetable juice	1.4 L
1 (1 ounce) packet onion soup mix	30 g
1 (3 ounce) package beef-flavored ramen noodles	85 g
1 (16 ounce) package frozen mixed vegetables	455 g

- Cook beef in large soup pot over medium heat until no longer pink. Drain. Stir in cocktail juice, soup mix, contents of noodle seasoning packet and mixed vegetables.

- Heat mixture to boiling, reduce heat and simmer for 6 minutes or until vegetables are tender-crisp. Return to boiling, stir in noodles and cook for 3 minutes. Serves 6.

Italian Beefy Veggie Soup

1 pound lean ground beef	455 g
2 teaspoons minced garlic	10 ml
2 (15 ounce) cans Italian stewed tomatoes	2 (425 g)
2 (14 ounce) cans beef broth	2 (400 g)
2 teaspoons Italian seasoning	10 ml
1 (16 ounce) package frozen mixed vegetables	455 g
⅓ cup macaroni (tube) pasta	35 g
1 (8 ounce) package shredded Italian cheese	230 g

- Cook beef and garlic in large soup pot for 5 minutes. Stir in tomatoes, broth, 1 cup (250 ml) water, Italian seasoning, mixed vegetables, macaroni and a little salt and pepper.

- Boil, reduce heat and simmer for 10 to 15 minutes or until macaroni is tender.

- Ladle into individual serving bowls and sprinkle several tablespoons cheese over top of soup. Serves 4.

Mother's Beef-Veggie Soup

1 pound lean ground beef	455 g
1 (1 ounce) packet onion soup mix	30 g
2 (14 ounce) cans beef broth	2 (400 g)
2 (15 ounce) cans stewed tomatoes	2 (425 g)
2 (15 ounce) cans mixed vegetables with liquid	2 (425 g)
1 cup macaroni (tube) pasta	105 g

- Brown beef in soup pot over high heat and drain. Reduce heat to medium and add soup mix, broth, tomatoes, mixed vegetables and 1 cup (250 ml) water and cook for 5 minutes.

- Stir in macaroni and cook for 15 minutes or until macaroni is tender, stirring occasionally. Serves 6.

Rewards with Italian Soup

1 pound lean ground beef	455 g
2 green bell peppers, seeded, coarsely chopped	
1 large onion, coarsely chopped	
½ cup shredded carrots	35 g
2 teaspoons minced garlic	10 ml
1 (14 ounce) can beef broth	400 g
2 (15 ounce) cans Italian stewed tomatoes	2 (425 g)
1 tablespoon sugar	15 ml
1 tablespoon Italian seasoning	15 ml
1 (8 ounce) package conchiglie (medium shells) pasta	230 g

- Cook beef, bell peppers, onion, carrots and garlic in large soup pot over medium heat until beef is no longer pink; drain.

- Add beef broth, 4 cups (1 L) water, stewed tomatoes, sugar, Italian seasoning and a little salt and pepper. Bring to a boil, stir in pasta shells, reduce heat to medium and cook for about 15 minutes. Serves 10.

Soup in a Snap

1 pound lean ground beef	455 g
1 (3 ounce) package Oriental noodles with beef flavor	85 g
1 (32 ounce) carton beef broth	1 kg
1 (16 ounce) package frozen mixed vegetables	455 g
2 ribs celery, sliced	
2 tablespoons soy sauce	30 ml

- Brown beef in skillet on medium-high heat, drain and set aside.

- Break up noodles, add seasoning packet, beef broth, 1 cup (250 ml) water, mixed vegetables, celery and soy sauce in soup pot. Bring to a boil, stir in ground beef and simmer for 10 to 15 minutes or until vegetables are tender. Serves 6 to 8.

Down-Home Beefy Soup

1½ pounds lean ground beef	680 g
1 (16 ounce) package frozen onions and peppers	455 g
2 teaspoons minced garlic	10 ml
2 (14 ounce) cans beef broth	2 (400 g)
2 (15 ounce) cans Italian stewed tomatoes	2 (425 g)
3 teaspoons Italian seasoning	15 ml
1½ cups macaroni (tube) pasta	160 g
Shredded cheddar cheese	

- Brown and cook beef, onions and peppers, and garlic in soup pot on medium heat. Add beef broth, 2 cups (500 ml) water, stewed tomatoes and Italian seasoning and boil for 2 minutes.

- Add macaroni and cook, stirring occasionally on medium heat for about 15 minutes. When serving, sprinkle cheese over each serving. Serves 6.

Chunky Beefy Noodle Soup

1 pound beef round steak, cubed	455 g
1 onion, chopped	
2 ribs celery, sliced	
1 tablespoon olive oil	15 ml
1 tablespoon chili powder	15 ml
½ teaspoon dried oregano	2 ml
1 (15 ounce) can stewed tomatoes	425 g
2 (14 ounce) cans beef broth	2 (400 g)
½ (8 ounce) package fettuccini (medium egg noodles) pasta	½ (230 g)
1 green bell pepper, seeded, chopped	

- Cook and stir cubed steak, onion and celery in soup pot with oil for 15 minutes or until beef browns.

- Stir in 2 cups (500 ml) water, 1 teaspoon (5 ml) salt, chili powder, oregano, stewed tomatoes and beef broth. Boil, reduce heat and simmer for 1 hour 30 minutes to 2 hours or until beef is tender.

- Stir in noodles and green pepper and heat to boiling. Reduce heat and simmer for 10 to 15 minutes or until noodles are tender. Serves 4.

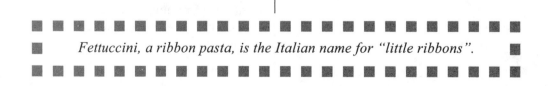

Fettuccini, a ribbon pasta, is the Italian name for "little ribbons".

Spaghetti Soup

1 (7 ounce) package ready-cut spaghetti pasta	200 g
1 (18 ounce) package frozen, cooked meatballs, thawed	510 g
1 (28 ounce) jar spaghetti sauce	795 g
1 (15 ounce) can Mexican stewed tomatoes	425 g

- Cook spaghetti in soup pot with 2 quarts (2 L) boiling water and a little salt for about 6 minutes (no need to drain).

- When spaghetti is done, add meatballs, spaghetti sauce and stewed tomatoes and cook until mixture heats through. Serves 6.

TIP: *If you want to garnish each soup bowl, sprinkle with 2 tablespoons (15 g) mozzarella cheese or whatever cheese you have in the refrigerator.*

Chicken-Noodle Soup Supper

1 (3 ounce) package chicken-flavored ramen noodles, broken	85 g
1 (10 ounce) package frozen green peas, thawed	280 g
1 (4 ounce) jar sliced mushrooms, drained	115 g
3 cups cooked, cubed chicken	420 g

- Heat 2¼ cups (560 ml) water in large saucepan to boiling. Add ramen noodles, contents of seasoning packet and peas. Heat to boiling, reduce heat to medium and cook for about 5 minutes.

- Stir in mushrooms and chicken and continue cooking over low heat until all ingredients are hot. To serve, spoon into soup bowls. Serves 6 to 8.

Plum Good Soup

2 tablespoons olive oil	30 ml
¾ pound beef round steak, cubed	340 g
1 onion, chopped	
2 ribs celery, chopped	
2 teaspoons minced garlic	10 ml
1 (32 ounce) carton beef broth	1 kg
1 (8 ounce) can tomato puree	230 g
1 (10 ounce) can tomatoes and green chilies	280 g
2 teaspoons Italian seasoning	10 ml
1 (10 ounce) package frozen Italian green beans	280 g
⅔ cup orzo or pastina (tiny) pasta	50 g
Grated parmesan cheese	

- Heat oil in soup pot over medium-high heat. Add beef cubes, onion, celery and garlic. Cook and stir until meat is crusty brown and onion and celery are tender.

- Stir in beef broth, tomato puree, tomatoes and green chilies and Italian seasoning. Simmer for 45 minutes.

- Add green beans, orzo and a little salt and pepper; bring to a boil. Cook and stir often for 5 minutes. Sprinkle 1 tablespoon (15 ml) parmesan cheese over top of each serving. Serves 6 to 8.

Tiny pastas like orzo are good to use in soups.

Chicken-Pasta Soup

1½ pounds boneless, skinless chicken thighs, cubed	680 g
1 onion, chopped	
3 carrots, sliced	
½ cup halved, pitted ripe olives	65 g
1 teaspoon minced garlic	5 ml
3 (14 ounce) cans chicken broth	3 (400 g)
1 (15 ounce) can Italian stewed tomatoes	425 g
1 teaspoon Italian seasoning	5 ml
½ cup gnocchi (small shells) pasta	55 g
Parmesan cheese	

- Combine all ingredients in slow cooker except shell pasta and parmesan cheese.

- Cover and cook on LOW for 8 to 9 hours. About 30 minutes before serving, add pasta and stir.

- Increase heat to HIGH and cook for additional 20 to 30 minutes. Garnish with parmesan cheese. Serves 6 to 8.

Feel-Better Chicken-Noodle Soup

1 (3 ounce) package chicken-flavored ramen noodles, broken	85 g
1 (10 ounce) package frozen green peas, thawed	280 g
2 teaspoons butter	10 ml
1 (4 ounce) jar sliced mushrooms, drained	115 g
3 cups cooked, cubed chicken	420 g

- Heat 2¼ cups (540 ml) water in large saucepan to boiling.

- Add ramen noodles, contents of seasoning packet, peas and butter. Heat to boiling, reduce heat to medium and cook about 5 minutes.

- Stir in mushrooms and chicken and continue cooking over low heat until all ingredients heat through. To serve, spoon into serving bowls. Serves 6.

Old-Fashioned Chicken-Noodle Soup

1 (3 - 4 pound) whole
   chicken   1.3 kg - 1.8 kg
1 carrot, chopped
2 ribs celery with leaves,
   chopped
½ - ¾ cup tagliatelle
   (thin egg noodles)
   pasta, cooked   95 - 145 g

- Wash whole chicken and giblets
  and put in large soup pot. Add
  7 to 8 cups (1.6 to 2 L) water,
  carrot and celery and bring to a
  boil. Reduce heat and simmer,
  partially covered, for 45 minutes
  to 1 hour or until meat is tender.

- Remove chicken from soup pot
  and cool. Continue simmering and
  spoon off fat from top of liquid
  when needed.

- Bone chicken and put all bones and
  skin back into soup pot. Continue
  to simmer for 3 to 4 hours. Turn
  heat off and strain chicken stock in
  large bowl. Add chopped chicken
  and cooked egg noodles. Add a
  little salt and pepper. Serves 4.

Oriental Chicken-Noodle Soup

1 (3 ounce) package
   chicken-flavor ramen
   noodles   85 g
1 rotisserie chicken, boned,
   skinned, cubed
2 medium stalks bok choy
   with leaves, thinly sliced
1 (8 ounce) can sliced
   carrots, drained   230 g
1 red bell pepper, seeded,
   chopped

- Break apart noodles, place in
  3 cups (750 ml) water and heat in
  soup pot. Stir in chicken, bok choy,
  carrots and bell pepper.

- Boil, reduce heat and simmer for
  3 minutes; stir occasionally. Stir
  in flavor packet from noodles and
  serve immediately. Serves 6.

Quick Chicken-Noodle Soup

2 (14 ounce) cans chicken
     broth   2 (400 g)
2 boneless, skinless
     chicken breast halves,
     cubed
1 (8 ounce) can sliced
     carrots, drained   230 g
2 ribs celery, sliced
½ (8 ounce) package
     fettuccini (medium
     egg noodles) pasta   230 g

- Combine broth, chicken, carrots, celery and generous dash of pepper in large saucepan. Boil and cook for 3 minutes.

- Stir in noodles, reduce heat and cook for 10 minutes or until noodles are done; stir often. Serves 4.

Turkey and Mushroom Soup

Another great way to use leftover chicken or turkey.

2 cups sliced shitake
     mushrooms   145 g
2 ribs celery, sliced
1 small onion, chopped
2 tablespoons butter   30 g
1 (15 ounce) can sliced
     carrots   425 g
2 (14 ounce) cans chicken
     broth   400 g
½ cup orzo (tiny) pasta   55 g
2 cups cooked, chopped
     turkey or chicken   280 g

- Saute mushrooms, celery and onion with butter in skillet.

- Transfer vegetables to slow cooker and add carrots, broth, orzo and turkey. (Do not use smoked turkey.)

- Cover and cook on LOW for 2 to 3 hours or on HIGH for 1 to 2 hours. Serves 4 to 6.

Tortellini Soup

1 (1 ounce) packet white sauce mix	30 g
3 boneless, skinless chicken breast halves	
1 (14 ounce) can chicken broth	400 g
1 teaspoon minced garlic	5 ml
½ teaspoon dried basil	2 ml
½ teaspoon oregano	2 ml
½ teaspoon cayenne pepper	2 ml
1 (8 ounce) package cheese tortellini pasta	230 g
1½ cups half-and-half cream	465 g
6 cups fresh baby spinach	180 g

- Place white sauce mix in sprayed 5 to 6-quart (5 to 6 L) slow cooker.

- Stir in 4 cups (1 L) water and stir gradually until mixture is smooth.

- Cut chicken into 1-inch (2.5 cm) pieces. Add chicken, broth, garlic, basil, oregano, cayenne pepper and ½ teaspoon (2 ml) salt to mixture.

- Cover and cook on LOW for 6 to 7 hours or on HIGH for 3 hours.

- Stir in tortellini, cover and cook for additional 1 hour on HIGH.

- Stir in half-and-half cream and fresh spinach. Cook just enough for soup to get hot. Serves 4 to 6.

TIP: Sprinkle a little shredded parmesan cheese on top of each serving.

Beans and Pasta Soup

2 tablespoons olive oil	30 ml
1 onion, chopped	
2 ribs celery, sliced	
2 teaspoons minced garlic	10 ml
1 (15 ounce) can pinto beans	425 g
1 (15 ounce) can kidney beans, rinsed, drained	425 g
1 (8 ounce) can lima beans	230 g
1 cup cooked, shredded ham	140 g
2 (32 ounce) cartons chicken broth	2 (910 g)
2 bay leaves	
1 cup rigatoni (large tubes) pasta	105 g

- Heat oil in large soup pot and cook onion, celery and garlic on medium heat for about 5 minutes.

- Stir in pinto beans, kidney beans, lima beans, ham, broth and bay leaves. Bring to a boil, reduce heat and simmer for about 30 minutes.

- Bring bean mixture back to boiling, add pasta, reduce heat to medium, cover and cook for about 12 to 14 minutes or until pasta is tender. Remove bay leaves before serving. Serves 8.

Pasta made from spelt can sometimes be tolerated by those allergic to gluten. Spelt is a different variety of wheat with a lower gluten content than common wheat, and has been cultivated for at least 4,000 years.

Ham, Bean and Pasta Soup

1 onion, finely chopped
2 ribs celery, chopped
2 teaspoons minced garlic   10 ml
2 (14 ounce) cans chicken
    broth   2 (400 g)
2 (15 ounce) cans pork
    and beans with liquid   2 (425 g)
3 cups cooked, cubed ham   420 g
⅓ cup macaroni (tube)
    pasta   35 g
Bacon cooked crisp,
    crumbled

- Combine onion, celery, garlic, chicken broth, beans, ham and 1 cup (250 ml) water in 5 to 6-quart (5 to 6 L) slow cooker.

- Cover and cook on LOW for 4 to 5 hours.

- Turn cooker to HIGH heat, add pasta and cook for additional 35 to 45 minutes or until pasta is tender.

- Garnish each serving with cooked, crisp and crumbled bacon. Serves 6 to 8.

Italian Vegetable Soup

1 pound bulk Italian
    sausage   455 g
2 onions, chopped
2 teaspoons minced garlic   10 ml
1 (1 ounce) packet beefy
    recipe soup mix   30 g
1 (15 ounce) can sliced
    carrots, drained   425 g
2 (15 ounce) cans Italian
    stewed tomatoes   2 (425 g)
2 (15 ounce) cans garbanzo
    beans (chickpeas),
    drained   2 (425 g)
1 cup elbow macaroni
    (tube) pasta   105 g

- Brown sausage, onions and garlic in large soup pot. Pour off fat and add 4 cups (1 L) water, soup mix, carrots, tomatoes and garbanzo beans. Bring to a boil, reduce heat to low and simmer for 25 minutes.

- Add elbow macaroni and continue cooking for additional 15 to 20 minutes or until macaroni is tender. Serves 8.

Sausage-Tortellini Soup

1 pound Italian sausage	455 g
1 onion, chopped	
3 ribs celery, sliced	
2 (14 ounce) cans beef	
broth	2 (400 g)
½ teaspoon dried basil	2 ml
1 (15 ounce) can sliced	
carrots, drained	425 g
1 medium zucchini,	
halved, sliced	
1 (10 ounce) can Italian	
stewed tomatoes	280 g
1 (9 ounce) package	
refrigerated meat-	
filled tortellini pasta	255 g
Mozzarella cheese	

- Cook and stir sausage, onion and celery in soup pot on medium heat until sausage is light brown.

- Drain and stir in beef broth, 1½ cups (375 ml) water, basil, carrots, zucchini, tomatoes, tortellini and a little salt and pepper.

- Boil, reduce heat and simmer for 20 minutes or until tortellini are tender.

- Ladle into individual soup bowls and sprinkle each serving with cheese. Serves 4 to 6.

The first known written recipe for pasta dates to about the year 1000 in a cookbook written in Sicily.

Mama Mia Chicken Chowder

2 (12 ounce) cans chicken breasts with liquid	2 (340 g)
¼ cup Italian salad dressing	60 ml
1 (15 ounce) can stewed tomatoes	425 g
1 (10 ounce) can chicken broth	280 g
2 small zucchini, chopped	
½ cup elbow macaroni (tube) pasta	55 g
1 teaspoon dried basil	5 ml
1 cup shredded mozzarella cheese	115 g

- Combine chicken, salad dressing, tomatoes, broth, zucchini, macaroni, basil, ½ cup (125 ml) water and a little salt and pepper in large soup pot.

- Boil, reduce heat and simmer for 10 minutes or until macaroni is tender. Serve in individual soup bowls and sprinkle cheese over each serving. Serves 6.

Vegetarian Chili

2 (15 ounce) cans stewed tomatoes	2 (425 g)
1 (15 ounce) can kidney beans, rinsed, drained	425 g
1 (15 ounce) can pinto beans with liquid	425 g
1 onion, chopped	
1 green bell pepper, seeded, chopped	
1 tablespoon chili powder	15 ml
1 (12 ounce) package elbow macaroni (tube) pasta	340 g
¼ cup (½ stick) butter, sliced	60 g

- Combine tomatoes, kidney beans, pinto beans, onion, bell pepper, chili powder and 1 cup (250 ml) water in soup pot. Cover and cook on medium heat for 1 hour.

- Cook macaroni in saucepan according to package directions, drain and add butter. Stir until butter melts. Add macaroni to chili and mix well. Serves 6.

Turkey-Veggie Chili

1 pound ground turkey	455 g
Olive oil	
2 (15 ounce) cans pinto beans with liquid	2 (425 g)
1 (15 ounce) can great northern beans with liquid	425 g
1 (14 ounce) can chicken broth	400 g
2 (15 ounce) cans Mexican stewed tomatoes	2 (425 g)
1 (8 ounce) can whole kernel corn	230 g
1 large onion, chopped	
1 red bell pepper, seeded, chopped	
2 teaspoons minced garlic	10 ml
2 teaspoons ground cumin	10 ml
½ cup elbow macaroni (tube) pasta	55 g

- Cook and brown turkey in skillet with a little oil before placing in large slow cooker.

- Add beans, broth, tomatoes, corn, onion, bell pepper, garlic, cumin and a little salt and stir well.

- Cover and cook on LOW for 4 to 5 hours.

- Stir in macaroni and continue cooking for about 15 minutes. Stir to make sure macaroni does not stick to cooker and cook for additional 15 minutes or until macaroni is tender. Serves 6 to 8.

TIP: Top each serving with dab of sour cream or 1 tablespoon (15 ml) shredded cheddar cheese.

Italian-Vegetable Stew

1½ - 2 pounds Italian sausage	680 - 910 g
2 (16 ounce) packages frozen vegetables	2 (455 g)
2 (15 ounce) cans Italian stewed tomatoes	2 (425 g)
1 (14 ounce) can beef broth	400 g
1 teaspoon Italian seasoning	5 ml
½ cup gnocchi (small shells) pasta	50 g

- Brown sausage in skillet and cook for about 5 minutes and drain.

- Combine sausage, vegetables, stewed tomatoes, broth, Italian seasoning and shells in 5 to 6-quart (5 to 6 L) slow cooker and mix well.

- Cover and cook on LOW for 3 to 5 hours. Serves 4 to 6.

Chicken-Tortellini Stew

1 (9 ounce) package cheese-filled tortellini pasta	255 g
2 medium yellow squash, halved, sliced	
1 red bell pepper, seeded, coarsely chopped	
1 onion, chopped	
2 (14 ounce) cans chicken broth	2 (400 g)
1 teaspoon dried rosemary	5 ml
½ teaspoon dried basil	2 ml
2 cups cooked, chopped chicken	280 g

- Place tortellini, squash, bell pepper and onion in slow cooker. Stir in broth, rosemary, basil and chicken.

- Cover and cook on LOW for 2 to 4 hours or until tortellini and vegetables are tender. Serves 4.

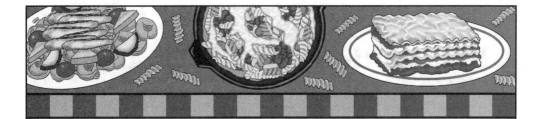

Scrumptious Salads

*Veggie salads and meat salads
that can be a complete meal
are filling, tasty and easy.*

Scrumptious Salads Contents

A Unique Salad Blend

2 (3 ounce) packages
Asian ramen noodles,
crushed   2 (85 g)
1 cup slivered almonds,
toasted   170 g
¼ cup sunflower kernels   30 g
¼ cup (1 slick) butter,
melted   60 g
1 head napa cabbage,
finely shredded
1 red bell pepper, seeded,
finely chopped
1 bunch fresh green
onions, sliced

Dressing:

¾ cup olive oil   175 ml
¼ cup white vinegar   60 ml
½ cup sugar   100 g
2 tablespoons light soy
sauce   30 ml

- Brown ramen noodles, almonds and sunflower kernels with melted butter in large skillet over low heat. Remove from heat and cool.

- Combine olive oil, vinegar and sugar in small saucepan on high heat. Boil for 1 minute and add soy sauce.

- Combine noodle-almond mixture, napa cabbage, bell pepper and green onions in large bowl. Drizzle dressing over salad and toss to coat well. Serves 8 to 10.

Broccoli-Noodle Crunch Salad

Who thought up the idea of grating broccoli "stems" for a salad? It was pure genius! This salad is different – and very good. It will last and still be "crispy" in the refrigerator for days!

1 cup slivered almonds, toasted	**170 g**
1 cup sunflower seeds, toasted	**130 g**
2 (3 ounce) packages chicken-flavored ramen noodles	**2 (85 g)**
1 (12 ounce) package broccoli slaw	**340 g**

- Preheat oven to 275° (135° C).

- Toast almonds and sunflower seeds in oven for 15 minutes. Break up ramen noodles (but do not cook) and mix with slaw, almonds and sunflower seeds.

Dressing:

¾ cup olive oil	**175 ml**
½ cup white vinegar	**125 ml**
½ cup sugar	**100 g**
Ramen noodles seasoning packets	

- In separate bowl, combine dressing ingredients and noodle seasoning packet. Pour over slaw mixture and mix well. Prepare at least 1 hour before serving. Serves 10 to 12.

TIP: Add a handful of broccoli florets just to make it prettier!

Fusilli pasta gets its name from the Italian for "rifle" because its shape resembles the device that rifles the inside of the barrel of a firearm.

Color-Coded Salad

1 (16 ounce) package
    tri-colored fusilli (spiral)
    pasta, cooked, drained   455 g
1 red bell pepper, julienne
1 cup chopped zucchini   125 g
1 cup broccoli florets   70 g
1 cup Caesar salad dressing   250 ml

- Combine all ingredients except dressing in bowl.

- Toss with dressing. Refrigerate. Serves 4.

Colorful Garden Salad

1 (8 ounce) package
    multi-color tortellini
    pasta   230 g
1 tablespoon olive oil
1 (8 ounce) can cut green
    beans, drained   230 g
1 cup diced carrots   130 g
1 cup cherry tomato halves   150 g
1 yellow bell pepper,
    seeded, julienned
1 (8 ounce) package cubed
    cheddar cheese   230 g
1 (8 ounce) bottle zesty
    Italian dressing   230 g

- Cook tortellini in saucepan according to package directions, drain and rinse in cold water. Transfer to bowl and drizzle a little oil over tortellini. Add green beans, carrots, tomatoes, bell pepper and cheese and toss.

- Pour dressing over salad and toss to make sure dressing coats all ingredients. Cover and refrigerate for several hours before serving. Serves 8.

Fusilli Pasta Salad

1 (16 ounce) package fusilli
   (spiral) pasta   455 g
1 (16 ounce) package frozen
   broccoli-cauliflower
   combination   455 g
1 (8 ounce) package cubed
   mozzarella cheese   230 g
1 (8 ounce) bottle of
   Catalina salad dressing 230 g

- Cook pasta in saucepan according to package directions. Drain and cool.

- Cook vegetables in microwave according to package directions. Drain and cool.

- Combine pasta, vegetables and cheese chunks in large bowl.

- Toss with Catalina dressing. Refrigerate several hours before serving. Serves 6.

Macaroni-Vegetable Salad

1 (16 ounce) package
   tri-colored macaroni
   (tube) pasta   455 g
1 red bell pepper, seeded,
   julienned
1 small zucchini, sliced
2 cups small broccoli florets 140 g
1 cup refrigerated Caesar
   salad dressing   250 ml

- Cook macaroni in saucepan according to package directions and drain. Place in container with lid and add bell pepper, zucchini, broccoli and a little salt and pepper.

- Toss with salad dressing. Use more if needed to coat salad well. Cover and refrigerate for several hours before serving. Serves 6 to 8.

Harvest Pasta Salad

1 (9 ounce) package
  refrigerated cheese-
  stuffed tortellini pasta   255 g
1 (16 ounce) bottle zesty
  Italian salad dressing   455 g
2 cups fresh broccoli florets   140 g
2 cups fresh cauliflower
  florets   200 g
2 cups cherry tomato
  halves, drained   300 g
1 yellow bell pepper,
  seeded, julienned
1 (4 ounce) can ripe olives,
  drained   115 g
½ cup grated parmesan
  cheese   50 g
⅓ cup toasted sunflower
  seeds   40 g

- Cook tortellini in saucepan according to package directions; drain, rinse in cold water and drain again. Place in bowl with lid and pour about ½ cup (125 ml) salad dressing over pasta and toss.

- Add broccoli, cauliflower, tomatoes, bell pepper, olives and cheese to tortellini. Add another ½ cup (125 ml) dressing and toss. Keep adding a little more dressing until vegetables and pasta coat well.

- Cover and refrigerate for 2 to 3 hours before serving. Sprinkle sunflower seeds over top of salad before serving. Serves 10.

Nutty Noodle Slaw

1 (8 ounce) package fettuccini (medium egg noodles) pasta	230 g
½ cup peanut sauce	125 ml
½ cup vegetables broth	125 ml
1 tablespoon finely chopped, peeled fresh ginger	15 ml
1 tablespoon olive oil	15 ml
1 (16 ounce) package broccoli slaw mix	455 g
1 cup shredded carrots	110 g
2 tablespoons olive oil	30 ml

- Cook pasta in saucepan according to package directions, drain and return to pot. Using kitchen scissors, snip pasta in small pieces with kitchen scissors. Cover and keep warm.

- Whisk peanut sauce and vegetable broth in small bowl and set aside. Stir-fry ginger in hot oil in large skillet on medium heat for just 15 seconds.

- Add broccoli slaw, carrots and olive oil, cook and stir for 1 minute. Stir in peanut-broth mixture to coat vegetables well and cook for additional 2 minutes.

- Add pasta and use tongs to toss mixture well. Serve warm. Serves 4 to 6.

Most pasta recipes are designed for using dried pastas. Fresh pastas cook faster than dried pasta but are best used with lighter sauces with cream or cheese. Dried pastas work better with heavier sauces, casseroles and salads.

Pasta-Veggie Salad

1 (16 ounce) package
   cavatappi (corkscrew)
   pasta   455 g
1 (16 ounce) package
   frozen broccoli-
   cauliflower mixture,
   thawed   455 g
1 (8 ounce) block
   mozzarella cheese,
   cubed   230 g
1 (8 ounce) bottle Catalina
   salad dressing   230 g

- Cook pasta in saucepan according to package directions, drain and cool. Cook vegetables in microwave according to package directions, drain and cool.

- Combine pasta, vegetables and cheese in large bowl and toss with salad dressing. Refrigerate for several hours before serving. Serves 10.

Pasta Plus

1 (16 ounce) package rainbow
   rotini (spiral) pasta   455 g
2 cups small fresh broccoli
   florets   140 g
2 cups small cauliflower
   florets   200 g
1 cup baby carrots, halved
   lengthwise   135 g
1 red bell pepper, seeded,
   julienned
¾ - 1 (16 ounce) bottle
   peppercorn ranch
   salad dressing   ¾ - 1 (455 g)

- Cook pasta in saucepan according to package directions; drain and rinse in cold water.

- Place pasta in large salad bowl and add broccoli, cauliflower, carrots and bell pepper.

- Pour about three-fourths dressing over salad, add more if needed and toss. Cover and refrigerate for 2 to 3 hours. Serves 8.

Pasta Plus Salad

1 (16 ounce) package farfalle
   (bow-tie) pasta   455 g
1 (10 ounce) package frozen
   green peas, thawed   280 g
1 red bell pepper, seeded,
   cut in strips
1 (8 ounce) package cubed
   Swiss cheese   230 g
1 small yellow summer
   squash, sliced

- Cook pasta in saucepan according to package directions and add peas last 2 minutes of cooking time. Drain pasta and peas, rinse in cold water and drain again. Transfer to large salad bowl and add cheese and squash.

Dressing:

¾ cup mayonnaise   170 g
2 tablespoons lemon juice 30 ml
1 tablespoon sugar   15 ml
½ cup whipping cream   40 g

- Combine dressing ingredients in bowl and mix well. Spoon over salad with a little salt and pepper. Toss salad and refrigerate for several hours before serving. Serves 8.

Quinoa pasta is a substitute for pasta for people with wheat allergies. Quinoa [keen WAH] is a grain from South America that has been in use for 6,000 years.

Pasta-Packed Supper Salad

1 (8 ounce) package whole-grain penne (tube) pasta	230 g
1 (15 ounce) can black beans, rinsed, drained	425 g
1½ cups cooked, chopped chicken	210 g
1 small red bell pepper, seeded, julienned	
½ red onion, cut into thin wedges	
2 cups lightly packed arugula leaves, shredded	70 g
2 tablespoons snipped fresh cilantro	2 g

- Cook pasta in saucepan according to package directions; drain and rinse in cold water and drain again. Place pasta in large salad bowl and add black beans, chicken, bell pepper and red onion; set aside.

Dressing:

½ cup orange juice	125 ml
1 (8 ounce) carton light sour cream	230 g
½ teaspoon lemon pepper	2 ml
1 teaspoon salt-free table seasoning blend	5 ml

- Combine orange juice, sour cream, lemon pepper and seasoning blend in small bowl. Spoon over salad mixture and toss to coat well. Cover and refrigerate for 3 hours or overnight.

- When ready to serve, mix in 1 tablespoon (15 ml) orange juice if needed for desired consistency. Add arugula and cilantro and toss well. Serves 6.

Perfect Pasta Salad

1 (8 ounce) package
    cavatappi (corkscrew)
    pasta   230 g
2 cups fresh broccoli florets   140 g
1 (8 ounce) can sliced
    carrots, drained   230 g
½ cup chopped red bell
    pepper   75 g
½ cup chopped red onion   80 g

- Cook pasta in large saucepan according to package directions. Add broccoli to pasta cooking water during last 2 minutes. Drain pasta and broccoli and rinse with cold water to cool quickly.

Dressing:

¾ cup mayonnaise   170 g
2 tablespoons white wine
    vinegar   30 ml
1 tablespoon dijon-style
    mustard   15 ml
1 teaspoon sugar   5 ml
1 teaspoon minced garlic   5 ml

- Combine mayonnaise, vinegar, mustard, sugar, garlic and a little salt and pepper in large bowl. Add pasta, broccoli, carrots, bell pepper and onion and toss to coat well. Cover and refrigerate. Serves 8.

In the 17th century, a pasta machine was invented in Naples. This technological advance revolutionized production and made pasta much less expensive.

Protein Plus Pasta Salad

1 (8 ounce) package macaroni (tube) pasta	230 g
1 (15 ounce) can kidney beans, rinsed, drained	425 g
1 (10 ounce) package frozen green peas, thawed, drained	280 g
1 cup shredded carrots	70 g
1 (8 ounce) package cubed cheddar cheese	230 g
1 red bell pepper, seeded, chopped	

- Cook macaroni in saucepan according to package directions, drain and rinse in cold water. Transfer macaroni to large bowl.

- Combine mayonnaise, olive oil, parsley, garlic, lemon pepper and a little salt in small bowl and mix well.

- Place beans, peas, carrots, cheese and bell pepper in bowl with macaroni.

Dressing:

¾ cup mayonnaise	170 g
2 tablespoons olive oil	30 ml
¼ cup fresh chopped parsley	15 g
1 teaspoon minced garlic	5 ml
1 teaspoon lemon pepper	5 ml

- Combine all dressing ingredients in bowl. Stir in dressing and toss. Make sure dressing coats all ingredients. Add a little more oil if salad needs to be creamer. Refrigerate for 2 to 3 hours before serving. Serves 8

15-Minute Macaroni-Chicken Salad

1 (12 ounce) package
  conchiglie (small shells)
  pasta   340 g
1 (10 ounce) package frozen
  baby green peas, thawed 280 g
1 (12 ounce) can chicken,
  drained   340 g
1 (4 ounce) can sliced ripe
  olives   115 g
2 ribs celery, chopped
4 fresh green onions, sliced
1 cup mayonnaise   225 g

- Cook macaroni in large pot of salted water according to package directions; drain and rinse in cold water.

- Combine macaroni, peas, chicken, olives, celery, green onions and a little salt and pepper in large bowl. Add mayonnaise and toss to mix well. If salad seems too dry, add a little more mayonnaise. Refrigerate until time to serve. Serves 8.

Sesame-Broccoli Salad

1 (16 ounce) package
  broccoli rabe slaw   455 g
1 red bell pepper, seeded,
  chopped
2 (9 ounce) packages
  refrigerated tortellini
  pasta, cooked   2 (255 g)
1 (8 ounce) bottle
  vinaigrette salad
  dressing   230 g
2 tablespoons olive oil   30 ml
¼ cup sesame seeds,
  toasted   30 g

- Combine broccoli rabe, bell pepper and cooked tortellini in salad bowl. Drizzle salad dressing and olive oil over salad and toss. Refrigerate just before serving, sprinkle sesame seeds over salad. Serves 8.

TIP: *Toasting bring out the flavors of nuts and seeds. Place nut or seeds on baking sheet and bake at 225° (110° C) for 10 minutes. Be careful not to burn them.*

Pool Party Pasta Salad

½ cup pine nuts, toasted	65 g
1 (8 ounce) bunch trimmed asparagus	230 g
1 (16 ounce) package farfalle (bow-tie) pasta	455 g
¾ pound deli turkey, cut in 2-inch strips	340 g/5 cm
1 red bell pepper, seeded, chopped	
1 (14 ounce) can artichoke hearts, drained, sliced	400 g
3 fresh green onions, sliced	
1 (8 ounce) bottle creamy ranch dressing	230 g

- Toast pine nuts in small skillet over low heat for about 5 minutes or until golden. Set aside.

- Cut asparagus into 1-inch (2.5 cm) pieces. Cook pasta in saucepan according to package directions but add asparagus last minute of cooking time. Drain thoroughly and transfer to large baking sheet to cool.

- Place all salad ingredients, except pine nuts, in large bowl and refrigerate for at least 1 hour. When ready to serve, add dressing and pine nuts and toss well to coat all ingredients. Serves 8 to 10.

Pasta is one of the most versatile dishes we know. It is very quick and simple to prepare and it easily takes on the flavors of sauces and seasonings. Deliciously satisfying!

Ready-To-Go Pasta Salad

1 (16 ounce) package salad
   rotini (spiral) pasta   455 g
12 cherry tomatoes, halved,
   drained
4 fresh green onions, sliced
1 (4 ounce) can sliced ripe
   olives   115 g
¾ cup chopped green bell
   pepper   110 g
¾ cup sliced pepperoni,
   halved   100 g
1 (8 ounce) package cubed
   mozzarella cheese   230 g

- Cook pasta in saucepan according
  to package directions and drain.
  Rinse in cold water and drain again.

- Combine pasta, tomatoes, green
  onions, olives, bell pepper,
  pepperoni and cheese in large bowl
  and gently mix.

Dressing:

½ cup olive oil   125 ml
½ cup red wine vinegar   125 ml
1 tablespoon sugar   15 ml
1 teaspoon minced garlic   5 ml
2 teaspoons dried basil   10 ml

- Whisk oil, vinegar, sugar, garlic,
  basil and a little salt and pepper in
  bowl. Drizzle dressing over salad
  and gently toss.

- Cover and refrigerate for at least
  2 hours or overnight. Serves 6 to 8.

*Pasta became popular very quickly from an early date not only because
it is delicious and nutritious, but because it has a long shelf life.*

Special Macaroni Salad

1 (16 ounce) carton prepared
   macaroni salad   455 g
1 (8 ounce) can whole kernel
   corn, drained   230 g
2 small zucchini, diced
⅔ cup chunky salsa   175 g

- Combine macaroni salad, corn,
  zucchini and salsa in salad bowl
  with lid and mix well. Cover and
  refrigerate until ready to serve.
  Serves 6.

Terrific Tortellini Salad

2 (14 ounce) packages
   refrigerated cheese
   tortellini pasta   2 (400 g)
1 green bell pepper,
   seeded, diced
1 red bell pepper, seeded,
   diced
1 cucumber, chopped
1 (14 ounce) can artichoke
   hearts, rinsed, drained 400 g
1 (8 ounce) bottle creamy
   Caesar salad dressing   230 g

- Prepare tortellini in saucepan
  according to package directions
  and drain.

- Rinse with cold water, drain
  and refrigerate.

- Combine tortellini, bell peppers,
  cucumber, artichoke hearts and
  dressing in large bowl. (You may
  want to add a little black pepper).

- Cover and refrigerate for at least
  2 hours before serving. Serves 6.

Summer Picnic Salad

1 (8 ounce) package cavatelli (shell) pasta	230 g
1 cup shredded cheddar cheese	115 g
2 cups fresh broccoli florets	140 g
½ cup chopped pepperoni	70 g
8 cherry tomatoes, halved	
¼ cup shredded mozzarella cheese	30 g

Dressing:

½ cup olive oil	125 ml
3 tablespoons red wine vinegar	45 ml
1 teaspoon dried basil	5 ml
2 teaspoons sugar	10 ml
Crushed red pepper flakes	

- Cook macaroni in large saucepan according to package directions, drain and rinse under cold water. Place in bowl.

- Combine all dressing ingredients in small bowl and stir until they blend well.

- Pour over macaroni and toss; stir in cheddar cheese and toss again. Cover and refrigerate for 2 to 3 hours.

- Add broccoli, pepperoni and tomato halves and toss well. Transfer to serving bowl and sprinkle mozzarella cheese over top. Serves 6.

If you do not use enough water when boiling pasta, the pasta will not cook evenly.

Tailgate Tortellini Salad

2 (9 ounce) packages
   refrigerated meat-
   filled tortellini pasta   2 (255 g)
1 red bell pepper, seeded,
   cubed
1 seedless cucumber,
   peeled, cubed
1 (8 ounce) package cubed
   mozzarella cheese   230 g
1 (4 ounce) can sliced
   ripe olives, drained   115 g
1 teaspoon dried basil   5 ml
¼ cup olive oil   60 ml
2 tablespoons white wine
   vinegar   30 ml
1 tablespoon balsamic
   vinegar   15 ml
1 tablespoon sugar   15 ml
Shredded lettuce

- Cook tortellini in saucepan according to package directions and drain immediately. Rinse with cold water and drain again. Place pasta in large bowl and add bell pepper, cucumber, mozzarella cheese, olives and a little salt and pepper.

- Combine basil, olive oil, white wine vinegar, balsamic vinegar and sugar in screw-top jar. Cover and shake well.

- Pour dressing over pasta mixture and gently toss to coat all ingredients. Serve on bed of shredded lettuce. Serves 6.

Tri-Color Pasta Salad

3 cups tri-color fusilli (spiral) pasta	315 g
1 tablespoon olive oil	15 ml
1 large bunch broccoli, cut into small florets	
1 cup chopped celery	100 g
1 cup peeled, thinly sliced cucumber	120 g
1 (1 pound) block Swiss cheese, cubed	455 g
1 (8 ounce) bottle ranch dressing	230 g

- Cook pasta in saucepan according to package directions and drain. Stir in olive oil and transfer to large salad bowl. Add broccoli florets, celery, cucumber, cheese and a little salt and pepper.

- Pour dressing over salad and toss. Refrigerate for several hours for flavors to blend. Serves 10.

Chicken or Turkey Salad

3 cups cooked, chopped chicken	420 g
1 cup celery	100 g
1½ cups green grapes, halved	225 g
¾ cup cashew nuts	100 g
¾ cup mayonnaise	170 g
1 cup chow mein noodles	55 g
Cabbage leaves	

- Combine chopped chicken, celery, grapes and cashew nuts in bowl and toss with mayonnaise. Just before serving, mix in noodles and serve on cabbage leaves. Serves 6.

Fruity Summer Macaroni Salad

1 (12 ounce) package elbow macaroni (tube) pasta	340 g
½ cup slivered almonds, toasted	85 g
2 ribs celery, chopped	
1 red bell pepper, seeded, chopped	
1 red apple with peel, diced	
1 green apple with peel, diced	
1 (11 ounce) can mandarin oranges, drained	315 g
1 cup pineapple tidbits, drained	250 g
1 tablespoon chopped fresh chives	15 ml

- Cook macaroni in saucepan according to package directions; drain and rinse in cold water. Set aside. Toast almonds for 10 minutes at 325° (160° C).

- Combine celery, bell pepper, apples, oranges, pineapple, chives and a little salt and pepper in large bowl.

Dressing:

1 cup mayonnaise	225 g
1 tablespoon lemon juice	15 ml
1 tablespoon sugar	15 ml

- Combine all dressing ingredients in bowl.

- Add macaroni and almonds to celery-orange mixture and toss with dressing mixture to blend well. If salad seems too dry, add another tablespoon or 2 mayonnaise and toss. Cover and refrigerate until ready to serve. Serves 8.

Chicken Salad Meal

1 (12 ounce) package farfalle or tripolini (bow-tie) pasta	340 g
2 (15 ounce) cans three-bean salad with liquid, chilled	2 (425 g)
2½ cups bite-size chunks rotisserie chicken	350 g
1 cup cherry tomatoes, halved	150 g
2 ribs celery, chopped	

- Cook pasta in saucepan according to package directions with 1 teaspoon (5 ml) salt; drain and rinse under cold water. Shake any excess water off pasta and place in large bowl.

- Drain juice from three-bean salad and set aside. Add three-bean salad, chicken, tomatoes and celery; stir well to combine; transfer to salad bowl.

Dressing:

½ cup from bean salad juice	125 ml
¼ cup olive oil	60 ml
1 tablespoon dijon-style mustard	15 ml
¼ cup mayonnaise	60 g
1 tablespoon sugar	15 ml
1 teaspoon dried dill weed	5 ml

- Place all dressing ingredients in jar and shake well to blend. Drizzle about half dressing over salad and toss gently to mix well. Refrigerate for about 20 minutes.

- When ready to serve, add more dressing as needed and toss again. Serves 8.

Chicken Pasta Joy

1 (12 ounce) package ziti
   (thin tubes) pasta   340 g
2 ribs celery, sliced
1 (4 ounce) can chopped
   pimento, drained   115 g
1 red bell pepper, seeded,
   cut into 1-inch strips   2.5 cm
1 onion, chopped
6 boneless, skinless chicken
   breast halves, cooked
1 cup cashew halves   140 g

- Cook pasta in saucepan according to package directions; drain and rinse under cold water. Transfer to large bowl. Cut chicken into bite-size pieces. Add celery, pimento, bell pepper, onion, chicken and a little salt and pepper. Toss to mix well.

Dressing:

1¼ cups mayonnaise   280 g
⅓ cup packed brown sugar   75 g
1 tablespoon lemon juice   15 ml
1 tablespoon white vinegar   15 ml

- Combine mayonnaise, brown sugar, lemon juice, vinegar and a little salt in small bowl. Pour over salad, toss, cover and refrigerate until ready to serve. Stir in cashews just before serving. Serves 8.

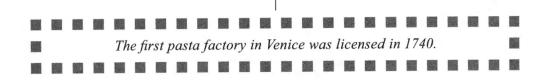

The first pasta factory in Venice was licensed in 1740.

Chicken-Curry Salad

1 (14 ounce) can chicken
   broth   400 g
2 - 3 boneless, skinless
   chicken breast halves
1 (8 ounce) package
   conchiglie (medium
   shells) pasta   230 g
1 (4 ounce) can chopped
   ripe olives, drained   115 g
1 red bell pepper, seeded,
   chopped
1 apple, peeled, cored, sliced
2 ribs celery, chopped

- Place chicken broth and chicken in large saucepan and cook on medium-high heat for about 12 to 14 minutes. Remove chicken and leave broth in saucepan. Cool chicken, cut into bite-size chunks and set aside.

- With remaining broth, add enough water to cook macaroni according to package directions. Drain and rinse in cold water. Discard remaining broth.

Dressing:

½ cup sour cream   120 g
½ cup mayonnaise   115 g
1 teaspoon minced garlic   5 ml
¾ teaspoon curry powder 4 ml

- Combine sour cream, mayonnaise, garlic, curry powder and a little salt and pepper in small bowl. Combine cooled pasta, chicken, dressing, olives, bell pepper, apple and celery in large bowl.

- Mix well and refrigerate for at least 3 hours before serving. Serves 4 to 6.

Colorful Salad that Packs a Punch

1 (8 ounce) package cavatappi (corkscrew) pasta	230 g
2½ cups bite-size pieces rotisserie chicken without skin	600 ml
½ cup grated carrots	120 ml
2 ribs celery, chopped	
1 red bell pepper, seeded, chopped	
1 bunch fresh green onions, sliced	
1 (10 ounce) bag torn romaine lettuce	280 g

- Cook pasta in saucepan according to package directions; drain and rinse in cold water.

- Place in large bowl. Add chicken, carrots, celery, bell pepper and onions. Refrigerate for about 20 minutes.

Dressing:

1 (8 ounce) bottle blue cheese dressing	250 ml
½ cup sour cream	120 g
¼ cup bottled chili sauce	70 g
1 tablespoon liquid pepper sauce	15 ml
2 teaspoons paprika	10 ml
⅓ teaspoon cayenne pepper	3 ml

- Combine all dressing ingredients plus 1 teaspoon salt in bowl and mix well. Dressing can be made ahead of time.

- Pour dressing over salad and toss to coat well. Line serving platter with romaine lettuce and spoon salad on top. Serves 8.

Exciting Grilled Chicken Salad

6 boneless, skinless chicken
    breast halves
Creole seasoning
1 (12 ounce) package rotini
    (short spirals) pasta   **340 g**
1 (12 ounce) package cubed
    mozzarella cheese   **340 g**
1 red onion, chopped
1 yellow bell pepper,
    seeded, chopped
1 (10 ounce) package frozen
    baby green peas, thawed **280 g**
1 head romaine lettuce, torn
1 - 1½ cups refrigerated
    honey-mustard
    dressing   **250 - 360 ml**

- Preheat grill to high heat. Season both sides of chicken breasts with ample amount of Creole seasoning. Grill chicken for 6 to 8 minutes (according to size) on each side or until juices run clear.

- Remove from heat and place on plate to cool. When chicken is cool enough, cut into strips. Refrigerate.

- Cook pasta in saucepan according to package directions, drain and rinse in cold water; set aside.

- Mix cheese, onion, bell pepper, peas and lettuce in large bowl. When chicken and pasta chill, add to cheese-lettuce mixture and toss.

- Pour in 1 cup (250 ml) honey-mustard dressing and toss again. Add more dressing, if needed. Refrigerate until time to serve. Serves 6 to 8.

Mandarin Chicken Salad

2 tablespoons butter	30 g
1 (3 ounce) package Oriental-flavor ramen noodle soup mix	85 g
3 cups cooked, cubed chicken	420 g
⅓ cup dry-roasted peanuts	50 g
1 (16 ounce) bag of coleslaw mix	455 g
1 (11 ounce) can mandarin orange slices, drained	310 g

- Melt butter in large skillet over medium heat. Stir in seasoning packet from soup mix. Break up block of noodles into bite-sized pieces and stir into butter mixture.

- Cook noodles for 3 to 4 minutes, stirring often, until noodles are golden brown. Remove from heat and place in large bowl. Stir in chicken, peanuts, coleslaw and orange slices and mix well.

Dressing:

⅓ cup sugar	70 g
⅓ cup white vinegar	75 ml
¼ cup olive oil	60 ml

- Combine dressing ingredients in small bowl and pour over salad and toss. Serves 8 to 10.

It takes one and one-half pounds of fresh pasta to cook the same quantity as one pound of dried pasta.

New Classic Caesar Pasta

1 (16 ounce) package penne
   (tube) pasta   455 g
2 tablespoons butter   30 g
4 boneless, skinless chicken
   breast halves, cut in
   strips
1 (8 ounce) package cubed
   cheddar cheese   230 g
1 red bell pepper, seeded,
   chopped
1 head romaine lettuce, torn
1 large tomato, chopped, drained

- Cook pasta in saucepan according to package directions and drain; transfer to large bowl.

- Melt butter in large skillet over medium-high heat and cook chicken for about 10 minutes or until juices run clear. Remove skillet from heat.

Dressing:

1 (8 ounce) bottle Caesar
   salad dressing   250 ml
¼ cup red wine vinegar 60 ml
1 tablespoon sugar   15 ml

- Combine dressing ingredients in jar and mix well. Add chicken, cheese, bell pepper and lettuce to pasta and toss.

- Pour dressing over mixture and toss again. Garnish with chopped tomato and serve immediately. Serves 8.

Corn pasta works well for those allergic to wheat;
however, it tends to have a "mushy" consistency.

Chicken Rotini Salad

1 (7.5 ounce) box Caesar
   Suddenly Pasta Salad
   mix   210 g
3 tablespoons olive oil   45 ml
1½ cups cooked, cubed
   chicken   210 g
3 fresh green onions, sliced
1 medium tomato, chopped,
   drained
1 (7 ounce) container
   refrigerated basil pesto   200 g

- Bring two-thirds full of water in
  3-quart (3 L) saucepan to a boil
  and add contents of pasta pouch.
  Boil for about 13 minutes, stirring
  occasionally until pasta is tender;
  drain. Rinse with cold water until
  pasta is slightly cool; drain.

- Combine seasoning mix,
  3 tablespoons (45 ml) water and
  olive oil in large bowl. Stir in pasta
  mixture, chicken, onions, tomato
  and pesto. Toss with topping (from
  the salad mix) just before serving.
  Serves 8.

Quick-Fix Salad

½ (8 ounce) package
   spaghetti pasta   ½ (230 g)
1 cup cooked, shredded
   chicken breast   140 g
½ cup peeled, diced
   cucumber   60 g
½ cup sliced baby carrots 60 g
½ cup green peas   50 g

- Cook spaghetti in saucepan
  according to package directions,
  drain and rinse in cold water.
  Drain again.

- Combine spaghetti, chicken,
  cucumber, carrots, peas and a little
  salt and pepper in bowl.

Dressing:

1 tablespoon white vinegar   15 ml
1 tablespoon light soy sauce 15 ml
1 tablespoon olive oil   15 ml
1 teaspoon sugar   5 ml
½ teaspoon minced garlic   2 ml

- Combine vinegar, soy sauce, oil,
  sugar and garlic in small saucepan.
  Bring to a boil, remove from heat
  and drizzle over spaghetti mixture.
  Toss to coat well. Serves 2 to 3.

Noodle-Turkey Salad

1 (3 ounce) package
   oriental-flavor ramen
   noodle soup mix   85 g
1 (16 ounce) package finely
   shredded coleslaw mix   455 g
¾ pound smoked turkey,
   cut into strips   340 g
½ cup vinaigrette salad
   dressing   125 ml

- Coarsely crush noodles and place
  in bowl with lid. Add coleslaw mix
  and turkey strips.

- Combine vinaigrette salad dressing
  and seasoning packet from noodle
  mix in small bowl, pour over
  noodle-turkey mixture and toss
  to coat mixture well. Refrigerate
  before serving. Serves 4.

Pasta Salad Supper

1 (12 ounce) package
   tri-color fusilli (spiral)
   pasta   340 g
1 (4 ounce) can sliced ripe
   olives, drained   115 g
2 cups fresh broccoli florets,
   chopped   140 g
2 small yellow squash, sliced
1 (8 ounce) bottle
   cheddar-parmesan
   ranch dressing   230 g
1 (3 pound) package hickory-
   smoked cracked pepper
   turkey breast, sliced   1.4 kg

- Cook pasta in saucepan according
  to package directions, drain and
  rinse in cold water. Place in large
  salad bowl and add olives, broccoli
  and squash.

- Pour dressing over salad mixture
  and toss. Place turkey on top of
  salad. Serves 8.

TIP: *You won't need all the turkey,
       but what's left will make
       great sandwiches!*

Perky Party Pasta

1 pound ground turkey	455 g
¼ cup seasoned breadcrumbs	30 g
1 teaspoon minced garlic	5 ml
1 large egg	
1 cup grated romano cheese, divided	100 g
1 (16 ounce) package farfalle (bow-tie) pasta	455 g
1 tablespoon cornstarch	15 ml
1 cup milk	250 ml
1 (14 ounce) can chicken broth	400 g
1 (9 ounce) package baby spinach	255 g

- Preheat oven to 375° (190° C).

- Combine ground turkey, breadcrumbs, garlic, egg and ¼ cup (60 ml) cheese in medium bowl. Mix just until they blend well and shape into 36 (1-inch/2.5 cm) meatballs.

- Place meatballs on foil-lined 10 x 15-inch (25 x 38 cm) jellyroll pan and bake for 20 minutes.

- Cook pasta in large saucepan according to package directions, drain and return to saucepan.

- Whisk cornstarch into milk in 2-cup (500 ml) measuring cup. Add broth and pour into saucepan with pasta. Bring mixture to boiling, stir often and cook for 1 minute to thicken sauce slightly.

- Remove saucepan from heat and stir in spinach, ½ cup (50 g) cheese and meatballs. Gently toss to blend. Spoon into sprayed 3-quart (3 L) baking dish. Sprinkle with remaining cheese and bake for 20 minutes. Serves 6.

Picnic Pasta Salad

1 (8 ounce) package maruzze
   (shell) pasta   230 g
1 cup cubed cheddar cheese 130 g
2 ribs celery, sliced
1 red bell pepper, seeded,
   chopped
1 (10 ounce) package frozen
   green peas, thawed   280 g
¼ cup sweet pickle relish   60 g

- Cook macaroni in saucepan
  according to package directions,
  rinse under cold water and drain.

- Combine macaroni, cheese, celery,
  bell pepper, peas, pickle relish and
  a little salt and pepper in bowl.

Dressing:

½ cup mayonnaise   110 g
⅔ cup ranch salad dressing   150 ml

- Stir in mayonnaise and ranch
  dressing and toss. Cover and
  refrigerate for at least 24 hours
  before serving. Serves 6.

Pasta-Turkey Salad Supper

1 (12 ounce) package
   tri-color fusilli (spiral)
   pasta   340 g
1 (4 ounce) can sliced ripe
   olives, drained   115 g
1 cup each fresh broccoli
   and cauliflower
   florets   70 g/100 g
2 small yellow squash,
   sliced
1 cup halved cherry
   tomatoes   150 g
1 (8 ounce) bottle
   cheddar-parmesan
   ranch dressing   230 g
1½ pounds hickory-smoked
   cracked-pepper turkey
   breast, sliced   680 g

- Cook pasta in saucepan according
  to package directions. Drain and
  rinse in cold water. Place in large
  salad bowl and add olives, broccoli,
  cauliflower, squash and tomatoes.

- Toss with dressing. Place thin
  slices of turkey breast, arranged
  in rows, over salad. Serve
  immediately. Serves 8.

Tuna-Veggie Salad

1 (8 ounce) package
   maruzze (shell) pasta   230 g
2 small yellow squash,
   chopped
2 small zucchini, chopped
1 (15 ounce) can pinto beans,
   rinsed, drained   425 g
1 (11 ounce) can
   Mexicorn®, drained   310 g
1 (12 ounce) can tuna,
   drained   340 g
1 cup creamy Italian
   salad dressing   250 ml

- Cook pasta in saucepan according to package directions, drain and rinse in cold water.

- Place squash and zucchini in saucepan with about ¾ cup (175 ml) water and cook on medium-high heat for 10 minutes or just until they are barely tender. Drain well.

- Combine pasta, squash, zucchini, beans, corn, tuna and a little salt and pepper in large bowl. Refrigerate for at least 1 hour. Add salad dressing and toss to mix well. Refrigerate. Serves 6 to 8.

What's the difference between pasta and noodles? Noodles are a form of pasta made of durum flour (more finely ground than semolina), water and eggs. Eggs are a required ingredient. All other forms of pasta are made from semolina flour and water and are generically referred to as macaroni.

Tuna-Tortellini Salad

1 (7 ounce) package ready-cut spaghetti pasta	200 g
¼ cup (½ stick) butter	60 g
1 (12 ounce) can tuna, drained	340 g
1 (4 ounce) can sliced ripe olives	115 g

- Cook spaghetti in saucepan according to package directions, drain, add butter and stir until butter melts. Add tuna and olives.

Dressing:

¾ cup whipping cream	55 g
1 teaspoon dried basil leaves	5 ml
2 tablespoons grated parmesan cheese	10 g

- Combine dressing ingredients with 1 teaspoon (5 ml) salt in bowl. Pour over spaghetti-tuna mixture and toss. Serves 4.

Garden Crab Salad

1 (12 ounce) package tri-color fusilli or rotini (spiral) pasta	340 g
1 head fresh broccoli, cut into small florets	
1 small head cauliflower, cut into small florets	
1 red bell pepper, seeded, chopped	
1 (16 ounce) carton imitation crabmeat, flaked	455 g
1 (8 ounce) bottle vinaigrette salad dressing	230 g
2 tablespoons dry roasted sunflower kernels	15 g

- Cook pasta in saucepan according to package directions; drain and rinse in cold water.

- Combine broccoli, cauliflower, bell pepper and crabmeat in large bowl. Pour vinaigrette dressing over salad and toss. Sprinkle sunflower kernels over top.

- Refrigerate for at least 1 to 2 hours before serving. Serves 6 to 8.

Easy Macaroni-Tuna Salad

3 cups elbow macaroni (tube) pasta	315 g
1 (12 ounce) can tuna, drained, flaked	340 g
1 red onion, chopped	
2 ribs celery, chopped	
1 (4 ounce) jar chopped pimento, drained	115 g
1 (4 ounce) can chopped ripe olives	115 g

- Cook macaroni in saucepan according to package directions. (Macaroni can be cooked ahead of time.)

- Drain, rinse in cold water and drain again. Transfer to large bowl and add tuna, onion, celery, pimento and olives; mix well.

Dressing:

½ cup creamy Italian salad dressing	125 ml
½ cup sour cream	120 g
½ cup mayonnaise	110 g
½ teaspoon garlic powder	2 ml

- Combine Italian dressing, sour cream, mayonnaise, garlic powder, 1 teaspoon salt and ½ teaspoon black pepper in bowl.

- Stir into macaroni-tuna mixture and toss. Refrigerate for several hours before serving. Refrigerate any leftover salad. Serves 6.

Lemony Crab Salad

1 (8 ounce) package farfalle
   (bow-tie) pasta   230 g
1 seedless cucumber,
   peeled, sliced
1 rib celery, chopped
1 red bell pepper, seeded,
   chopped
4 fresh green onions, sliced
1 (16 ounce) package
   imitation crabmeat,
   flaked   455 g
1 lemon, sliced thinly

Dressing:

½ cup sour cream   120 g
⅔ cup mayonnaise   150 g
2 tablespoons lemon juice   30 ml
1 teaspoon sugar   5 ml
½ teaspoon dried dill weed   2 ml

- Cook pasta in saucepan according to package directions; drain and rinse with cold water. Rinse again with cold water and set aside.

- Combine all dressing ingredients plus a little salt and pepper in large bowl; mix well.

- Add farfalle pasta, cucumber, celery, bell pepper and onion and toss. Stir in crabmeat and gently toss again.

- Cover and refrigerate for at least 1 hour before serving. Garnish with lemon slices. Serves 6.

Linguine-Crab Reward

1 (16 ounce) package linguine
    (thin egg noodles) pasta   455 g
1 (9 ounce) package mixed
    salad greens   255 g
1 (16 ounce) package
    imitation crabmeat,
    flaked   455 g
1 (4 ounce) jar chopped
    pimentos, drained   115 g
¼ cup chopped dill pickles   40 g

- Cook linguine in saucepan according to package directions and drain.

- Combine all dressing ingredients in jar with lid and shape to mix well. Refrigerate.

- Toss linguine, salad greens, crabmeat, pimentos, pickles and a little salt and pepper in large bowl.

Dressing:

¾ cup light soy sauce   175 ml
½ cup extra-virgin olive oil   125 ml
½ cup sugar   100 g
⅓ cup white vinegar   75 ml
1 tablespoon sesame seeds   15 ml

- Combine all dressing ingredients in bowl. Pour about half dressing over salad, toss and add more dressing as needed. Refrigerate until serving. Serves 8 to 10.

Pasta nera or black pasta is sometimes known as squid-ink pasta because it is flavored with squid "ink". This gives it its distinctive black color. It is usually served with shellfish.

Angel Shrimp Supreme

1 (16 ounce) package capelli
    d'angelo (angel hair)
    pasta   455 g
1 (16 ounce) package frozen
    salad shrimp, thawed,
    drained   455 g
1 bunch fresh green onions
    with tops, chopped
1 red bell pepper, seeded,
    finely chopped
2 ribs celery, sliced
1 (16 ounce) bottle creamy
    ranch salad dressing,
    divided   455 g

- Break strands of pasta in half; then cook in saucepan according to package directions, drain and rinse under cold water. Place in large bowl.

- Stir in shrimp, onions, bell pepper and celery and toss. Add 1½ cups (375 ml) salad dressing and toss again. Refrigerate for at least 2 hours before serving.

- After salad stands, you may want to add a little more dressing before serving. Serves 6 to 8.

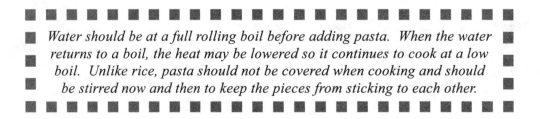

Water should be at a full rolling boil before adding pasta. When the water returns to a boil, the heat may be lowered so it continues to cook at a low boil. Unlike rice, pasta should not be covered when cooking and should be stirred now and then to keep the pieces from sticking to each other.

Seafood Medley Salad

1 (16 ounce) package macaroni (shell) pasta	455 g
1 (6 ounce) can crabmeat, drained	170 g
1 (6 ounce) can tuna, drained	170 g
1 (6 ounce) can shrimp, drained	170 g
½ cup dill pickle, chopped	80 g
2 ribs celery, sliced	
2 carrots, grated	

- Cook shell macaroni in saucepan according to package directions. Drain and rinse with cold water. Combine crabmeat, tuna, shrimp, dill pickles, celery and carrots in large bowl.

Dressing:

1 cup mayonnaise	225 g
⅓ cup French salad dressing	75 ml
¼ cup milk	60 ml
1 tablespoon lemon juice	15 ml
1 tablespoon sugar	15 ml

- Combine all dressing ingredients in small bowl and mix well. Add macaroni to seafood mixture, spoon on dressing and toss well. Cover and refrigerate until cold or overnight. Serves 8 to 10.

Superb Seafood Salad

1 (16 ounce) package
   macaroni (tube) pasta   455 g
3 eggs, hard-boiled, chopped
1 (10 ounce) package frozen
   baby green peas, thawed 280 g
1 red bell pepper, seeded,
   finely chopped
2 ribs celery, chopped
1 (8 ounce) package frozen
   salad shrimp, thawed   230 g
1 (16 ounce) package
   imitation crabmeat,
   flaked   455 g
Paprika

- Cook pasta in saucepan according to package directions, drain and rinse with cold water. Transfer to large bowl and add eggs, peas, bell pepper, celery, shrimp and crabmeat. Cover and refrigerate.

Dressing:

1 pint mayonnaise   455 g
1 tablespoon lemon juice   15 ml
2 teaspoons sugar   10 ml
1 teaspoon dried parsley   5 ml
1 teaspoon Creole seasoning 5 ml

- Combine all dressing ingredients in bowl and mix well. Spoon over salad ingredients and toss until they mix well.

- If salad seems a little dry, stir in 1 tablespoon (15 ml) milk. Refrigerate for at least 1 to 2 hours before serving. Garnish with sprinkles of paprika. Serves 10 to 12.

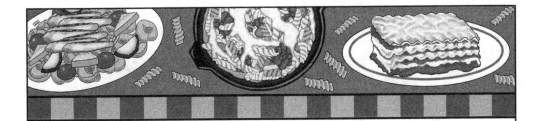

Pasta with Beef

Appetizing and hearty recipes with beef at the center make pasta a family favorite.

Pasta with Beef Contents

Bold Chili over Pasta

2 pounds lean ground beef	1 kg
1 onion, chopped	
2 teaspoons minced garlic	10 ml
1 (15 ounce) can Mexican stewed tomatoes	425 g
1 (4 ounce) can chopped green chilies	115 g
1 (15 ounce) can pinto beans, drained	425 g
1 (8 ounce) can tomato sauce	230 g
1 (10 ounce) can beef broth	280 g
2 tablespoons chili powder	30 ml
1 tablespoon ground cumin	15 ml
½ teaspoon ground allspice	2 ml
1 (12 ounce) package cavatappi (corkscrew) pasta	340 g

- Saute beef, onion and garlic in large skillet over medium-high heat for 5 minutes.

- Drain fat and stir in tomatoes, green chilies, beans, tomato sauce, broth, chili powder, cumin, allspice and a little salt and pepper. Bring mixture to a boil, reduce heat and simmer, for 20 to 25 minutes.

- Cook corkscrew pasta in saucepan according to package directions, drain and place in 6 soup bowls. Top with beef-tomato mixture and serve immediately. Serves 6.

Cheesy Beefy Gnocchi

1 pound lean ground beef	455 g
1 (10 ounce) can cheddar cheese soup	280 g
1 (10 ounce) can tomato bisque soup	280 g
2 cups gnocchi (small shells) pasta	210 g

- Cook beef in skillet until brown and drain.

- Add soups, 1½ cups (375 ml) water and pasta. Bring mixture to a boil.

- Cover and cook over medium heat for 10 to 12 minutes or until pasta is done and stir often. Serves 6.

Chili with Spaghetti

1 pound lean ground beef	455 g
2 (14 ounce) cans Mexican stewed tomatoes	2 (400 g)
1 (15 ounce) can kidney beans, drained	425 g
1 (8 ounce) can tomato sauce	230 g
2 tablespoons chili powder	30 ml
2 teaspoons ground cumin	10 ml
1 (8 ounce) package spaghetti pasta, cooked, drained	230 g
½ - 1 cup shredded 4-cheese blend	60 - 115 g

- Cook and stir ground beef in large sprayed saucepan or soup pot over medium-high heat until crumbly and brown. Stir in tomatoes, beans, tomato sauce, chili powder, cumin and a little salt; bring to a boil.

- Reduce heat, cover and simmer for about 15 minutes, stirring occasionally.

- Place cooked spaghetti in serving bowl and spoon beef-bean mixture over top. Garnish with cheese. Serves 8.

Chili-Pasta Bowl

1 (12 ounce) package genelli (twisted) pasta	340 g
1 (16 ounce) package frozen chopped onion and bell pepper	455 g
1 tablespoon olive oil	15 ml
1 pound lean ground beef	455 g
2 tablespoons chili powder	30 ml
1 teaspoon cocoa	5 ml
1 teaspoon ground cumin	5 ml
1 (15 ounce) can Mexican stewed tomatoes	425 g
1 (15 ounce) can kidney beans, rinsed, drained	425 g
1 cup shredded 4-cheese blend	115 g

- Cook pasta in saucepan according to package directions (drain later). Cook onion and bell peppers in oil in skillet over medium-high heat for about 10 minutes or until light brown. Transfer onion mixture to small bowl.

- In same skillet, cook ground beef over medium-high heat until brown and crumbly; discard any fat. Stir in chili powder, cocoa, cumin and ½ teaspoon (2 ml) salt; cook for 2 minutes.

- Return onion mixture to skillet and stir in tomatoes, beans and 1 cup (250 ml) water; bring to a boil. Reduce heat to medium, cook for 6 minutes and break up tomatoes with side of spoon.

- Drain pasta and return to saucepan. Add chili mixture to pasta in saucepan and stir until they blend well. Transfer to serving bowl and sprinkle cheese over top of dish. Serves 6.

Classic Beefy Noodles

1½ pounds lean ground
beef   680 g
2 (10 ounce) cans
tomatoes and green
chilies   2 (280 g)
2 teaspoons minced garlic 10 ml
1 (8 ounce) package
fettuccini (medium
egg noodles) pasta   230 g
1 (3 ounce) package
cream cheese   85 g
1 (8 ounce) carton sour
cream   230 g
1 (8 ounce) package
shredded cheddar
cheese   230 g

- Preheat oven to 350° (175° C).

- Brown beef in skillet. Drain and stir in tomatoes and green chilies, garlic and a little salt and pepper. Bring to a boil, reduce heat and simmer for 25 minutes.

- While beef mixture cooks, place noodles in large saucepan and cook according to package directions. Drain, stir in cream cheese and stir until cream cheese melts. Fold in sour cream and stir in beef mixture.

- Spoon into sprayed 9 x 13-inch (23 x 33 cm) baking dish. Cover and bake for 30 minutes. Remove from oven, sprinkle cheese over top and return to oven for 5 minutes. Serves 8.

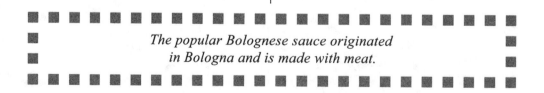

*The popular Bolognese sauce originated
in Bologna and is made with meat.*

Company Beef and Pasta

2 pounds lean, ground beef   910 g
2 onions, chopped
1 green bell pepper, chopped
¾ teaspoon garlic powder   4 ml
1 (14 ounce) jar spaghetti
   sauce   400 g
1 (15 ounce) can Italian
   stewed tomatoes   425 g
1 (4 ounce) can sliced
   mushrooms, drained   115 g
1 (8 ounce) package rotini
   (short spirals) pasta   230 g
1½ pints sour cream,
   divided   750 ml
1 (8 ounce) package sliced
   provolone cheese   230 g
1 (8 ounce) package
   shredded mozzarella
   cheese   230 g

- Preheat oven to 325° (160° C).

- Brown and cook beef in deep skillet or soup pot and stir often to break up pieces. Drain off excess fat.

- Add onions, bell pepper, garlic powder, spaghetti sauce, stewed tomatoes and mushrooms and mix well. Simmer for 20 minutes.

- Cook rotini in saucepan according to package directions and drain. Pour half rotini into sprayed deep 10 x 15-inch (25 x 38 cm) baking dish.

- Cover with half meat-tomato mixture and half sour cream. Top with slices of provolone cheese. Repeat process once more ending with mozzarella cheese.

- Cover and bake for 35 minutes.

- Uncover and continue baking for additional 10 to 15 minutes or until mozzarella cheese melts. Serves 8 to 10.

Delicious Stuffed Shells

24 lumache (large shells) pasta	
1 pound lean ground beef	455 g
1 (26 ounce) can spaghetti sauce	740 g
1 (8 ounce) container cream cheese with chives, softened	230 g
2 teaspoons dried parsley	10 ml
1 (8 ounce) package shredded Italian cheese blend, divided	230 g
1 cup grated parmesan cheese, divided	100 g
1 egg, beaten	

- Preheat oven to 350° (175° C).

- Cook pasta shells in saucepan according to package directions, drain and place on a large sheet of wax paper.

- Cook ground beef in skillet over medium-high heat for about 7 or 8 minutes, stir until crumbly and brown and drain thoroughly. Let cool for about 5 minutes.

- Combine spaghetti sauce and ¼ cup (60 ml) water in large bowl and pour 1 cup (250 ml) in 9 x 13-inch (23 x 33 cm) baking pan.

- In separate bowl, combine cream cheese, parsley, 1½ cups (170 g) Italian cheese, ½ cup (50 g) parmesan cheese, egg and cooked beef; mix well.

- Carefully place heaping tablespoonfuls of mixture into each shell and arrange stuffed shells over sauce in baking pan. Pour remaining sauce over top and cover shells completely. Cover with foil and bake for 40 minutes.

- Uncover and sprinkle with remaining Italian and parmesan cheeses and cook for additional 10 minutes. Serves 8.

Dinner with the Italian Touch

Baked Italian dishes are famous for their rich, flavorful sauces. This recipe is creamy, cheesy and delicious.

2 pounds ground round beef	**910 g**
1 onion, chopped	
1 red bell pepper, chopped	
2 teaspoons minced garlic	**10 ml**
1 (26 ounce) jar chunky spaghetti sauce	**740 g**
2 (8 ounce) jars sliced mushrooms, drained	**2 (230 g)**
1 teaspoon oregano	**5 ml**
2 teaspoons Italian seasoning	**10 ml**
1 (12 ounce) package fettuccini (medium egg noodles) pasta	**340 g**
1 (15 ounce) package ricotta cheese	**425 g**
1 (1 pint) carton sour cream	**500 ml**
1 (5 ounce) package grated parmesan cheese	**145 g**
1 (16 ounce) package shredded mozzarella cheese, divided	**455 g**

- Preheat oven to 325° (160° C).

- Brown beef, onion, bell pepper and garlic in very large skillet; drain well. Add spaghetti sauce, mushrooms, oregano, Italian seasoning and dash of salt and pepper. Heat to a boil, reduce heat and simmer about 15 minutes.

- Cook noodles in saucepan according to package directions and drain.

- Combine ricotta cheese, sour cream, parmesan cheese and half mozzarella cheese in large bowl.

- Layer half noodles, half beef mixture and half cheese mixture in sprayed 10 x 15-inch (25 x 38 cm) baking dish. Repeat layers.

- Cover and bake for 40 minutes. Remove covering and sprinkle with remaining mozzarella cheese. Bake for additional 5 to 10 minutes. Serves 20.

Family OK Casserole

1½ pounds lean ground beef	680 g
1 (15 ounce) can stewed tomatoes	425 g
1 (10 ounce) can tomatoes and green chilies	280 g
1 (12 ounce) package tagliatelle (thin egg noodles) pasta	340 g
1 (8 ounce) package cream cheese, softened	230 g
1 (8 ounce) carton light sour cream	230 g
1 (16 ounce) package shredded mozzarella cheese, divided	455 g

- Preheat oven to 350° (175° C).

- Brown beef in large saucepan on medium heat and drain fat. Add stewed tomatoes and tomatoes and green chilies; reduce heat and simmer 20 minutes.

- Cook noodles in saucepan according to package directions and drain. Beat cream cheese in bowl until smooth, add sour cream and mix until they blend well.

- Spread half noodles into sprayed 9 x 13-inch (23 x 33 cm) baking pan. Cover with half cream cheese mixture and half mozzarella cheese. Spread all meat-tomato mixture over cheese.

- Layer remaining noodles, cream cheese mixture and cheese. Cover and bake for 35 minutes. Let stand for 10 minutes before serving. Serves 12.

Fettuccini Italian

*Adding broccoli to this classic
Italian recipe dresses it up
and adds wonderful flavor.*

6 ounces fettuccini (medium egg noodles) pasta	**170 g**
½ pound lean ground beef	**230 g**
1 teaspoon minced garlic	**5 ml**
1 onion, minced	
1 (8 ounce) can tomato sauce	**230 g**
1 (15 ounce) can Italian stewed tomatoes, with liquid	**425 g**
1 teaspoon Italian seasoning	**5 ml**
2 eggs, divided	
2 tablespoons butter	**30 g**
1 (8 ounce) package shredded mozzarella cheese	**230 g**
1 cup small curd cottage cheese, drained	**230 g**
1 cup chopped fresh broccoli, stemmed	**225 g**
1 (5 ounce) package grated parmesan cheese	**145 g**

- Preheat oven to 350° (175° C).

- Cook fettuccini in saucepan according to package directions, drain and set aside.

- Brown beef in large skillet and stir to crumble. Add garlic and onion, stir to mix and reduce heat. Cook for 5 minutes.

- Add tomato sauce, stewed tomatoes with liquid and Italian seasoning. Stir and bring to boil. Reduce heat, cover and simmer for 10 to 12 minutes, stirring occasionally.

- Beat 1 egg and melted butter in mixing bowl. Stir in fettuccini and mozzarella cheese.

- Spoon mixture into deep 10-inch (25 cm) pie pan and press down on bottom and sides of pan to pack fettuccini mixture.

- In separate bowl, mix remaining egg and cottage cheese. Pour over fettuccini in pie pan and smooth over surface. Sprinkle with broccoli.

- Spoon beef mixture evenly over top. Sprinkle parmesan evenly over top and remove any cheese from edges of the pie pan.

- Bake for 30 minutes or until thoroughly hot. Let stand for 10 minutes to set before cutting. Serves 6 to 8.

Garden Spaghetti

1 (12 ounce) package spaghetti pasta	340 g
1 tablespoon olive oil	15 ml
1 pound lean ground beef	455 g
3 small zucchini, cubed	
1 onion, chopped	
1 green bell pepper, seeded, chopped	
1 (10 ounce) package frozen sliced carrots, thawed	280 g
1 teaspoon minced garlic	5 ml
1 (26 ounce) can chunky garden pasta sauce	740 g
½ cup grated parmesan cheese	50 g

- Cook spaghetti in saucepan according to package directions; drain, cover and keep warm.

- Heat oil in large skillet, cook beef for about 5 minutes and stir well to crumble. Stir in zucchini, onion, bell pepper, carrots, garlic and a little salt and pepper. Stir occasionally and cook for 10 minutes or until vegetables are tender-crisp.

- Stir in pasta sauce, bring to a boil; reduce heat, simmer for about 8 minutes and stir often. Place warm spaghetti on serving platter, spoon vegetable-beef sauce over top and sprinkle with parmesan cheese. Serves 8 to 10.

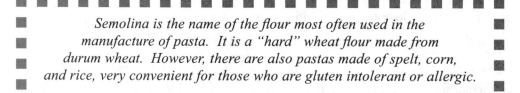

Semolina is the name of the flour most often used in the manufacture of pasta. It is a "hard" wheat flour made from durum wheat. However, there are also pastas made of spelt, corn, and rice, very convenient for those who are gluten intolerant or allergic.

Glorified Spaghetti

1 (8 ounce) package vermicelli
   (thin spaghetti) pasta,
   broken in half   230 g
2 tablespoons olive oil   30 ml
1 teaspoon minced garlic   5 ml
2 ribs celery, chopped
1½ pounds lean ground
   beef   680 g
1 teaspoon sugar   5 ml
2 (8 ounce) cans tomato
   sauce   2 (225 g)
1 (6 ounce) can tomato
   paste   170 g
1 (8 ounce) carton sour
   cream   230 g
1 (3 ounce) package
   cream cheese, softened   85 g
1 bunch green onions,
   chopped
½ cup grated parmesan
   cheese   50 g

- Preheat oven to 350° (175° C).

- Cook spaghetti in saucepan according to package directions; drain and set aside.

- Place oil in large skillet over medium heat and cook garlic, celery, beef, sugar and a little salt and pepper. Cook and stir until beef is no longer pink; drain fat. Add tomato sauce, tomato paste and ¼ cup (60 ml) water and simmer for 15 minutes.

- Beat sour cream and cream cheese in bowl until smooth and stir in green onions. Spread about ½ cup (125 ml) meat sauce into sprayed 3-quart (3 L) baking dish.

- Layer half spaghetti, half sour cream mixture and half meat mixture. Repeat layers, cover and bake for 40 minutes.

- Sprinkle parmesan cheese over top of casserole and serve hot. Serves 8.

Hearty Tortellini Bake

2 (9 ounce) packages
   refrigerated cheese
   tortellini pasta   2 (255 g)
1 pound lean ground beef   455 g
1 small onion, chopped
2 teaspoons minced garlic 10 ml
1 teaspoon dried oregano   5 ml
1 (26 ounce) can chunky
   spaghetti sauce with
   herbs   740 g
3 small zucchini, cut in
   thick slices
½ cup grated parmesan
   cheese   50 g

- Cook tortellini in saucepan according to package directions and drain.

- Cook beef, onion and garlic in large skillet on medium-high heat. Add oregano, spaghetti sauce and zucchini slices and bring to a boil. Reduce heat to medium-low and cook for about 15 minutes, stirring occasionally.

- Transfer half tortellini into sprayed 9 x 13-inch (23 x 33 cm) baking dish and top with half sauce and half cheese. Repeat layers. Serves 3 to 4.

Cooked pasta does not freeze well. Baked casseroles which include pasta can be frozen.

Impressive Baked Ziti

1 (16 ounce) package ziti (thin tubes) pasta	455 g
1 tablespoon olive oil	15 ml
1 large onion, chopped	
1 red bell pepper, seeded, chopped	
1 pound lean ground beef	455 g
1 tablespoon minced garlic	15 ml
1 (26 ounce) jar pasta sauce	740 g
1 (8 ounce) package shredded mozzarella cheese, divided	230 g
1 (15 ounce) carton ricotta	425 g
1 (10 ounce) box frozen spinach, thawed, well drained*	280 g

- Preheat oven to 375° (190° C).

- Cook ziti in saucepan according to package directions; drain and keep warm

- Place oil, onion, bell pepper, beef and garlic in soup pot over medium heat. Cook for 10 to 15 minutes, stirring often or until there is no trace of pink in beef.

- Add pasta sauce and heat 5 minutes. Stir pasta into beef-onion mixture and toss to coat. Add half mozzarella cheese, ricotta and spinach and toss again.

- Spread mixture into sprayed 9 x 13-inch (23 x 33 cm) baking dish, cover and bake for 15 minutes. Uncover and sprinkle remaining mozzarella cheese over top and return to oven for 5 minutes. Serves 10 to 12.

TIP: Squeeze spinach between paper towels to completely remove excess moisture.

Italian Dinner

Baked Italian dishes are famous for their rich, flavorful sauces. This recipe tastes wonderful on the first night and is even better the next day served as leftovers.

2 pounds ground round
   beef   910 g
1 onion, chopped
1 red bell pepper, seeded,
   chopped
2 ribs celery, chopped
2 garlic cloves, finely minced
1 (32 ounce) jar spaghetti
   sauce   910 g
3 (6 ounce) jars sliced
   mushrooms, drained   3 (170 g)
½ teaspoon oregano   2 ml
1 teaspoon Italian
   seasoning   5 ml
1 (8 ounce) package
   fettuccini (medium
   egg noodles) pasta   230 g
1 (8 ounce) package
   cream cheese, softened 230 g
1 (1 pint) carton sour
   cream   500 ml
1 cup grated parmesan
   cheese   100 g
1 (16 ounce) package
   shredded mozzarella
   cheese   455 g

- Preheat oven to 325° (160° C).

- Brown beef, onion, bell pepper, celery and garlic in very large skillet and drain well.

- Add spaghetti sauce, mushrooms, oregano, Italian seasoning and dash of salt and pepper. Heat to boiling, turn heat down and simmer for about 15 minutes.

- Cook noodles in saucepan according to package directions and drain.

- Beat cream cheese in bowl until creamy and add sour cream and cheeses.

- Layer half noodles, half beef mixture and half cheeses in sprayed deep 10 x 15-inch (25 x 38 cm) baking dish. Repeat layers.

- Cover and bake for 30 minutes. Remove covering and bake for additional 10 to 15 minutes. Serves 10 to 12.

Italian Manicotti

1 pound lean ground beef 455 g
2 teaspoons minced garlic 10 ml
2 onions, chopped
1 (28 ounce) can diced
    tomatoes with juice 795 g
1 (8 ounce) package fresh
    mushrooms, sliced 230 g
1 teaspoon fennel seed 5 ml
2 teaspoons basil 10 ml
1 teaspoon Italian
    seasoning 5 ml
2 (10 ounce) boxes frozen
    spinach, thawed,
    drained 2 (280 g)
½ cup grated parmesan
    cheese, divided 50 g
1 (16 ounce) carton small
    curd cottage cheese,
    drained 455 g
¼ teaspoon ground
    nutmeg 1 ml
14 manicotti (large tubes)
    pasta, cooked al dente

- Preheat oven to 325° (160° C).

- Brown ground beef in large skillet, add garlic and onion and reduce heat to low. Simmer for 10 minutes and drain.

- Add tomatoes with juice, mushrooms, fennel seed, basil, Italian seasoning, ½ teaspoon

- (2 ml) each of salt and pepper and stir to mix well. Bring to a boil, reduce heat and simmer for 10 minutes, stir occasionally.

- Squeeze spinach between paper towels to complete remove excess moisture.

- Combine spinach, half parmesan, cottage cheese, nutmeg and ½ teaspoon (2 ml) pepper in bowl.

- Spoon about one-third of beef sauce evenly in sprayed 9 x 13-inch (23 x 33 cm) baking dish.

- Fill manicotti shells with spinach mixture and place on beef layer in baking dish. Repeat until all spinach mixture is in manicotti shells.

- Pour remaining beef sauce evenly over manicotti shells to cover. Sprinkle remaining parmesan cheese over top.

- Cover and bake for 1 hour 30 minutes or until shells are tender. Serves 8 to 12.

Lasagna Roll Ups

12 lasagna noodles
1 pound lean ground beef   455 g
1 onion, finely chopped
1 (14 ounce) jar spaghetti
    sauce   400 g
1 (15 ounce) container
    ricotta cheese   425 g
1 (10 ounce) package frozen,
    chopped spinach,
    thawed, drained*   280 g
1½ cups shredded
    mozzarella cheese,
    divided   175 g

- Preheat oven to 350° (175° C).

- Cook noodles according to package directions and drain.

- Cook beef and onion in skillet on high for about 3 minutes, stirring constantly, drain.

- Stir in spaghetti sauce and heat to boiling, stirring constantly. Pour into 7 x 11-inch (18 x 28 cm) baking pan.

- Mix ricotta cheese, spinach, 1 cup (115 g) mozzarella cheese and a little salt and pepper. Spread 3 tablespoons (20 g) cheese-spinach mixture over each noodle. Roll each noodle; cut roll crosswise in half.

- Place rolls, cut-side down in beef mixture. Cover and bake for about 30 minutes. To serve, sprinkle with remaining cheese. Serves 6 to 8.

TIP: Squeeze spinach between paper towels to completely remove excess moisture.

■ *The word "lasagna" (or lasagne) actually means "cooking pot" in Italian.* ■

Mac Cheese Supper

1½ pounds lean ground
   beef   680 g
2 (7 ounce) packages
   macaroni and cheese
   dinners   2 (200 g)
1 (15 ounce) can whole
   kernel corn, drained   425 g
1½ cups shredded
   Monterey Jack cheese 175 g

- Sprinkle ground beef with
  1 teaspoon (5 ml) salt in large
  skillet, brown until no longer
  pink and drain.

- Prepare macaroni and cheese
  in saucepan according to
  package directions.

- Spoon in beef, macaroni and corn
  in sprayed 5-quart (5 L) slow
  cooker and mix well.

- Cover and cook on LOW for
  4 to 5 hours.

- When ready to serve, sprinkle Jack
  cheese over top and leave in cooker
  until cheese melts. Serves 4 to 6.

Quick Skillet Supper

1½ pounds lean ground
   beef   680 g
⅔ cup stir-fry sauce   150 ml
1 (16 ounce) package
   frozen stir-fry
   vegetables   455 g
2 (3 ounce) packages
   Oriental-flavor
   ramen noodles   2 (85 g)

- Brown and crumble ground beef in
  large skillet. Add 2⅓ cups (575 ml)
  water, stir-fry sauce, vegetables and
  both seasoning packets contained in
  noodle package.

- Cook and stir on medium heat for
  about 5 minutes

- Break up noodles, add to beef-
  vegetable mixture and cook for
  about 6 minutes. Stir to separate
  noodles as they soften. Serve hot.
  Serves 4 to 6.

Make-Believe Lasagna

1 pound lean ground beef	455 g
1 onion, chopped	
½ teaspoon garlic powder	2 ml
1 (18 ounce) can spaghetti sauce	510 g
½ teaspoon oregano	2 ml
6 - 8 lasagna noodles, divided	
1 (12 ounce) carton cottage cheese, divided	340 g
½ cup grated parmesan cheese, divided	50 g
1 (12 ounce) package shredded mozzarella cheese, divided	340 g

- Brown ground beef and onion in large skillet. Add garlic powder, spaghetti sauce and oregano. Cook just until thoroughly warm.

- Spoon layer of meat sauce in sprayed, oval slow cooker. Add layer of lasagna noodles (break to fit slow cooker).

- Top with layer of half remaining meat sauce, half cottage cheese, half parmesan cheese and half mozzarella cheese. Repeat layers and start with more lasagna noodles.

- Cover and cook on LOW for 6 to 8 hours. Serves 4 to 6.

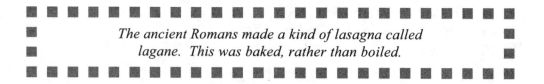

The ancient Romans made a kind of lasagna called lagane. This was baked, rather than boiled.

Mexican Beef and Noodles

This is ideal to make ahead of time for a quick and easy supper and it will serve about 14 people. These blended flavors create a delicious dish that people always remember.

1½ -2 pounds lean ground beef	680 - 910 g
1 onion, chopped	
1 green bell pepper, chopped	
1 (16 ounce) package cubed Mexican Velveeta® cheese	455 g
1 (10 ounce) can fiesta nacho cheese soup	280 g
1 (15 ounce) can stewed tomatoes	425 g
1 (10 ounce) can tomatoes and green chilies	280 g
1 (8 ounce) can whole kernel corn, drained	230 g
½ teaspoon chili powder	2 ml
¼ teaspoon ground mustard	1 ml
1 (8 ounce) package fettuccini (medium egg noodles) pasta	230 g
¼ cup (½ stick) butter, cut into 4 - 5 slices	60 g
1 cup shredded cheddar cheese	115 g

- Preheat oven to 350° (175° C).

- Cook beef, onion and bell pepper in skillet until beef is no longer pink and vegetables are tender. Drain.

- Remove from heat, add Velveeta® cheese and stir until cheese melts.

- Combine fiesta nacho cheese, stewed tomatoes, tomatoes and green chilies, corn, chili powder, mustard and 1½ teaspoons (7 ml) salt and ½ teaspoon (2 ml) pepper in large bowl. Add beef mixture and mix well.

- Cook egg noodles in saucepan according to package directions and drain well.

- While noodles are still very hot, add butter and stir until it melts.

- Stir noodles in with tomato-beef mixture. Transfer to sprayed 10 x 15-inch (25 x 38 cm) baking dish.

- Cover and bake for 45 minutes. Uncover and sprinkle cheese over casserole and return to oven for 4 to 10 minutes. Serves 10.

Oriental Beef and Noodles

1 pound lean ground beef	455 g
2 (3 ounce) packages Oriental ramen noodles, crumbled	2 (85 g)
1 (16 ounce) package frozen broccoli stir-fry vegetables	455 g
1 (10 ounce) box frozen green peas, thawed	280 g
¼ teaspoon ground ginger	1 ml
3 fresh green onions, thinly sliced	

- Cook beef in large skillet over medium heat for 6 minutes or until no longer pink. Stir in 1 flavoring packet from ramen noodles and mix well. Transfer to warm plate.

- In same skillet, combine stir-fry vegetables, peas, ginger, noodles, 2⅔ cups (650 ml) water and remaining flavoring packet. Bring to boil. Reduce heat, cover and simmer 5 minutes, stirring occasionally.

- Return beef to skillet and cook for additional 3 minutes or until thoroughly hot. Just before serving, stir in sliced onions. Serves 8.

Pasta-Beef Skillet

1 pound lean ground beef	455 g
1 small onion, chopped	
1 teaspoon minced garlic	5 ml
1 (15 ounce) can Italian stewed tomatoes	425 g
1 (12 ounce) package penne (tube) pasta	340 g
1 (8 ounce) package shredded cheddar cheese	230 g
1 cup crushed tortilla chips	55 g

- Cook beef, onion and garlic in large sprayed skillet over medium-high heat, stirring often, until beef is crumbly and brown. Stir in tomatoes, 1 cup (250 ml) water and pasta. Cover and cook for about 15 minutes or until pasta is tender.

- Sprinkle cheese over top, cover and cook over medium-low heat just until cheese melts. Sprinkle with chips and serve immediately. Serves 8.

Peanuts, Beef and Pea Pods

1 (8 ounce) package capelli
   d'angelo (angel hair)
   pasta   230 g
1 pound lean ground beef 455 g
1 small onion, finely
   chopped
2 ribs celery, cut in 1-inch
   pieces   2 (2.5 cm)
1 red bell pepper, seeded,
   julienned
1 (8 ounce) package frozen
   pea pods, thawed   230 g
1 (14 ounce) can chicken
   broth   400 g
¼ teaspoon cayenne
   pepper   1 ml
1 tablespoon cornstarch 15 ml
½ cup peanut butter   145 g
⅓ cup chopped, salted
   peanuts   55 g

- Cook angel hair pasta in saucepan according to package directions, drain and keep warm.

- Cook ground beef over medium-high heat for 7 minutes, stir until crumbly and drain. Add onion, celery, bell pepper and pea pods. Cook and stir for 4 minutes or until vegetables are tender-crisp.

- Combine broth, cayenne pepper and cornstarch in saucepan. Cook and stir on medium heat until slightly thick. Stir in cooked beef, vegetables and peanut butter. Cook for 2 minutes, stirring frequently, until thick and bubbly.

- Place pasta in serving plate, spoon beef-vegetable mixture over pasta and sprinkle top with peanuts. Serves 6 to 8.

Ravioli and More

1 pound lean ground beef	455 g
1 teaspoon garlic powder	5 ml
1 large onion, chopped	
2 zucchini squash, grated	
¼ cup (½ stick) butter	60 g
1 (28 ounce) jar spaghetti sauce	795 g
1 (25 ounce) package ravioli with portobello mushrooms pasta, cooked	710 g
1 (12 ounce) package shredded mozzarella cheese	340 g

- Preheat oven to 350° (175° C).

- Brown ground beef in large skillet until no longer pink and drain. Add garlic powder and ½ teaspoon (2 ml) each of salt and pepper.

- Cook onion and zucchini with butter in saucepan just until tender-crisp and stir in spaghetti sauce.

- Spread ½ cup (125 ml) sauce in sprayed 9 x 13-inch (23 x 33 cm) baking dish. Layer half of ravioli, half spaghetti sauce, half beef and half cheese. Repeat layers, but omit remaining cheese. Cover and bake for 35 minutes.

- Uncover and sprinkle remaining cheese. Let stand for 10 minutes before serving. Serves 8.

Historians believe that the Etruscans were making pasta of spelt wheat as early as 400 B.C. The Etruscans lived in central and northern Italy before the founding of Rome.

Seriously Good Stuffed Rigatoni

1 (8 ounce) package rigatoni (large tubes) macaroni pasta	230 g
1 (10 ounce) block cheddar cheese	280 g
1 pound lean ground beef	455 g
1 (15 ounce) jar spaghetti sauce	425 g
½ cup shredded mozzarella cheese	60 g
½ cup seasoned breadcrumbs	60 g

- Preheat oven to 350° (175° C).

- Cook rigatoni in saucepan according to package directions. Drain, rinse thoroughly and place on baking sheet covered with wax paper. Cut cheese into strips about 1¼ x ¼-inch (3 x .6 cm). Insert strip of cheese in each cooked rigatoni and place in sprayed 2-quart (2 L) baking dish.

- Brown beef in non-stick skillet, stirring often, for about 10 minutes. Stir in spaghetti sauce and heat on medium-high until thoroughly hot. Pour over stuffed rigatoni and sprinkle mozzarella cheese over top.

- Cover and bake for 20 minutes. Uncover and sprinkle breadcrumbs over top and return to oven for 10 minutes. Serves 8.

Simple Spaghetti Bake

8 ounces spaghetti pasta	230 g
1 pound lean ground beef	455 g
1 green bell pepper, finely chopped	
1 onion, chopped	
1 (10 ounce) can tomato bisque soup	280 g
1 (15 ounce) can tomato sauce	425 g
2 teaspoons Italian seasoning	10 ml
1 (8 ounce) can whole kernel corn, drained	230 g
1 (4 ounce) can black sliced olives, drained	115 g
1 (12 ounce) package shredded cheddar cheese	340 g

- Cook spaghetti in saucepan according to package directions, drain and set aside.

- Cook beef, bell pepper and onion in skillet and drain.

- Add remaining ingredients, ⅓ cup (75 ml) water and ½ teaspoon (2 ml) salt and spaghetti to beef mixture and stir well. Pour into sprayed 9 x 13-inch (23 x 33 cm) baking dish and cover.

- Refrigerate for 2 to 3 hours.

- When ready to bake, preheat oven to 350° (175° C).

- Cover and bake for 45 minutes. Serves 8 to 10.

Skillet Beef and Pasta

1 (8 ounce) package rotini
    (spiral) pasta   230 g
1 (14 ounce) can beef
    broth   400 g
1 pound lean ground beef 455 g
2 (11 ounce) cans
    Mexicorn®, drained   2 (310 g)
1 (16 ounce) package
    cubed Mexican
    Velveeta® cheese   455 g

- Cook pasta in saucepan according to package directions and substitute beef broth for 1¾ cups (425 ml) water. (Usually an 8 ounce/230 g package pasta will call for 6 cups/1.4 L water, so use 4¼ cups/1.1 L water plus 1¾ cups/425 ml beef broth.)

- While pasta cooks, brown beef in large skillet and drain.

- Stir in corn and cheese and cook on low heat until cheese melts. Gently stir cooked pasta into beef mixture until pasta coats well. Spoon mixture into serving bowl and garnish with sprigs of parsley, if desired. Serves 8.

Southwest Spaghetti

1½ pounds lean ground beef 680 g
2½ teaspoons chili powder   12 ml
1 (15 ounce) can tomato
    sauce   425 g
1 (7 ounce) package
    spaghetti pasta   200 g
1 heaping tablespoon beef
    seasoning   15 ml
Shredded cheddar-Jack
    cheese

- Brown ground beef in skillet until no longer pink. Place in 4 to 5-quart (4 to 5 L) slow cooker.

- Add chili powder, tomato sauce, spaghetti, 2⅓ cups (575 ml) water and beef seasoning and mix well.

- Cover and cook on LOW for 6 to 7 hours.

- When ready to serve, cover with lots of shredded cheddar-Jack cheese. Serves 4 to 6.

Skillet Lasagna

1½ pounds lean ground beef	680 g
1 onion, finely chopped	
2 teaspoons minced garlic	10 ml
1 (26 ounce) jar spaghetti sauce	740 g
5 lasagna noodles, broken into 2-inch pieces	5 (5 cm)
1 (15 ounce) carton ricotta cheese	425 g
2 eggs, beaten	
½ cup grated parmesan cheese	50 g
2 teaspoons dried parsley	10 ml
1 (8 ounce) package shredded Italian cheese blend, divided	230 g

- Cook ground beef, onion and garlic in large nonstick skillet over medium-high heat for about 8 minutes, stirring occasionally, until beef is thoroughly cooked; drain.

- Stir in spaghetti sauce, 1 cup (250 ml) water and noodles. Reduce heat to medium-low. Cover and cook for about 20 minutes, stirring often, until pasta is almost tender.

- Combine ricotta cheese, 2 tablespoons (30 ml) water, eggs, parmesan cheese and parsley in bowl. Spread over partially cooked pasta mixture.

- Sprinkle with half Italian cheese, cover and cook for additional 10 to 15 minutes or until cottage cheese mixture sets and pasta is tender.

- Sprinkle with remaining cheese and serve right from the skillet. Serves 8.

Spaghetti Pie Special

6 ounces spaghetti pasta,
   cooked, drained   170 g
⅓ cup grated parmesan
   cheese   25 g
1 egg, beaten
1 cup small curd cottage
   cheese, drained   225 g
1 pound lean ground beef   455 g
½ cup chopped onion   80 g
1 (15 ounce) can tomato
   sauce   425 g
1 teaspoon minced garlic   5 ml
1 teaspoon dried oregano   5 ml
1 tablespoon sugar   15 ml
½ cup mozzarella cheese   60 g

- Preheat oven to 350° (175° C).

- Mix spaghetti while still warm with parmesan and egg in large bowl.

- Spoon into sprayed 10-inch (25 cm) pie pan (or pizza pan) and pat mixture up and around sides with spoon to form crust. Spoon cottage cheese over spaghetti layer.

- Brown meat and onion in skillet. Drain and add tomato sauce, garlic, oregano, sugar and a little salt and pepper. Simmer for 15 minutes.

- Spoon meat mixture over cottage cheese and bake for 30 minutes. Sprinkle mozzarella on top and return to oven for 5 minutes or just until cheese melts. To serve, cut into wedges. Serves 8.

If the water is not at a full rolling boil when the pasta is added, the outside of the pasta will not "set" and the pasta will be mushy.

Spicy Beef and Noodles

This is an ideal casserole to make ahead of time for a quick-and-easy supper. The flavors blend to create a delicious dish that people will always remember.

2 pounds lean ground beef	910 g
1 large onion, chopped	
1 green bell pepper, seeded, chopped	
1 (16 ounce) package shredded Mexican Velveeta® cheese	455 g
1 (10 ounce) can fiesta nacho cheese soup	280 g
1 (15 ounce) can Mexican stewed tomatoes	425 g
1 (15 ounce) can whole kernel corn, drained	425 g
1 teaspoon chili powder	5 ml
1 (12 ounce) package fettuccini (medium egg noodles) pasta	340 g
1 (8 ounce) package shredded cheddar cheese	230 g

- Preheat oven to 350° (175° C).

- Cook beef, onion and bell pepper in skillet until beef is no longer pink and vegetables are tender. Drain. Remove from heat, add Velveeta® cheese and stir until cheese melts.

- Combine fiesta nacho cheese, stewed tomatoes, corn, chili powder and a little salt in large mixing bowl. Add beef mixture and mix well.

- Cook egg noodles in saucepan according to package directions and drain well. Stir noodles into tomato-beef mixture. Transfer to sprayed 10 x 15-inch (25 x 30 cm) baking dish.

- Cover and bake for 50 to 55 minutes.

- Uncover and sprinkle cheddar cheese over casserole and return to oven for 5 minutes. Serves 20.

Spicy Beef Noodle

1 pound lean ground beef	455 g
1 (1 ounce) packet taco seasoning mix	30 g
1 (15 ounce) can Mexican stewed tomatoes	425 g
1 (15 ounce) can pinto beans with liquid	425 g
1 (16 ounce) package fettuccini (medium egg noodles) pasta	455 g
1 bunch fresh green onions, sliced	

- Cook beef in large skillet and drain. Add taco seasoning with ½ cup (125 ml) water and simmer for 15 minutes.

- Stir in stewed tomatoes, pinto beans and a little salt and pepper.

- Cook noodles in saucepan according to package directions and place on serving platter. Spoon spicy beef over noodles and sprinkle with sliced green onions. Serves 8.

Yummy Creamy Pasta Shells

1¼ pounds lean ground beef	570 g
1 onion, chopped	
Garlic salt	
1 (10 ounce) can cream of celery soup	280 g
1 (12 ounce) box Velveeta® shells and cheese sauce	340 g

- Brown beef and onion in skillet and stir until beef crumbles.

- Add a little pepper and garlic salt, if desired. Add soup and mix.

- Prepare shells and cheese in saucepan according to package directions. Stir into beef mixture.

- Simmer for 20 minutes. Serve hot. Serves 8.

Spinach Manicotti

1 (8 ounce) package
   manicotti (large tubes)
   pasta   **230 g**
1 (10 ounce) package frozen
   chopped spinach,
   thawed, drained*   **280 g**
1 pound lean ground beef   **455 g**
1 teaspoon dried onion
   flakes   **5 ml**
1 cup shredded mozzarella
   cheese   **115 g**
½ cup pesto   **250 g**
1 egg
1 (26 ounce) jar tomato
   pasta sauce   **740 g**

- Preheat oven to 375° (190° C).

- Cook manicotti according to package directions; drain and rinse with cold water. Place manicotti on large piece of wax paper to cool

- Combine spinach, ground beef, onion flakes, cheese, pesto, egg and a little salt and pepper in bowl.

- Fill each manicotti by carefully stuffing beef-spinach mixture into each manicotti. Place manicotti on sprayed 9 x 13-inch (23 x 33 cm) glass baking dish. Pour pasta sauce over manicotti.

- Cover and bake for 35 to 40 minutes or until filling is no longer pink in center. Serves 8.

TIP: *Squeeze spinach between paper towels to completely remove excess moisture.*

Asian Beef and Noodles

1½ pounds lean ground
    beef   680 g
2 (3 ounce) packages
    Oriental-flavored
    ramen noodles   2 (85 g)
1 (16 ounce) frozen
    Oriental stir-fry
    vegetables, thawed   455 g
½ teaspoon ground ginger   2 ml
1 bunch fresh green
    onions, sliced

- Cook ground beef in large skillet and drain. Add ½ cup (125 ml) water and simmer 10 minutes. Transfer to separate bowl.

- In same skillet, combine 2 cups (500 ml) water, broken up noodles, vegetables, ginger and both seasoning packets from ramen noodles. Bring to a boil, reduce heat, cover and simmer for 3 minutes, stirring occasionally.

- Return beef to skillet and stir in green onions. Serve right from skillet. Serves 8.

Beef and Macaroni Supper

1 (10 ounce) package
    macaroni (tube) pasta,
    cooked, drained   280 g
3 tablespoons olive oil   45 ml
1½ pounds lean ground beef,
    browned, drained   680 g
1 onion, chopped
3 ribs celery, chopped
2 (10 ounce) cans tomato
    soup   2 (280 g)
1 (6 ounce) can tomato
    paste   170 g
1 teaspoon beef bouillon
    granules   5 ml
1 (8 ounce) package cubed
    Velveeta® cheese   230 g

- Toss cooked macaroni with oil to make sure macaroni does not stick.

- Place in sprayed slow cooker.

- Add beef, onion, celery, tomato soup, tomato paste, beef bouillon and ⅔ cup (150 ml) water and stir to mix well.

- Cover and cook on LOW for 4 to 6 hours. Before last hour of cooking time, stir in cubed cheese. Serves 4 to 6.

Beef and Mushrooms over Spaghetti

1 pound lean ground beef	455 g
3 tablespoons olive oil	45 ml
1 onion, chopped	
1 cup chopped green bell pepper	150 g
1 (8 ounce) carton mushrooms, sliced	230 g
2 teaspoons minced garlic	10 ml
1 (15 ounce) can stewed tomatoes	425 g
1 (8 ounce) can tomato paste	230 g
1 (12 ounce) package vermicelli (thin spaghetti) pasta	340 g
⅓ cup grated parmesan cheese	35 g

- Cook beef in large skillet over medium-high heat for 4 to 5 minutes; break up lumps with fork. Remove beef from skillet with slotted spoon and set aside. Discard pan drippings.

- Heat oil on medium-high heat and cook onion, bell pepper, mushrooms and garlic for about 5 minutes; stir often.

- Return beef to skillet and stir in stewed tomatoes, tomato paste, ¼ cup (60 ml) water and a little salt and pepper. Bring to a boil, reduce heat to low and simmer sauce for 30 minutes, stirring occasionally.

- While sauce simmers, cook spaghetti in saucepan according to package directions; drain and place in serving dish. Spoon beef sauce over spaghetti and top with grated parmesan cheese. Serves 6 to 8.

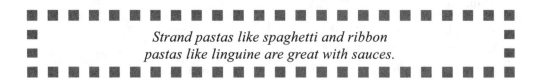

Strand pastas like spaghetti and ribbon pastas like linguine are great with sauces.

Beef and Noodles

3 pounds lean beef, cubed 1.4 kg
2 (10 ounce) cans golden
    mushroom soup 2 (280 g)
½ cup cooking sherry 125 ml
1 (1 ounce) packet onion
    soup mix 30 g
Fettuccini (medium egg
    noodles) pasta, cooked

- Preheat oven to 325° (160° C).

- Mix all ingredients and add ¾ cup (175 ml) water.

- Pour into 3-quart (3 L) baking dish.

- Bake for about 2 hours. Serve over noodles. Serves 8.

Spiced Beef

1 pound lean ground beef 455 g
1 (1 ounce) packet taco
    seasoning mix 30 g
1 (16 ounce) can Mexican
    stewed tomatoes with
    liquid 455 g
1 (16 ounce) can kidney
    beans with liquid 455 g
1 (1 pound) package
    linguine (thin egg
    noodles) pasta 455 g

- Cook beef in skillet and drain. Add taco seasoning and ½ cup (125 ml) water and simmer for 15 minutes.

- Add stewed tomatoes and kidney beans. (You may need to add ¼ teaspoon/1 ml salt.)

- Cook egg noodles in saucepan according to package directions and serve beef over noodles. Serves 6.

Beef and Noodles al Grande

1½ pounds lean ground beef	680 g
1 (16 ounce) package frozen onions and bell peppers, thawed	455 g
1 (16 ounce) box cubed Velveeta® cheese	455 g
2 (15 ounce) cans Mexican stewed tomatoes with liquid	2 (425 g)
2 (15 ounce) cans whole kernel corn, drained	2 (425 g)
1 (8 ounce) package fettuccini (medium egg noodles) pasta	230 g
1 cup shredded cheddar cheese	115 g

- Brown ground beef in skillet and drain fat.

- Place beef in sprayed 5 to 6-quart (5 to 6 L) slow cooker, add onions and peppers, cheese, tomatoes, corn and about 1 teaspoon (5 ml) salt and mix well.

- Cover and cook on LOW for 4 to 5 hours.

- Cook noodles in saucepan according to package direction, drain and fold into beef-tomato mixture. Cook for additional 30 minutes to heat thoroughly.

- When ready to serve, top with cheddar cheese, several sprinkles of chopped fresh parsley or chopped fresh green onions. Serves 4 to 6.

The Chinese were making noodles, one of the two forms of pasta, by 2000 B.C.

Spaghetti and Meatballs

1 (18 ounce) package frozen
   meatballs, thawed   510 g
1 (28 ounce) jar spaghetti
   sauce   795 g
1 (8 ounce) package
   spaghetti pasta   230 g
1 (5 ounce) package fresh
   shredded parmesan
   cheese   145 g

- Heat meatballs on HIGH in large microwave-safe dish for 10 to 12 minutes. Stir twice.

- Cook spaghetti in saucepan according to package directions and drain well. Pour onto serving plate and spoon meatball sauce over spaghetti. Top with cheese. Serves 4 to 5.

Meatballs and Orzo Casserole

1 (10 ounce) package frozen
   onions and bell peppers   280 g
2 ribs celery, sliced
2 tablespoons Italian salad
   dressing   30 ml
1 (14 ounce) can beef broth   400 g
1 cup orzo (tiny) pasta   105 g
18 cooked, frozen Italian
   meatballs, thawed
2 tomatoes, chopped,
   drained
1 teaspoon dried parsley   5 ml
⅓ cup grated parmesan
   cheese   35 g

- Stir-fry vegetables and dressing in large sprayed skillet over medium-high heat for about 2 minutes.

- Add broth and heat to boiling. Stir in orzo and meatballs and bring to a boil. Cover and cook for 10 minutes, stirring occasionally.

- Stir in tomatoes and parsley; cover and cook for additional 5 minutes or until most of liquid absorbs and orzo is tender. Spoon into serving bowl and top with parmesan cheese. Serves 6.

Beef Tips over Pasta

2 pounds lean beef stew meat	910 g
2 cups frozen, small whole onions, thawed	320 g
1 green bell pepper	
1 (6 ounce) jar pitted Greek olives or ripe olives	170 g
½ cup sun-dried tomatoes in oil, drained, chopped	30 g
1 (28 ounce) jar marinara sauce	795 g
1 (8 ounce) package cavatappi (corkscrew) pasta	230 g

- Place beef and onions in sprayed 4 or 5-quart (4 to 5 L) slow cooker.

- Cut bell pepper in 1-inch (2.5 cm) cubes and add to slow cooker.

- Add olives, tomatoes and bell pepper and pour marinara sauce over top.

- Cover and cook on LOW for 8 to 10 hours.

- Serve over hot, cooked pasta. Serves 4 to 6.

Beef and Gravy

2 pounds sirloin steak or thick round steak	910 g
Olive oil	
1 (1 ounce) packet onion soup mix	30 g
1 (10 ounce) can golden mushroom soup	280 g
1 (4 ounce) can sliced mushrooms, drained	115 g
Fettuccini (medium egg noodles) pasta, cooked	

- Cut steak in ½-inch (1.2 cm) pieces. Brown beef in skillet in a little oil and place in 5 to 6-quart (5 to 6 L) slow cooker.

- Combine onion soup mix, mushroom soup, mushrooms and ½ cup (125 ml) water and mix well. Spoon over top of beef.

- Cover and cook on LOW for 7 to 8 hours. Serve over noodles. Serves 4 to 6.

Beef Tips over Noodles

3 pounds beef tips	1.4 kg
½ cup plus 3 tablespoons flour, divided	70 g
1 (8 ounce) carton fresh mushrooms, sliced	230 g
1 bunch fresh green onions, chopped	
1 small red bell pepper, seeded, chopped	
¼ cup ketchup	70 g
1 (14 ounce) can beef broth	400 g
1 tablespoon Worcestershire sauce	15 ml
1 (12 ounce) package fettuccini (medium egg noodles) pasta, cooked	340 g

- Coat beef tips with ½ cup (60 g) flour in bowl and transfer to sprayed slow cooker.

- Add mushrooms, onion, bell pepper, ketchup, broth, Worcestershire sauce and a little salt and pepper.

- Cover and cook on LOW for 8 to 9 hours. About 1 hour before serving, turn heat to HIGH.

- Combine remaining flour with ¼ cup (60 ml) water in small bowl, stir into cooker and cook until liquid thickens.

- Serve over hot, buttered noodles. Serves 6 to 8.

Pasta lisce refers to pasta with a smooth finish.

Beef Tips and Mushrooms Supreme

2 (10 ounce) cans golden
   mushroom soup   2 (280 g)
1 (14 ounce) can beef
   broth   400 g
1 tablespoon beef
   seasoning   15 ml
2 (4 ounce) cans sliced
   mushrooms, drained   2 (115 g)
2 pounds round steak   910 g
Fettuccini (medium egg
   noodles) pasta, cooked
Butter
1 (8 ounce) carton sour
   cream   230 g

- Combine soups, beef broth, beef seasoning and sliced mushrooms in bowl. Place in slow cooker and stir to blend.

- Add slices of beef and stir well.

- Cover and cook on LOW for 4 to 5 hours.

- When ready to serve, cook noodles, drain, add salt and a little butter.

- Stir sour cream into sauce in slow cooker. Spoon sauce and beef over noodles. Serves 4 to 6.

Thomas Jefferson introduced pasta to the United States. He discovered it when visiting Italy while he was serving as ambassador to France. He purchased a pasta-making machine and a shipment of macaroni to go to his home in the United States.

Thai Beef, Noodles And Veggies

**2 (4.4 ounce) packages Thai
   sesame noodles   2 (130 g)
1 pound sirloin steak, cut
   in strips   455 g
Olive oil
1 (16 ounce) package
   frozen stir-fry
   vegetables, thawed 455 g
½ cup chopped peanuts 85 g**

- Cook noodles in saucepan according to package directions, remove from heat and cover.

- Season sirloin strips with a little salt and pepper.

- Brown half sirloin strips in a little oil in skillet and cook for about 2 minutes. Remove from skillet and drain. Brown remaining sirloin strips in skillet with a little oil and cook for about 2 minutes. Remove from skillet and drain.

- In same skillet, place vegetables and ½ cup (125 ml) water, cover and cook for 5 minutes or until tender-crisp.

- Remove from heat, add steak strips and toss to mix. To serve, sprinkle with chopped peanuts. Serves 6 to 8.

Stroganoff over Spinach Noodles

1 (12 ounce) package spinach
    fettuccini (medium egg
    noodles) pasta   340 g
2 tablespoons olive oil   30 ml
1½ pounds sirloin steak,
    sliced in thin strips   680 g
1 (8 ounce) package
    mushrooms   230 g
1 small onion, finely
    chopped
1 (1 ounce) packet brown
    gravy mix   28 g
¼ cup white wine   60 ml
1 (8 ounce) carton sour
    cream   230 g
1 teaspoon dried parsley   5 ml

- Cook fettuccini noodles in saucepan according to package directions, drain and place on warmed serving platter.

- Heat oil in large skillet and sear half beef strips for about 1 minute. (Beef should be rare.) Season with a little salt and pepper and set aside.

- Sear remaining beef and add to first batch.

- In same skillet, saute mushrooms and onion just until softened and add to beef.

- In same skillet, stir gravy mix into 1 cup (250 ml) water and mix well. Add white wine, bring to a boil, reduce heat to medium and stir until it thickens.

- Stir in sour cream and parsley and remove from heat. Fold in beef, sauce, onion-mushroom mixture and spoon over warm platter of noodles. Serve 4 to 6.

Stroganoff Made Easy

1 pound beef sirloin, cut
    into 1-inch squares 455 g/2.5 cm
2 tablespoons olive oil   30 ml
1 onion, chopped
1 (10 ounce) can cream of
    mushroom soup   280 g
1 tablespoon tomato paste   15 ml
¼ cup sour cream   60 g
1 (12 ounce) package
    fettuccini (medium egg
    noodles) pasta, cooked,
    drained   340 g

- Sprinkle beef with ample black pepper and place in large skillet with oil. Cook on medium-high heat until beef browns on all sides and stir often. Remove beef with slotted spoon and set aside.

- Reduce heat to medium and saute onion for about 5 minutes. Stir in soup, tomato paste and ½ cup (125 ml) water; bring to a boil.

- Return beef to skillet, mix well and cook on high just until mixture is thoroughly hot. Stir in sour cream and spoon over hot, cooked noodles. Serves 4.

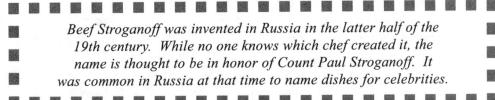

Beef Stroganoff was invented in Russia in the latter half of the 19th century. While no one knows which chef created it, the name is thought to be in honor of Count Paul Stroganoff. It was common in Russia at that time to name dishes for celebrities.

Spicy Swiss Steak

1½ pounds boneless, beef round steak	680 g
4 ounces spicy bratwurst	115 g
2 small onions	
2 tablespoons quick-cooking tapioca	35 g
1 teaspoon dried thyme	5 ml
2 (15 ounce) cans Mexican stewed tomatoes	2 (425 g)
1 (8 ounce) package fettuccini (medium egg noodles) pasta, cooked	230 g

- Trim fat from steak and cut into 4 serving-size pieces.

- Brown steak and bratwurst in skillet. Drain and place in sprayed 4 to 5-quart (4 to 5 L) slow cooker.

- Slice onions and separate into rings. Cover meat with onions and sprinkle with tapioca, thyme, a little salt and pepper. Pour stewed tomatoes over onion and seasonings.

- Cover and cook on LOW for 5 to 8 hours.

- Serve over noodles. Serves 4 to 6.

Classy Beef and Noodles

2 pounds lean round steak, cut in strips	910 g
Olive oil	
2 (10 ounce) cans golden mushroom soup	2 (280 g)
½ cup cooking sherry	125 ml
1 (1 ounce) packet onion-mushroom soup mix	30 g
1 (12 ounce) package fettuccini (medium egg noodles) pasta	340 g
¼ cup (½ stick) butter	60 g

- Preheat oven to 325° (160° C).

- Brown steak strips in skillet with a little oil and drain off fat. Stir in mushroom soup, sherry, onion-mushroom soup mix and ¾ cup (175 ml) water. Spoon into sprayed 3-quart (3 L) baking dish, cover and bake for 1 hour or until steak is tender.

- Cook noodles in saucepan according to package directions, drain and stir in butter. Spoon onto serving platter and spoon steak mixture over noodles. Serves 8 to 10.

Ready Noodles

1 (8 ounce) package fettuccini (medium egg noodles) pasta	230 g
2 (12 ounce) cans corned beef	2 (340 g)
2 (10 ounce) cans cream of celery soup	2 (280 g)
¾ cup mayonnaise	170 g
½ cup milk	125 ml
1 (10 ounce) package frozen green peas, thawed	280 g
1 (4 ounce) jar chopped pimentos, drained	115 g
¼ cup chopped onion	40 g
½ cup shredded cheddar cheese	60 g

- Preheat oven to 350° (175° C).

- Cook noodles in saucepan according to package directions, drain and place in large bowl. Break up corned beef until crumbly.

- Add beef and remaining ingredients, except cheese; mix until they blend well.

- Transfer to sprayed 3-quart (3 L) baking dish; cover and bake for 25 minutes. Uncover and sprinkle cheese over top and return to oven for 5 minutes. Serves 8 to 10.

Pasta needs a lot of water to cook properly. Use at least two quarts for every eight ounces of dried pasta.

Pantry Corned Beef Bake

1 (15 ounce) can corned beef, diced	425 g
1 cup shredded cheddar cheese	115 g
1 (10 ounce) can cream of mushroom soup	280 g
1 cup milk	250 ml
1 small onion, finely chopped	
1 red bell pepper, seeded, chopped	
1 (8 ounce) package pappardelle (wide egg noodles) pasta, cooked, drained	230 g

- Preheat oven to 350° (175° C).

- Combine corned beef, cheese, mushroom soup, milk, onion, bell pepper and a little black pepper in large bowl; mix well. Stir in cooked noodles and mix until all ingredients blend well.

- Spoon into sprayed 3-quart (3 L) baking dish, cover and bake for 45 minutes or until mixture is thoroughly hot. Serves 6.

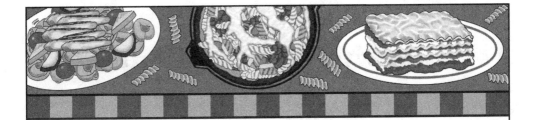

Pasta with Chicken

Chicken is so versatile and when you add pasta, it's great for everyday meals – and entertaining.

Pasta with Chicken Contents

Pasta with Chicken Contents

Naples, Italy, became a center for mass-producing pasta in the 1800's because its climate was perfect for the drying process. Now, modern equipment makes it possible to make dried pasta anywhere and everywhere and pasta is the most well-known Italian food all around the world.

A Twist on Tetrazzini

3 boneless skinless chicken
   breast halves
1 rib celery, sliced
½ cup (1 stick) butter   115 g
1 (4 ounce) can sliced
   mushrooms, drained   115 g
1 (12 ounce) can evaporated
   milk   340 g
1 (8 ounce) package
   shredded Velveeta®
   cheese   230 g
1 (8 ounce) package
   fettuccini (medium egg
   noodles) pasta, cooked,
   drained   230 g
⅓ cup crushed corn flake
   crumbs   10 g

- Preheat oven to 350° (175° C).

- Boil chicken and celery in large saucepan with boiling, salted water for about 30 minutes. Remove chicken and celery from water and cool. When chicken cools enough, shred and set aside.

- Melt butter in large skillet and add mushrooms and a little salt and pepper. Add evaporated milk, cheese and a little salt and pepper on medium heat; stir until cheese melts. Stir in shredded chicken and bring to a slow boil. Remove from heat.

- Spoon cooked noodles into sprayed 9 x 13-inch (23 x 33 cm) baking dish and spread with back of large spoon. Spoon mushroom-chicken mixture over noodles and stir just slightly, not thoroughly.

- Sprinkle corn flake crumbs over top, cover and bake for 25 minutes. Uncover and cook for additional 10 minutes. Serves 6 to 8.

Alfredo-Chicken Spaghetti

1 (8 ounce) package
    vermicelli (thin spaghetti)
    pasta, broken in thirds   230 g
2 teaspoons minced garlic   10 ml
1 (16 ounce) jar alfredo
    sauce   455 g
¼ cup milk   60 ml
1 (10 ounce) box broccoli
    florets, thawed   280 g
2 cups cooked, diced
    chicken   280 g

- Cook spaghetti in saucepan according to package directions and drain. Place back in saucepan and stir in garlic, alfredo sauce and milk and mix well.

- Add drained broccoli florets and cook on medium heat for about 5 minutes and stir several times or until broccoli is tender.

- Add more milk if mixture gets too dry. Stir in diced chicken and spoon into serving bowl. Serves 6.

Artichoke-Chicken Pasta

1½ pounds boneless chicken
    breast tenders   680 g
1 (15 ounce) can artichoke
    hearts, quartered   425 g
¾ cup roasted red peppers,
    chopped   100 g
1 (8 ounce) package
    American cheese,
    shredded   230 g
1 tablespoon white wine
    Worcestershire sauce   15 ml
1 (10 ounce) can cream
    of chicken soup   280 g
1 (8 ounce) package
    shredded cheddar
    cheese   230 g
4 cups hot, cooked farfalle
    (bow-tie) pasta   300 g

- Combine chicken tenders, artichoke, roasted peppers, American cheese, Worcestershire sauce and soup in slow cooker and mix well.

- Cover and cook on LOW for 6 to 8 hours. About 20 minutes before serving, fold in cheddar cheese, hot pasta, and a little salt and pepper. Serves 8.

Bright Broccoli over Fettuccini

1 (8 ounce) package cream cheese, cubed	230 g
¼ cup (½ stick) butter	60 g
⅔ cup half-and-half cream	210 g
2 boneless, skinless chicken breast halves, cooked, cubed	
1 (16 ounce) package frozen chopped broccoli, thawed	455 g
1 red bell pepper, seeded, chopped	
1 (8 ounce) package fettuccini (medium egg noodles) pasta, cooked, drained	230 g

- Melt cream cheese and butter in large skillet over low heat and stir until smooth.

- Add half-and-half cream, chicken, broccoli and bell pepper; cook, stirring often, over medium heat for 3 minutes. Reduce heat and cook for additional 5 minutes.

- Serve broccoli mixture over cooked fettuccini. Serves 6 to 8.

Busy Day Chicken Casserole

6 boneless, skinless chicken breast halves, cooked	
1 (1 pint) carton sour cream	480 g
1 (7 ounce) package ready-cut spaghetti pasta	200 g
2 (10 ounce) cans cream of chicken soup	2 (280 g)
1 (4 ounce) can mushrooms, drained	115 g
½ cup (1 stick) butter, melted	115 g
1 cup grated fresh parmesan cheese	100 g

- Preheat oven to 350° (175° C).

- Cut chicken into strips and combine all ingredients, except parmesan cheese with ⅛ teaspoon (.5 ml) pepper and mix well.

- Pour into sprayed 9 x 13-inch (23 x 33 cm) baking dish and sprinkle cheese on top. Cover and bake for 50 minutes. Serves 8.

Broccoli-Fusilli in Cream Sauce

1 (16 ounce) package broccoli florets	455 g
1 (12 ounce) package fusilli (spiral) pasta	340 g
½ cup olive oil	125 ml
4 teaspoons minced garlic	20 ml
4 boneless, skinless chicken breast halves, cut into strips	
1 cup cooking white wine	250 ml
1 (10 ounce) can chicken broth	280 g
1 (8 ounce) carton whipping cream	230 g
½ cup shredded mozzarella cheese	60 g

- Cook broccoli in boiling water for about 4 minutes or until tender-crisp. Drain and transfer broccoli to large bowl. Add fusilli to pot with broccoli water and cook just until tender; drain.

- Heat oil in large skillet and cook garlic and chicken strips for about 5 minutes. Drain and transfer chicken-garlic to bowl with broccoli.

- Stir in wine, broth and cream in skillet and bring to a boil. Reduce heat to medium and cook for 8 minutes, stirring constantly, until sauce thickens slightly.

- Add pasta, broccoli, chicken and cheese to sauce and toss until mixture coats evenly with sauce. Serve immediately. Serves 6.

Rice pasta and brown rice pasta are available for people allergic to gluten (wheat).

Champion Chicken with Chives

1 pound boneless, skinless chicken breast halves	455 g
1 teaspoon seasoned salt	5 ml
1 teaspoon lemon pepper	5 ml
1 tablespoon olive oil	15 ml
1 (10 ounce) package frozen chopped bell peppers and onions	280 g
¾ cup milk	175 ml
2 tablespoons butter	30 g
1 (5 ounce) package Pasta Roni® with sour cream and chives	145 g
1 (4 ounce) can chopped green chilies	115 g
2 tablespoons chopped fresh chives	30 ml

- Cut chicken into thin strips. Season strips with seasoned salt and lemon pepper.

- Heat oil in large skillet over medium-high heat and cook chicken strips, bell pepper and onions for about 5 minutes or until chicken is no longer pink. Remove from skillet and set aside.

- In same skillet, bring 1¼ cups (310 ml) water, milk and butter to a boil. Reduce heat to medium, cook pasta and special seasoning for about 10 minutes and stir often.

- Stir in chicken strips and green chilies, spoon into serving bowl and sprinkle with chopped chives. Let stand for 5 minutes before serving. Serves 4.

Cheesy Fettuccini and Chicken

1 (9 ounce) package refrigerated fettuccini (medium egg noodles) pasta	255 g
2 cups small fresh broccoli florets	140 g
⅓ cup Italian salad dressing, divided	75 ml
1 pound chicken breast strips for stir-fry	455 g
½ red onion, cut into wedges	
1 (7 ounce) jar roasted red bell peppers, drained, sliced	200 g
1 (5 ounce) package grated parmesan cheese	145 g

- Cook fettuccini with broccoli florets according to package directions on fettuccini. Drain and toss with 2 tablespoons (30 ml) salad dressing. Cover and keep warm.

- Spray large skillet and heat over medium-high heat. Add chicken strips, onion and a little salt and pepper. Cook for about 5 minutes, stirring often until chicken is no longer pink in center.

- Stir in bell peppers and remaining salad dressing and cook for about 3 minutes, stirring often until mixture is warm. Serve chicken mixture over fettuccini and broccoli. Sprinkle with parmesan cheese when ready to serve. Serves 8

Cheesy, Cheesy Chicken

Cheese lovers dig in!
This is a real winner!

1 onion, chopped
1 red and ½ green bell pepper,
    seeded chopped
½ cup (1 stick) butter,
    divided   115 g
1 (10 ounce) can cream of
    chicken soup   280 g
1 (4 ounce) can sliced
    mushrooms   115 g
½ teaspoon dried cilantro 2 ml
½ teaspoon dried basil   2 ml
1 teaspoon celery salt   5 ml
½ teaspoon garlic pepper 2 ml
1 (8 ounce) package
    fettuccini (medium
    egg noodles) pasta,
    cooked al dente, drained 230 g
4 - 5 boneless, skinless
    chicken breast halves,
    cooked, cubed
1 (15 ounce) carton ricotta
    cheese   425 g

1 (16 ounce) package
    shredded cheddar
    cheese   455 g
⅓ cup grated parmesan
    cheese   35 g
1 cup breadcrumbs   60 g

- Preheat oven to 350° (175° C).

- Saute onion and bell peppers with 5 tablespoons (75 g) butter in skillet. Remove from heat and stir in soup, mushrooms, cilantro, basil, celery salt, garlic pepper and a little salt.

- Combine noodles, chicken, cheeses and soup-mushroom mixture in large bowl. Mix well.

- Spoon into sprayed 9 x 13-inch (23 x 33 cm) baking dish.

- Melt 3 tablespoons (45 g) butter and combine with breadcrumbs. Sprinkle over casserole.

- Cover and bake for 45 minutes. Serves 8.

Chicken Alfredo

1½ pounds boneless chicken
    thighs   680 g
2 ribs celery, sliced diagonally
1 red bell pepper, seeded,
    julienned
1 (16 ounce) jar alfredo
    sauce   455 g
3 cups fresh broccoli florets   215 g
1 (8 ounce) package
    linguine (thin egg
    noodles) pasta   230 g
1 (5 ounce) package grated
    parmesan cheese   145 g

- Cut chicken into strips. Layer chicken, celery and bell pepper in 4 to 5-quart (4 to 5 L) slow cooker. Pour alfredo sauce evenly over vegetables. Cover and cook on LOW for 5 to 6 hours.

- About 30 minutes before serving, turn heat to HIGH and add broccoli florets to chicken-alfredo mixture. Cover and cook for additional 30 minutes.

- Cook pasta according to package directions and drain. Just before serving pour pasta into cooker, mix and sprinkle parmesan cheese on top. Serves 8.

Chicken and Noodles

2 pounds boneless, skinless
    chicken breast halves   910 g
¼ cup cornstarch   30 g
⅓ cup soy sauce   75 ml
2 onions, chopped
3 ribs celery, sliced diagonally
1 red bell pepper, seeded,
    julienned
2 (14 ounce) cans mixed
    Chinese vegetables,
    drained   2 (400 g)
¼ cup molasses   60 ml
2 cups chow mein noodles,
    cooked   110 g

- Place chicken breasts and 2 cups (500 ml) water in sprayed slow cooker. Cover and cook on LOW for 3 to 4 hours. At least 1 hour before serving, remove chicken and cut into bite-size pieces.

- Combine cornstarch and soy sauce in bowl and mix well. Stir into slow cooker. Add onions, celery, bell pepper, mixed vegetables and molasses. Turn heat to HIGH and cook for 1 to 2 hours.

- Serve over chow mein noodles. Serves 4 to 6.

Chicken and Pasta

1 (16 ounce) package frozen
    whole green beans,
    thawed   **455 g**
1 onion, chopped
1 cup fresh mushroom
    halves   **70 g**
3 boneless, skinless
    chicken breast halves
1 (15 ounce) can Italian
    stewed tomatoes   **425 g**
1 teaspoon chicken
    bouillon granules   **5 ml**
1 teaspoon minced garlic   **5 ml**
1 teaspoon Italian seasoning **5 ml**
1 (8 ounce) package
    fettuccini (medium
    egg noodles) pasta   **230 g**
1 (4 ounce) package grated
    parmesan cheese   **115 g**

- Place green beans, onion and mushrooms in sprayed 4-quart (4 L) slow cooker.

- Cut chicken into 1-inch (2.5 cm) pieces and place over vegetables.

- Combine stewed tomatoes, chicken bouillon, garlic and Italian seasoning in small bowl. Pour over chicken.

- Cover and cook on LOW for 5 to 6 hours.

- Cook fettuccini according to package directions and drain.

- Serve chicken over fettuccini sprinkled with parmesan cheese. Serves 4.

TIP: *Add ¼ cup (60 g) butter to make this dish have a richer taste.*

Chicken and Spaghetti

How could anything be easier?

4 boneless, skinless chicken
    breast halves, cooked,
    cubed
2 (8 ounce) cartons sour
    cream   **2 (230 g)**
1 (7 ounce) box ready-cut
    spaghetti pasta   **200 g**
2 (10 ounce) cans cream
    of chicken soup   **2 (280 g)**
1 (4 ounce) can
    mushrooms, drained **115 g**
½ cup (1 stick) butter,
    melted   **115 g**
1 cup grated parmesan
    cheese   **100 g**

- Preheat oven to 325° (160° C).

- Combine chicken, sour cream, spaghetti, chicken soup, mushrooms, butter and ¼ teaspoon (1 ml) pepper in large bowl.

- Pour into sprayed 9 x 13-inch (23 x 33 cm) baking dish.

- Sprinkle cheese on top of casserole.

- Cover and bake for 50 minutes. Serves 8.

There is a legend that Marco Polo, the explorer from Venice, brought pasta to Italy from China in the 13th century. But pasta existed in Italy even before Rome was founded.

Chicken and Spinach Fettuccini

1 (8 ounce) package spinach
fettuccini (medium egg
noodles) pasta   230 g
1 (6 ounce) jar marinated
artichoke hearts   170 g
1 small onion, finely
chopped
1 red bell pepper, seeded,
chopped
1 cup half-and-half cream   310 g
⅔ cup grated parmesan
cheese   70 g
2½ cups cooked, cubed
chicken breasts   350 g

- Cook fettuccini according to package directions; drain and keep warm.

- Cut artichokes in half; drain and set aside 2 tablespoons (30 ml) marinade. Heat marinade to boiling in large skillet and add onion and bell pepper. Cook for about 5 minutes, stirring often or until tender-crisp.

- Stir half-and-half cream into onion-bell pepper mixture and heat, but not boiling.

- Stir in artichoke hearts, cheese and chicken and mix until blended well. Add fettuccini and toss. Sprinkle with black pepper. Serves 8.

Dried pasta is called pasta secca in Italy; fresh pasta is called pasta fresca.

Chicken and Vegetables

1 (3 ounce) package
   chicken-flavored
   instant ramen noodles   85 g
1 (16 ounce) package
   frozen broccoli,
   cauliflower and carrots   455 g
⅔ cup sweet-and-sour sauce 150 ml
3 boneless, skinless chicken
   breast halves, cooked,
   cut into thin strips

- Reserve seasoning packet from noodles. Cook noodles and vegetables in 2 cups (500 ml) boiling water in saucepan for 3 minutes, stirring occasionally and drain.

- Combine noodle-vegetable mixture with seasoning packet, sweet-and-sour sauce and a little salt and pepper. (You may want to add 1 tablespoon/15 ml soy sauce.)

- Add chicken and heat thoroughly. Serves 8.

Chicken Delight

5 - 6 boneless, skinless
   chicken breast halves
1 teaspoon chicken
   seasoning   5 ml
1 (10 ounce) can cream
   of chicken soup   280 g
1 (10 ounce) can broccoli-
   cheese soup   280 g
½ cup white cooking wine   125 ml
1 (12 ounce) package
   fettuccini (medium
   egg noodles) pasta,
   cooked   340 g

- Cut chicken breasts in half if they are unusually large. Place breast halves, sprinkled with pepper and chicken seasoning in sprayed slow cooker.

- Combine soups and wine in saucepan and heat enough to mix well. Pour over chicken. Cover and cook on LOW for 5 to 6 hours. Serve chicken and sauce over hot, cooked noodles. Serves 8 to 10.

Chicken Chow Mein

3½ cups cooked, cubed
   chicken breasts   490 g
2 (10 ounce) cans cream
   of chicken soup   2 (280 g)
2 (15 ounce) cans chop
   suey vegetables,
   drained   2 (425 g)
1 (8 ounce) can sliced
   water chestnuts,
   drained   230 g
¾ cup chopped cashews   100 g
1 green bell pepper,
   seeded, chopped
1 onion, chopped
1 cup chopped celery   100 g
¼ teaspoon hot sauce   1 ml
1¼ cups chow mein
   noodles   125 g

- Preheat oven to 350° (175° C).

- Combine chicken, soup, vegetables, water chestnuts, cashew nuts, bell pepper, onion, celery and hot sauce in large bowl. Stir to mix well.

- Spoon into sprayed 9 x 13-inch (23 x 33 cm) baking dish. Sprinkle chow mein noodles over top of casserole.

- Bake for 35 minutes or until it bubbles at edges of casserole. Let stand for 5 minutes before serving. Serves 8.

Because pasta has such a long shelf life, it was often used for ocean voyages in the days of sailing ships.

Chicken Dish, WOW!

1 (10 ounce) can cream of chicken soup	280 g
1 (10 ounce) can fiesta nacho cheese	280 g
1 (5 ounce) can evaporated milk	145 g
2 (15 ounce) cans French-style green beans, drained	2 (425 g)
1 teaspoon chicken bouillon granules	5 ml
4 cups cooked, cubed chicken breasts	560 g
1 red bell pepper, chopped	
2 ribs celery, sliced	
¼ cup chopped onion	40 g
1 cup chow mein noodles	55 g
½ cup slivered almonds	85 g
1 (3 ounce) can french-fried onions	85 g

- Preheat oven to 350° (175° C).

- Combine soup, fiesta nacho cheese and evaporated milk and mix well.

- Fold in green beans, chicken bouillon, chicken, bell pepper, celery, onion, noodles, almonds, and ½ teaspoon (2 ml) each of salt and pepper.

- Spoon into sprayed 9 x 13-inch (23 x 33 cm) baking dish.

- Cover and bake for 35 minutes. Remove from oven and sprinkle french-fried onions over casserole.

- Place back in oven and bake for additional 10 minutes. Serves 8 to 10.

TIP: *This casserole may easily be made ahead of time and baked the next day. Just wait to add the french-fried onions until called for.*

Chicken Elegant

This is rich, but worth the calories!

3 tablespoons butter	75 g
3 tablespoons flour	45 g
1¾ cups milk	425 ml
½ cup shredded sharp cheddar cheese	115 g
½ cup shredded Swiss cheese	110 g
½ teaspoon Worcestershire sauce	2 ml
1 cup cooked, diced chicken	140 g
1 cup cooked, diced ham	140 g
1 (4 ounce) can sliced mushrooms, drained	115 g
2 tablespoons chopped pimento	30 ml
Fettuccini (medium egg noodles) pasta, cooked	

- Melt butter in saucepan and blend in flour. Add milk all at once, cook and stir until sauce is thick and bubbly. Remove from heat, add cheeses and stir until they melt.

- Stir in Worcestershire sauce, chicken or turkey, ham, mushrooms and pimento. Heat thoroughly and serve over noodles. Serves 6 to 8.

Chicken Supper

5 boneless, skinless chicken breast halves	
1 (16 ounce) jar alfredo sauce	455 g
1 (16 ounce) package frozen green peas, thawed	455 g
1½ cups shredded mozzarella cheese	175 g
1 (8 ounce) package pappardelle (wide egg noodles) pasta, cooked	230 g
2 tablespoons butter	30 g

- Cut chicken into strips and place in sprayed slow cooker.

- Combine alfredo sauce, peas and cheese in bowl and mix well. Spoon over chicken strips.

- Cover and cook on LOW for 5 to 6 hours.

- When ready to serve, spoon over hot, cooked noodles with butter. Serves 4 to 5.

TIP: If you want chicken supper in 1 casserole, cook 1 (8 ounce/230 g) package noodles and mix with chicken and peas. Sprinkle a little extra cheese over top and serve.

Chicken Lasagna

1 (16 ounce) jar alfredo
   sauce   455 g
1 (4 ounce) can diced
   pimentos, drained   115 g
⅓ cup cooking white wine 75 ml
1 (10 ounce) box frozen
   chopped spinach,
   thawed   280 g
1 (15 ounce) carton ricotta
   cheese   425 g
½ cup grated parmesan
   cheese   50 g
1 egg, beaten
8 lasagna noodles
3 cups cooked, shredded
   chicken   420 g
1 (12 ounce) package
   shredded cheddar
   cheese   340 g

- Preheat oven to 350° (175° C).

- Combine alfredo sauce, pimentos and wine in large bowl; reserve ½ cup (125 ml) for top of lasagna.

- Squeeze spinach between paper towels to completely remove excess moisture. In separate bowl, combine spinach, ricotta, parmesan cheese and egg. Mix well.

- Place 4 noodles in sprayed 9 x 13-inch (23 x 33 cm) baking dish. Layer with half remaining sauce, half spinach-ricotta mixture and half chicken. (Spinach-ricotta mixture will be fairly dry so you will need to "spoon" it on and spread out.)

- Sprinkle with half cheese. For last layer, place noodles, remaining sauce, remaining spinach-rocotta mixture, remaining chicken and reserved sauce on top.

- Cover and bake for 45 minutes. Uncover and sprinkle remaining cheese over top and return to oven for 6 minutes. Let casserole stand for 10 minutes before serving. Serves 10 to 12.

Chicken Linguine

1 pound boneless, skinless
  chicken breast halves,
  cut into strips   455 g
Olive oil
1 (28 ounce) can garlic-
  onion spaghetti sauce   795 g
1 (16 ounce) package
  frozen broccoli, carrots
  and cauliflower, thawed   455 g
1 bell pepper, seeded,
  chopped
⅓ cup grated parmesan
  cheese   30 g
1 (12 ounce) package
  linguine (thin egg
  noodles) pasta, cooked,
  drained   340 g

- Cook half chicken strips with a little oil in large skillet over medium-heat until light brown. Remove and set aside. Repeat with remaining chicken and set aside.

- In same skillet combine spaghetti sauce, vegetables and cheese and bring to a boil. Reduce heat to medium-low, cover and cook for 10 minutes or until vegetables are tender. Stir occasionally.

- Return chicken to skillet and heat thoroughly.

- Place cooked linguine on serving platter and spoon chicken mixture over linguine. Serves 12.

TIP: *Break linguine into thirds before cooking to make serving a little easier.*

Linguine, like most pastas, gets its name from its shape; the word means "little tongues".

Chicken Meets Italy

1 (16 ounce) package frozen whole green beans, thawed	455 g
1 onion, chopped	
1 cup halved fresh mushrooms	70 g
3 boneless, skinless chicken breast halves	
1 (15 ounce) can Italian stewed tomatoes	425 g
1 teaspoon chicken bouillon granules	5 ml
1 teaspoon minced garlic	5 ml
1 teaspoon Italian seasoning	5 ml
1 (8 ounce) package fettuccini (medium egg noodles) pasta	230 g
1 (4 ounce) package parmesan cheese	145 g

- Place green beans, onion and mushrooms in sprayed 4 to 5-quart (4 to 5 L) slow cooker. Cut chicken into 1-inch (2.5 cm) pieces and place over vegetables.

- Combine stewed tomatoes, chicken bouillon, garlic and Italian seasoning in small bowl. Pour over chicken. Cover and cook on LOW for 5 to 6 hours.

- Cook fettuccini according to package directions and drain. Serve chicken over fettuccini and sprinkle with parmesan cheese. Serves 8.

TIP: *For added flavor, you can add ¼ cup (60 g) butter.*

Chicken Parmesan and Spaghetti

1 (14 ounce) package frozen,
    cooked, breaded
    chicken cutlets,
    thawed   400 g
1 (28 ounce) jar spaghetti
    sauce   795 g
2 (5 ounce) packages
    grated parmesan
    cheese, divided   2 (145 g)
1 (8 ounce) package
    vermicelli (thin
    spaghetti) pasta,
    cooked   230 g

- Preheat oven to 375° (190° C).

- Place cutlets in sprayed
  9 x 13-inch (23 x 33 cm) baking
  dish and top each with about
  ¼ cup (60 ml) spaghetti sauce
  and 1 heaping tablespoon (15 ml)
  parmesan. Bake for 15 minutes.

- Place cooked spaghetti on serving
  platter and top with cutlets.
  Sprinkle remaining cheese over
  cutlets. Heat remaining spaghetti
  sauce and serve with chicken and
  spaghetti. Serves 6 to 8.

Chicken Spaghetti

3 boneless, skinless chicken
    breasts, boiled
1 (10 ounce) can tomatoes
    and green chilies   280 g
1 (10 ounce) can cream
    of mushroom soup   280 g
1 (8 ounce) package
    shredded cheddar
    cheese   230 g
1 (8 ounce) package
    shredded Velveeta®
    cheese   230 g
1 (12 ounce) package
    spaghetti pasta   340 g

- Preheat oven to 350° (175° C).

- Shred cooked chicken into large
  bowl. Add tomatoes, soup, cheddar
  cheese and Velveeta® cheese. Boil
  spaghetti in saucepan according to
  package directions and drain.

- Add to chicken mixture and mix
  well. Pour into 3-quart (3 L)
  baking dish. Cover and bake for
  35 minutes. Serves 6.

Chicken Tarragon

*Tarragon works wonders
for this chicken.*

1 (8 ounce) package
    fettuccini (medium egg
    noodles) pasta   **230 g**
1 cup dry white wine   **250 ml**
1 teaspoon dried tarragon
    leaves   **5 ml**
1 (1 ounce) packet
    vegetable soup mix   **30 g**
4 boneless, skinless chicken
    breast halves
1 (8 ounce) carton sour
    cream   **230 g**

- Cook noodles in saucepan according to package directions, drain and set aside. Pour 2 cups (500 ml) water to large skillet. Over medium heat add wine and tarragon and bring to boil. Stir in dry soup mix and boil 5 minutes.

- Add chicken and reduce heat. Cover and simmer for 15 minutes or until juices run clear. Arrange noodles on serving dish. Use slotted spoon to remove chicken, place on top of noodles and cover with foil.

- Boil juices in skillet for about 5 to 10 minutes or until liquid reduces to ½ cup

- (125 ml). Turn heat to low and stir constantly while adding sour cream. Heat 3 to 4 minutes more and pour over chicken. Serves 6.

*It is better to measure dried pasta by weight
(ounces/grams) rather than by volume (cups/milliliters).*

Chicken with Mushrooms and Peppers

1 (16 ounce) carton fresh mushrooms, sliced, divided	455 g
2 red bell peppers, seeded, chopped, divided	
1½ cups seasoned breadcrumbs	90 g
6 boneless, skinless chicken breast halves	
2 eggs, beaten	
2 tablespoons butter	30 ml
6 slices Swiss cheese	
1 cup chicken broth	250 ml
1 (12 ounce) package fettuccini (medium egg noodles) pasta	340 g
2 tablespoons butter	30 g

- Preheat oven to 350° (175° C).

- Place half mushrooms and half bell peppers into sprayed 9 x 13-inch (23 x 33 cm) baking dish.

- Place breadcrumbs in shallow bowl. Dip each chicken breast in beaten eggs and dredge in breadcrumbs.

- Melt butter in large skillet, brown both sides of chicken and place chicken on top of mushroom-pepper mixture in baking dish. Arrange remaining mushroom-pepper mixture over chicken breast.

- Place cheese slices over chicken and pour broth in baking dish. Cover and bake for 35 minutes.

- Cook noodles according to package directions, drain and add butter. Stir until butter melts and place noodles on serving platter.

- Arrange chicken, mushrooms and peppers over noodles and serve hot. Serves 6.

Chicken-Broccoli Casserole

8 boneless, skinless chicken breast halves, sliced	
½ cup (1 stick) butter	115 g
½ cup flour	60 g
2 cups half-and-half cream	625 g
1 (14 ounce) can chicken broth	400 g
1 (8 ounce) package shredded cheddar cheese, divided	230 g
1 (5 ounce) package fresh grated parmesan cheese	145 g
2 tablespoons lemon juice	30 ml
1 tablespoon mustard	15 ml
2 tablespoons dried parsley	10 g
1 tablespoon dried onion flakes or 3 tablespoons fresh chopped onion	15 ml/30 g
¾ cup mayonnaise	170 g
2 (10 ounce) boxes frozen broccoli florets, slightly cooked	2 (280 g)
1 (7 ounce) package vermicelli (thin spaghetti) pasta	200 g

- Preheat oven to 350° (175° C).

- Wash chicken and dry well with paper towels. Melt butter in large saucepan or roasting pan and add flour.

- Add half-and-half cream and stir constantly over medium-low heat until thick. Add chicken broth, half cheddar cheese, parmesan cheese, lemon juice, ¼ teaspoon (1 ml) pepper, mustard, parsley, onion and 2 teaspoons (10 ml) salt.

- Heat on low until cheeses melt. Remove from heat and add mayonnaise. Add broccoli and chicken slices to sauce.

- Cook spaghetti according to package directions. Drain and pour into 10 x 15-inch (25 x 38 cm) glass dish. (This will not fit in 9 x 13-inch/23 x 33 cm glass dish.)

- Spread sauce and chicken mixture over spaghetti and sprinkle remaining cheese over top. Cook for 40 minutes. Serves 8 to 10.

Chicken-Ham Lasagna

1 (4 ounce) can chopped
    mushrooms, drained   115 g
1 large onion, chopped
¼ cup (½ stick) butter   60 g
½ cup flour   60 g
Ground nutmeg
1 (14 ounce) can chicken
    broth   400 g
1 (1 pint) carton half-and-
    half cream   500 ml
1 (3 ounce) package grated
    parmesan cheese   85 g
1 (16 ounce) package frozen
    broccoli florets   455 g
9 lasagna noodles, cooked,
    drained
1½ cups cooked, finely diced
    ham, divided   210 g
1 (12 ounce) package
    shredded Monterey
    Jack cheese, divided   340 g
2 cups cooked, shredded
    chicken breasts   280 g

- Preheat oven to 350° (175° C).

- Saute mushrooms and onion in butter in large skillet. Stir in flour, 1 teaspoon (5 ml) salt and ¼ teaspoon (1 ml) pepper and a dash of nutmeg and stir until they blend well.

- Gradually stir in broth and half-and-half cream, cook and stir for about 2 minutes or until it thickens. Stir in parmesan cheese.

- Cut broccoli florets into smaller pieces and add to cream mixture. Discard stems.

- Spread about ½ cup (125 ml) cream-broccoli mixture in sprayed 10 x 15-inch (25 x 38 cm) baking dish. Layer with 3 noodles, one-third of remaining broccoli mixture, ½ cup (120 ml) ham, 1 cup (240 ml) chicken and 1 cup (240 ml) Monterey Jack cheese.

- Top with 3 more noodles, one-third of broccoli mixture, 1 cup (240 ml) ham, 1 cup (240 ml) chicken and 1 cup (120 ml) Monterey Jack cheese. Pour in remaining noodles, chicken and cream-broccoli mixture.

- Cover and bake for 50 minutes or until it bubbles. Sprinkle with remaining cheese. Let stand for 15 minutes before cutting into squares to serve. Serves 8 to 10.

Chicken-Noodle Delight

This recipe is a hearty main dish and the bell peppers make it colorful as well. It's a great family supper.

2 ribs celery, chopped
½ onion, chopped
½ green bell pepper, seeded, chopped
½ red bell pepper, seeded, chopped
6 tablespoons (¾ stick) butter, divided   90 g
3 cups cooked, cubed chicken breasts   420 g
1 (4 ounce) can sliced mushrooms, drained   115 g
1 (16 ounce) jar sun-dried tomato alfredo sauce   455 g
½ cup half-and-half cream   155 g
1½ teaspoons chicken bouillon granules   7 ml
1 (8 ounce) package fettuccini (medium egg noodles) pasta, cooked, drained   230 g

- Preheat oven to 325° (160° C).

- Combine celery, onion, bell peppers and 4 tablespoons (60 g) butter in skillet or large saucepan and saute for about 5 minutes.

- Remove from heat and add chicken, mushrooms, alfredo sauce, half-and-half cream, chicken bouillon and noodles and mix well. Pour into sprayed 3-quart (3 L) baking dish.

Topping:

1 cup corn flake crumbs   30 g
½ cup shredded cheddar cheese   60 g

- Combine topping ingredients in bowl and sprinkle over casserole. Bake for 20 minutes or until casserole bubbles around edges. Serves 6.

Chicken-Orzo Florentine

4 boneless, skinless chicken
    breast halves
¾ cup orzo (tiny) pasta   130 g
1 (8 ounce) package fresh
    mushrooms, sliced   230 g
1 (10 ounce) package frozen
    spinach, thawed,
    drained*   280 g
1 (10 ounce) can golden
    mushroom soup   280 g
½ cup mayonnaise   110 g
1 tablespoon lemon juice   15 ml
1 (8 ounce) package
    shredded Monterey
    Jack cheese   230 g
½ cup seasoned Italian
    breadcrumbs   60 g

- Preheat oven to 350° (175° C).

- Cook chicken in boiling water for about 15 minutes and reserve broth. Cut chicken in bite-size pieces and set aside. Pour broth through strainer and cook orzo in remaining broth.

- Saute mushrooms in large, sprayed skillet until tender. Remove from heat and stir in chicken, orzo, spinach, soup, mayonnaise, lemon juice and ½ teaspoon (2 ml) pepper. Fold in half cheese and mix well.

- Spoon into sprayed 9 x 13-inch (23 x 33 cm) baking dish and sprinkle with remaining cheese and breadcrumbs. Bake for 35 minutes. Serves 6.

TIP: Squeeze spinach between paper towels to completely remove excess moisture.

Chicken-Orzo Supper

1 (5 ounce) box chicken-flavored orzo (tiny) pasta	145 g
1 (7 ounce) package cooked chicken strips	200 g
1 (10 ounce) package frozen corn	280 g
1 (10 ounce) package frozen cut green beans	280 g
¼ cup extra-virgin olive oil	60 ml
1 teaspoon minced garlic	5 ml

- Cook orzo in saucepan according to package directions. Add chicken strips, corn, green beans, olive oil, garlic, ¼ cup (60 ml) water and a little salt and pepper and mix well.

- Cook on low heat and stir several times until mixture is hot, for about 10 to 15 minutes. Serves 6.

Creamy Chicken Pasta

1 (10 ounce) package penne (tube) pasta	280 g
1 tablespoon olive oil	15 ml
2 (12 ounce) cans white chicken meat, drained	2 (340 g)
2 tablespoons prepared pesto	30 g
¾ cup whipping cream	60 g

- Cook penne pasta in large saucepan according to package directions. Drain and place back in saucepan. Gently stir in oil, chicken, pesto and whipping cream.

- Place saucepan over low heat, simmer just until cream is absorbed. Spoon into serving bowl and serve immediately. Serves 6.

Chicken-Pasta Supper Supreme

1 (10 ounce) package capelli
    d'angelo (angel hair)
    pasta   280 g
1 onion, chopped
1 red bell pepper, seeded,
    chopped
2 teaspoons minced garlic 10 ml
Olive oil
1 (10 ounce) package
    fresh baby spinach   280 g
2 tomatoes, chopped,
    drained
3 cups cooked, chopped
    chicken breasts   420 g
2 tablespoons, cooked,
    crumbled bacon   30 ml
½ (8 ounce) bottle creamy
    Italian salad dressing ½ (230 g)
¼ cup crumbled feta
    cheese   35 g

- Cook angle hair pasta in saucepan according to package directions. Drain and set aside.

- Saute onion, bell pepper and garlic in large skillet with little oil. Add spinach and ¼ cup (60 ml) water. Cover and cook for 3 minutes or until spinach wilts.

- Stir in tomatoes, chicken, bacon and salad dressing and cook until mixture heats thoroughly.

- Place pasta on serving platter and spoon chicken mixture over pasta. Sprinkle with feta cheese. Serves 8.

TIP: Leftover chicken or deli turkey may be substituted for chicken breasts.

Chicken-Spaghetti Bake

1 (10 ounce) package spaghetti pasta	280 g
1 onion, chopped	
1 rib celery, chopped	
1 bell pepper, seeded, chopped	
Olive oil	
1 (15 ounce) can Mexican stewed tomatoes	425 g
1 (4 ounce) can chopped mushrooms, drained	115 g
1 teaspoon minced garlic	5 ml
½ cup chicken broth	125 ml
4 cups cooked, cubed chicken	560 g
1 (12 ounce) package shredded Velveeta® cheese	340 g

- Preheat oven to 350° (175° C).

- Cook spaghetti in saucepan according to package directions.

- Saute onion, celery and bell pepper in saucepan with little oil. Add tomatoes, mushrooms, garlic, broth, chicken and a little salt and pepper.

- Stir in cheese and spoon into sprayed 4-quart (4 L) baking dish.

- Cover and bake for 45 minutes. Serves 8.

Pasta can be easily reheated in a microwave oven. Usually 1 to 3 minutes on HIGH will work and toss the pasta halfway through the cooking time. You can also put the pasta in a colander and pour very hot water over it.

Chicken-Spinach Lasagna

9 lasagna noodles, divided
½ cup (1 stick) butter   115 g
1 teaspoon minced garlic   5 ml
½ cup flour   60 g
1 (14 ounce) can chicken
    broth   400 g
1½ cups half-and-half
    cream   465 g
1 (16 ounce) package
    shredded mozzarella
    cheese, divided   455 g
1½ teaspoons oregano   7 ml
1 (15 ounce) carton ricotta
    cheese   425 g
2 cups cooked, shredded
    chicken   280 g
1 (16 ounce) package
    frozen chopped spinach,
    thawed, drained   455 g
¼ cup grated parmesan
    cheese   25 g

- Preheat oven to 350° (175° C).

- Cook lasagna noodles in saucepan according to package directions; drain and rinse with cold water. Place noodles (not touching) on sheet of wax paper.

- Melt butter in large saucepan on medium heat, add garlic and flour and stir until bubbly. Mix in broth and half-and-half cream, bring to a boil and stir constantly for 1 minute.

- Stir in half mozzarella and season with oregano, 1 teaspoon (15 ml) black pepper and a little salt. Remove from heat and set aside.

- Spread one-third broth-cream mixture in sprayed 9 x 13-inch (23 x 33 cm) baking pan. Layer with one-third noodles, ricotta, spinach and chicken.

- Place one-third noodles over chicken and layer broth-cream mixture, spinach and remaining mozzarella cheese.

- Arrange remaining 3 noodles over cheese and spread remaining broth-cream mixture evenly over noodles. Sprinkle with parmesan cheese and bake for 35 minutes. Let stand for 10 minutes before serving. Serves 10 to 12.

Chinese Chicken

3½ cups cooked, cubed
   chicken   490 g
2 (10 ounce) cans cream
   of chicken soup   2 (280 g)
1 (16 ounce) can chop
   suey vegetables,
   drained   455 g
1 (8 ounce) can sliced
   water chestnuts,
   drained   230 g
¾ cup cashew nuts   100 g
1 cup chopped green
   bell peppers   150 g
1 bunch green onions
   with tops, sliced
½ cup chopped celery   50 g
⅓ teaspoon hot sauce   2 ml
¼ teaspoon curry powder   1 ml
1 (5 ounce) can chow
   mein noodles   145 g

- Preheat oven to 350° (175° C).

- Combine chicken, soups, vegetables, water chestnuts, cashew nuts, bell pepper, green onions, celery, hot sauce and curry powder in large bowl. Stir to mix well.

- Spoon mixture into sprayed 9 x 13-inch (23 x 33 cm) glass baking dish and sprinkle chow mein noodles over casserole.

- Bake for 30 to 35 minutes or until bubbly at edges. Set aside for about 5 minutes before serving. Serves 6.

Americans eat about 20 pounds of pasta per person each year;
Italians, however, eat about 60 pounds per person every year.

Chinese Garden

*It is stretching a point to call
this Chinese, but the
combination of ingredients
makes a great tasting casserole.*

1 (6 ounce) package fried rice with almonds and oriental seasoning	170 g
2 tablespoons butter	30 g
1 onion, chopped	
2 cups chopped celery	200 g
1 (15 ounce) can Chinese vegetables, drained	425 g
1 (8 ounce) can sliced bamboo shoots	230 g
3½ cups cooked, chopped chicken	490 g
1 (10 ounce) can cream of chicken soup	280 g
1 cup mayonnaise	225 g
2 tablespoons soy sauce	30 ml
½ teaspoon garlic powder	2 ml
1 cup chop mein noodles	55 g

- Preheat oven to 350° (175° C).

- Cook rice in saucepan according to package directions and set aside.

- Heat butter in large skillet and saute onion and celery. Add Chinese vegetables, bamboo shoots and chicken and mix well.

- Heat chicken soup, mayonnaise, soy sauce, garlic powder and a little pepper in saucepan just enough to mix well.

- Combine rice, vegetable-chicken mixture and soup mixture in large bowl and mix well. Transfer to sprayed 3-quart (3 L) baking dish.

- Sprinkle chow mein noodles over casserole. Bake for 35 minutes. Serves 6 to 8.

Creamy Chicken Bake

1 (8 ounce) package fettuccini (medium egg noodles) pasta	230 g
1 (16 ounce) package frozen broccoli florets, thawed, trimmed	455 g
¼ cup (½ stick) butter, melted	60 g
1 (8 ounce) package shredded cheddar cheese	230 g
1 (10 ounce) can cream of chicken soup	280 g
1 cup half-and-half cream	310 g
¼ teaspoon ground mustard	1 ml
3 cups cooked, cubed chicken breasts	420 g
⅔ cup slivered almonds	110 g

- Preheat oven to 325° (160° C).

- Cook noodles in saucepan according to package directions, drain and keep warm.

- Combine noodles and broccoli in large bowl. Add butter and cheese and stir until cheese melts.

- Stir in chicken soup, half-and-half cream, mustard, chicken and 1 teaspoon (5 ml) each of salt and pepper. Spoon into sprayed 3-quart (3 L) baking dish.

- Cover and bake for about 25 minutes. Remove from oven, sprinkle with slivered almonds and cook for additional 15 minutes. Serves 6.

Creamy Lemon Fettuccini

1 (12 ounce) package fettuccini (medium egg noodles) pasta	340 g
2 bunches fresh asparagus, trimmed	
3 tablespoons olive oil	45 ml
2 cups bite-size chunks rotisserie chicken	280 g
¾ cup coarsely chopped walnuts	100 g
1 (16 ounce) jar light alfredo sauce	455 g
⅓ cup lemon juice	75 ml
½ cup shredded mozzarella cheese	60 g

• Preheat oven to 375° (190° C).

• Cook fettuccini in saucepan according to package directions, drain and return to pot, covered to keep warm. Cut asparagus into 2-inch (5 cm) pieces. Place asparagus in single layer in sprayed 9 x 13-inch (23 x 33 cm) baking dish and drizzle with oil; roast for 10 minutes.

• Add chicken, walnuts and a little salt and pepper and stir to blend well. Cook for an additional 5 minutes to toast walnuts lightly and stir often. Transfer fettuccini to serving bowl and spoon asparagus mixture over pasta. Toss to blend well.

• Pour alfredo sauce into microwave-safe bowl and heat on full power just until sauce begins to boil. Stir in lemon juice and pour over fettuccini-asparagus mixture. Toss well. Sprinkle with mozzarella cheese and serve immediately. Serves 6 to 8.

Delicious Chicken Pasta

1 pound chicken tenders	455 g
Lemon-herb chicken seasoning	
3 tablespoons butter	45 ml
1 onion, coarsely chopped	
1 (15 ounce) can diced tomatoes	425 g
1 (10 ounce) can golden mushroom soup	280 g
1 (8 ounce) box capelli d'angelo (angel hair) pasta	230 g

- Pat chicken tenders dry with several paper towels and sprinkle ample amount of chicken seasoning. Melt butter in large skillet, brown chicken and place in oval slow cooker. Pour remaining butter from skillet over chicken and cover with onion.

- In separate bowl, combine tomatoes and mushroom soup and pour over chicken and onions. Cover and cook on LOW for 4 to 5 hours.

- When ready to serve, cook pasta in saucepan according to package directions. Serve chicken and sauce over pasta. Serves 8.

Family-Night Spaghetti

6 frozen breaded, cooked chicken breast halves	
1 (8 ounce) package spaghetti pasta, cooked	230 g
1 (18 ounce) jar spaghetti sauce	510 g
1 (26 ounce) package shredded mozzarella cheese, divided	740 g

- Bake chicken breasts according to package directions and keep warm. Cook spaghetti in saucepan according to package directions, drain and arrange on platter.

- Place spaghetti sauce in saucepan with 1 cup (115 g) mozzarella cheese and heat slightly, but do not boil.

- Spoon about half sauce over spaghetti and arrange chicken breast over top. Spoon remaining spaghetti sauce on chicken and sprinkle remaining cheese over top. Serves 6.

Dijon-Tarragon Chicken

1 (8 ounce) package fettuccini (medium egg noodles) pasta	230 g
1 teaspoon seasoned salt	5 ml
2 tablespoons butter	30 g
1 pound boneless skinless chicken breasts, cut into ½-inch pieces	455 g/1.2 cm
1 (8 ounce) carton sour cream	230 g
2 tablespoons dijon-style mustard	30 g
1 teaspoon dried tarragon leaves	5 ml
½ cup frozen green peas, thawed	70 g
2 tablespoon chopped fresh parsley	10 g

- Cook fettuccini according to package directions, drain and cover to keep warm.

- Sprinkle seasoned salt over chicken. Melt butter in large skillet on medium-high heat. Cook chicken for 10 minutes, stirring frequently until center is no longer pink.

- Combine sour cream, mustard and tarragon leaves in small bowl, mix until smooth.

- Pour into skillet with chicken and add green peas. Cook for about 5 minutes, stirring frequently. Serve chicken mixture over fettuccini and sprinkle with parsley. Serves 6 to 8.

Extra Special Spaghetti

**4 - 5 boneless, skinless
chicken breast halves**
1 tablespoon olive oil   **15 ml**
**2 green bell peppers,
seeded, julienned**
1 onion, chopped
**1 (16 ounce) jar marinara
sauce**   **455 g**
**1 (8 ounce) package
shredded mozzarella
cheese, divided**   **230 g**
**1 (12 ounce) package
vermicelli (thin
spaghetti) pasta, cooked,
drained**   **340 g**

- Cut each chicken breast in 1-inch (2.5 cm) strips and sprinkle with salt and pepper. Place in large sprayed skillet and cook on medium-high heat for about 7 minutes on each side. Transfer chicken to plate and keep warm.

- In same skillet with oil, cook bell peppers and onion until tender for about 5 to 8 minutes. Add marinara sauce and chicken strips and bring to a boil. Reduce heat to medium-low and cook for 15 minutes. Add half mozzarella cheese and cook just until cheese melts.

- Place cooked spaghetti on serving platter and spoon chicken-sauce mixture over spaghetti. Sprinkle remaining cheese over top and serve immediately. Serves 8 to 10.

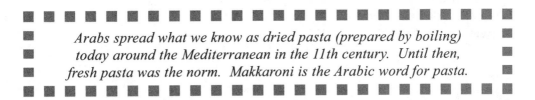

Arabs spread what we know as dried pasta (prepared by boiling) today around the Mediterranean in the 11th century. Until then, fresh pasta was the norm. Makkaroni is the Arabic word for pasta.

Family-Secret Chicken and Noodles

This is a great recipe to prepare ahead of time and freeze.

¼ cup (½ stick) butter	60 g
½ cup flour	60 g
½ teaspoon basil	2 ml
½ teaspoon parsley	2 ml
2 cups milk	500 ml
1 (4 ounce) can sliced mushrooms, drained	115 g
1 (10 ounce) can cream of mushroom soup	280 g
1 (2 ounce) jar diced pimentos	60 g
2 pounds boneless, skinless chicken breast halves, cooked, diced	
1 (14 ounce) can chicken broth	400 g
1 (16 ounce) package fettuccini (medium egg noodles) pasta	455 g
1 cup shredded cheddar or American cheese	115 g

- Preheat oven to 350° (175° C).

- Melt butter in saucepan, add flour, seasonings and ½ teaspoon (2 ml) salt and cook over medium heat. Add milk slowly and stir constantly until thick.

- Add mushrooms, mushroom soup, pimentos, chicken and chicken broth. Cook noodles in saucepan according to package directions. Drain.

- Mix noodles with sauce and stir gently. Pour mixture into 10 x 15-inch (25 x 38 cm) baking dish. Sprinkle with cheese and cover and refrigerate until baking time. Bake for 20 to 30 minutes until it heats thoroughly. Serves 8 to 10.

Farmhouse Supper

1 (8 ounce) package fettuccini (medium egg noodles) pasta	230 g
4 - 5 boneless, skinless chicken breast halves	
1 (14 ounce) can chicken broth	400 g
2 cups sliced celery	200 g
2 onions, chopped	
1 green and 1 red bell pepper, seeded, chopped	
1 (10 ounce) can cream of chicken soup	280 g
1 (10 ounce) can cream of mushroom soup	280 g
1 cup shredded 4-cheese blend	115 g

• Cook noodles in saucepan in boiling water until barely tender and drain well. Cut chicken into thin slices.

• Combine noodles, chicken and broth in large, sprayed slow cooker and mix. (Make sure noodles separate and coat with broth.)

• Combine remaining ingredients in saucepan and heat just enough to mix well and add to slow cooker. Cover and cook on LOW for 4 to 6 hours. Serves 6.

There is a pasta museum in Pontedassio, Italy, which includes exhibits of antique pasta-making machines and other tools as well as many examples of pasta.

Great Crazy Lasagna

*Chicken never got mixed up
with any better ingredients!*

1 tablespoon butter	15 ml
½ onion, chopped	
1 cup fresh mushrooms, sliced	70 g
1 (10 ounce) can cream of chicken soup	280 g
1 (16 ounce) jar alfredo sauce	455 g
1 (4 ounce) jar diced pimentos, drained	115 g
⅓ cup dry white wine	75 ml
½ teaspoon dried basil	2 ml
1 (10 ounce) package frozen chopped spinach, thawed	280 g
1 (15 ounce) carton ricotta cheese	425 g
⅓ cup grated parmesan cheese	35 g
1 egg, beaten	
9 lasagna noodles, cooked	
3 - 4 cups cooked chicken, shredded	420 - 560 g
1 (16 ounce) package shredded cheddar cheese	455 g

- Preheat oven to 350° (175° C).

- Melt butter and saute onion and mushrooms in large skillet. Stir in soup, alfredo sauce, pimentos, wine and basil. Reserve one-third sauce for top of lasagna.

- Squeeze spinach between paper towels to complete remove excess moisture.

- Combine spinach, ricotta, parmesan and egg in bowl and mix well.

- Place 3 noodles in sprayed 10 x 15-inch (25 x 38 cm) baking dish. Make sure 10 x 15-inch (25 x 38 cm) dish is full size with depth of 2½ inches (6.5 cm).

- Layer each with half of remaining sauce, spinach-ricotta mixture and chicken. (The spinach-ricotta mixture will be fairly dry and you will have to pour it over sauce and spread out.)

continued next page...

continued...

- Sprinkle with 1½ cups (360 ml) cheddar cheese. Repeat layering.

- Top with last 3 noodles and reserved sauce.

- Cover and bake for 45 minutes.

- Uncover and sprinkle remaining cheese on top.

- Bake for additional 5 minutes or just until cheese melts. Let casserole stand for 10 minutes before serving. Serves 10 to 12.

Favorite Budget Chicken

1 (10 ounce) can cream of chicken soup	280 g
3 green onions, chopped	
2 ribs celery, sliced	
3 cups white rice, cooked	710 ml
1 (4 ounce) can chopped pimentos, drained	115 g
1 (12 ounce) can chicken with liquid	340 g
1 (5 ounce) can evaporated milk	145 g
1½ cups chow mein noodles	85 g

- Preheat oven to 350° (175° C).

- Combine soup, onions, celery, rice, pimentos, chicken and evaporated milk in large bowl; mix until they blend well.

- Spoon into sprayed 2-quart (2 L) baking dish, cover and bake for 30 minutes. Serve over chow mein noodles. Serves 4 to 5.

Garden Chicken

This colorful, delicious casserole is not only flavor packed, but it is also a sight to behold! You can't beat this bountiful dish for family or company.

4 boneless, skinless chicken breasts halves, cut into strips	
1 teaspoon minced garlic	5 ml
5 tablespoons butter, divided	75 g
1 small yellow squash, thinly sliced	
1 small zucchini, thinly sliced	
1 red bell pepper, seeded, thinly sliced	
4 tablespoons flour	30 g
2 teaspoons pesto seasoning	10 ml
1 (14 ounce) can chicken broth	400 g
1 cup half-and-half cream	310 g
1 (8 ounce) package capelli d'angelo (angel hair) pasta, cooked al dente, drained	230 g
⅓ cup shredded parmesan cheese	335 g

- Preheat oven to 350° (175° C).

- Saute chicken and garlic with 2 tablespoons (30 g) butter in large skillet over medium heat for about 15 minutes. Remove chicken and set aside.

- With butter in skillet, saute squash, zucchini and bell pepper and cook just until tender-crisp.

- Melt 3 tablespoons (45 ml) butter and add flour, pesto seasoning and ½ teaspoon (2 ml) each of salt and pepper in small saucepan. Stir to form smooth paste.

- Gradually add broth, stirring constantly over medium-high heat until thick. Stir in half-and-half cream and heat thoroughly.

- Combine chicken, vegetables, broth-cream mixture and drained pasta in large bowl. Transfer to sprayed 9 x 13-inch (23 x 33 cm) baking dish.

- Cover and bake for 30 minutes.

- Uncover and sprinkle parmesan cheese over top of casserole and return to oven for additional 5 minutes. Serves 8.

Harmony with Linguine

1 (12 ounce) package linguine (thin egg noodles) pasta	340 g
2 teaspoons minced garlic	10 ml
2 tablespoons olive oil	30 ml
1 (16 ounce) package frozen broccoli, cauliflower and carrots	455 g
1 (10 ounce) package frozen baby green peas	280 g
1 pound chicken tenders	455 g
2 tablespoons butter	30 g
3 tablespoons light soy sauce	45 ml
½ cup fresh chopped cilantro	10 g

- Cook linguine in saucepan according to package directions. Drain and stir in garlic and oil. Allow to cool for about 10 minutes.

- Bring large pot of water to a boil. Immerse all vegetables in water for about 30 seconds. Drain and set aside.

- Cut chicken in strips and cook chicken with butter and soy sauce in skillet for about 10 to 15 minutes or until juices run clear.

- Combine linguine, vegetables and chicken tenders in large bowl and toss to mix well. Transfer to serving dish and garnish with fresh cilantro. Serves 8.

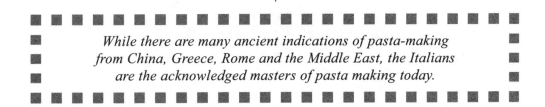

While there are many ancient indications of pasta-making from China, Greece, Rome and the Middle East, the Italians are the acknowledged masters of pasta making today.

Hearty Chicken-Noodle Casserole

1 (10 ounce) package frozen
chopped onions and bell
peppers   280 g
¼ cup (½ stick) butter   60 g
1 (10 ounce) can cream
of chicken soup   280 g
1 (4 ounce) jar chopped
pimentos   115 g
1 (8 ounce) package elbow
macaroni (tube) pasta,
cooked   230 g
3 cups cooked, diced
chicken   420 g
1 (15 ounce) carton ricotta
cheese   425 g
1 (8 ounce) package
shredded Mexican
4-cheese blend   230 g
¾ cup crushed round,
buttery crackers   45 g

- Preheat oven to 350° (175° C).

- Saute onions and bell peppers with butter in skillet. Stir in soup and pimentos and mix.

- Combine macaroni, chicken and cheeses in large bowl; mix until they blend well. Fold in soup-pimento mixture and mix well.

- Spoon into sprayed 9 x 13-inch (23 x 33 cm) baking dish and bake for 40 minutes. Remove from oven and sprinkle crushed crackers over top of casserole and cook for additional 15 minutes. Serves 10.

Lemony Chicken And Noodles

1 (8 ounce) package pappardelle (wide egg noodles) pasta	230 g
1 (10 ounce) package frozen sugar snap peas, thawed	280 g
1 (14 ounce) can chicken broth	400 g
1 teaspoon fresh grated lemon peel	5 ml
2 cups cubed, skinless rotisserie chicken meat	280 g
½ cup whipping cream	40 g

- Cook noodles in saucepan according to package directions. Add snap peas to noodles 1 minute before noodles are done. Drain and return to saucepan.

- Add chicken broth, lemon peel, chicken pieces and ½ teaspoon (2 ml) each of salt and pepper. Heat, stirring constantly, until thoroughly hot.

- Over low heat, gently stir in whipping cream. Serve hot. Serves 6.

Mac Cheese and Chicken

1½ cups elbow macaroni (tube) pasta	155 g
1 (12 ounce) can evaporated milk	340 g
½ - ⅔ cup hot chipotle salsa	120 - 175 g
2 cups skinned, cut-up rotisserie chicken	280 g
1 (8 ounce) package cubed Velveeta® cheese	230 g

- Cook macaroni in 2 cups (500 ml) water in saucepan according to package directions and drain well. Add evaporated milk and chipotle salsa and cook over medium heat for about 10 minutes, stirring frequently. (There will still be liquid in mixture.)

- Stir in rotisserie chicken and heat until chicken heats thoroughly. Fold in cheese, stir constantly and cook for 1 minute. Serve immediately. Serves 8.

Mr. Mozz's Spaghetti

This is a wonderful casserole to serve to family or for company. It has great flavor and taste with chicken, pasta and colorful vegetables all in one dish. It's a winner, I promise!

1 bunch fresh green onions
    with tops, chopped
1 cup celery, chopped   100 g
1 red bell pepper, seeded,
    chopped
1 yellow or orange bell pepper,
    seeded, chopped
¼ cup (½ stick) butter   60 g
1 tablespoon dried
    cilantro leaves   15 ml
1 teaspoon Italian seasoning 5 ml
1 (7 ounce) package
    vermicelli (thin
    spaghetti) pasta,
    cooked, drained   200 g
4 cups cooked chicken or
    turkey, chopped   560 g
1 (8 ounce) carton sour
    cream   230 g
1 (16 ounce) jar creamy
    alfredo sauce   455 g

1 (10 ounce) box frozen
    green peas, thawed   280 g
1 (8 ounce) package
    shredded mozzarella
    cheese, divided   230 g

- Preheat oven to 350° (175° C).

- Saute onions, celery and bell peppers in large skillet with butter.

- Combine onion-pepper mixture, cilantro, Italian seasoning, a little salt and pepper, spaghetti, chicken, sour cream and alfredo sauce in large bowl and mix well.

- Fold in peas and half mozzarella cheese.

- Spoon into sprayed 10 x 15-inch (25 cm x 38 cm) deep baking dish. Cover and bake for 45 minutes.

- Uncover and sprinkle remaining cheese over casserole. Return to oven for about 5 minutes. Serves 10 to 12.

TIP: *With spaghetti dishes like this, I like to break up the spaghetti before cooking it. It just makes it a little easier to serve and to eat.*

Mushrooms, Noodles and Chicken

½ cup (1 stick) butter	115 g
1 green bell pepper, seeded, chopped	
1 red bell pepper, seeded, chopped	
½ cup flour	60 g
1½ teaspoons seasoned salt	7 ml
1½ cups milk	375 ml
1 (14 ounce) can beef broth	400 g
1 (10 ounce) can cream of mushroom soup	280 g
1 (12 ounce) package fettuccini (medium egg noodles) pasta, cooked, drained	340 g
3 - 4 cups cooked, cubed chicken	420 - 560 g
1 (8 ounce) package shredded cheddar cheese	230 g

- Preheat oven to 350° (175° C).

- Melt butter in large skillet on medium-high heat. Cook and stir bell peppers for 10 minutes. Stir in flour and seasoned salt and mix well.

- While still on medium-high heat, slowly stir in milk, beef broth and 1 teaspoon pepper. Cook until mixture is thick and pour into large bowl.

- Fold in mushroom soup, noodles and chicken and transfer to sprayed 10 x 15-inch (25 x 38 cm) baking dish.

- Cover and bake for 35 minutes or until thoroughly hot. Uncover, sprinkle cheese over casserole and return to oven for additional 5 minutes. Serves 12.

Mushroom-Spaghetti Bake

1 (8 ounce) package spaghetti pasta	230 g
¼ cup olive oil	60 ml
2 teaspoons minced garlic	10 ml
1 (8 ounce) carton fresh mushrooms, sliced	230 g
2½ cups bite-size chunks rotisserie chicken	350 g
¼ cup capers, drained	30 g
1 cup roasted red bell peppers, drained	150 g
1 cup shredded mozzarella cheese	115 g

- Cook spaghetti in saucepan according to package directions. Use ladle to remove carefully ½ cup (125 ml) hot water from saucepan and set aside. Drain spaghetti and rinse in hot water; set aside.

- Heat oil in large skillet over medium heat and cook garlic for about 2 minutes. Add mushrooms and cook for an additional 4 minutes. Raise heat to high and add chicken, capers and a little salt and pepper; cook for about 2 minutes, stirring often.

- Add reserved pasta liquid, spaghetti and stir to blend well. Cook for about 3 minutes or until mixture is thoroughly hot. Remove from heat and stir in roasted bell peppers and cheese. Serve immediately. Serves 4 to 6.

Noodle Chicken

1 (3 ounce) package chicken-
   flavored, instant ramen
   noodles   85 g
1 (16 ounce) package
   frozen broccoli,
   cauliflower and carrots   455 g
⅔ cup sweet-and-sour sauce   150 ml
3 boneless, skinless chicken
   breast halves, cooked

- Cook noodles and vegetables in
  saucepan with 2 cups (500 ml)
  boiling water for 3 minutes, stir
  occasionally and drain.

- Combine noodle-vegetable mixture
  with seasoning packet, sweet-and-
  sour sauce and a little salt and
  pepper. Cut chicken in strips, add
  chicken to noodle mixture and heat
  thoroughly. Serves 6.

TIP: *You may want to add*
       1 tablespoon (15 ml) soy sauce,
       if you have it on hand.

Spaghetti Toss

1 (10 ounce) package
   vermicelli (thin
   spaghetti) pasta   280 g
1 (10 ounce) package
   frozen sugar snap peas   280 g
2 tablespoons butter   30 g
3 cups rotisserie-cooked
   chicken   420 g
1 (11 ounce) can mandarin
   oranges, drained   310 g
⅔ cup stir-fry sauce   150 ml

- Cook spaghetti in saucepan
  according to package directions.
  Stir in sugar snap peas and cook
  for an additional 1 minute.

- Drain and stir in butter until butter
  melts. Spoon into bowl. Cut
  chicken into strips and add strips,
  oranges and stir-fry sauce. Toss to
  coat. Serves 6 to 8.

Old-Fashioned Chicken Spaghetti

This is a great recipe for leftover turkey.

8 - 10 ounces spaghetti pasta	230 g
1 bell pepper, seeded, chopped	
1 onion, chopped	
1 cup chopped celery	100 g
½ cup (1 stick) butter	120 g
1 (10 ounce) can tomato soup	280 g
1 (10 ounce) can diced tomatoes and green chilies	280 g
1 (4 ounce) can chopped mushrooms	115 g
½ teaspoon garlic powder	2 ml
3 teaspoons chicken bouillon granules	15 ml
4 - 5 cups chopped chicken or turkey	560 - 700 g
1 (8 ounce) package cubed, Velveeta® cheese	230 g
1 (8 ounce) package shredded cheddar cheese	230 g

- Preheat oven to 325° (160° C).

- Cook spaghetti in saucepan according to package directions and drain.

- Saute bell pepper, onion and celery in butter in medium saucepan.

- Add soup, tomatoes and green chilies, mushrooms, garlic powder, bouillon and ½ cup (125 ml) water and mix well.

- Mix spaghetti, soup, tomato mixture, chicken and cheese in large mixing bowl. Place in sprayed 2 (2 quart/2 L) baking dishes.

- Cover and bake for 40 to 50 minutes. Serves 10 to 12.

TIP; Freeze one dish for later. To bake frozen dish, thaw first.

Pecan-Topped Fettuccini

1 pound boneless, skinless chicken breast halves	455 g
¾ cup (1½ sticks) butter, divided	170 g
1 (8 ounce) package mushrooms, sliced	230 g
1 bunch fresh green onions, sliced	
1 teaspoon minced garlic	5 ml
1 (8 ounce) package whole grain fettuccini (medium egg noodles) pasta	230 g
1 egg yolk	
⅔ cup half-and-half cream	210 g
1 teaspoon dried parsley	5 ml
½ cup grated parmesan cheese	50 g
¾ cup chopped pecans, toasted	85 g

- Cut chicken into 1-inch (2.5 cm) strips. Melt ¼ cup (55 g) butter in large skillet and cook chicken until light brown. Remove chicken from skillet and set aside.

- Leave pan drippings in skillet and cook mushrooms, onions, garlic and a little salt and pepper until vegetables are tender. Return chicken to skillet, mix well and simmer on low heat for 20 to 25 minutes or until chicken is done.

- Cook fettuccini in saucepan according to package directions and drain. Melt remaining butter and let cook before combining with egg yolk, half-and-half cream and parsley. Stir this mixture into stir into cooked fettuccini.

- Add cheese and toss until they blend well. Stir in chicken-vegetable mixture and toss. Spoon onto hot serving platter and sprinkle with toasted pecans. Serves 6.

Pop's Pleasing Pasta

1 (14 ounce) package
   frozen, cooked,
   breaded chicken
   cutlets, thawed   400 g
1 (28 ounce) jar spaghetti
   sauce, divided   795 g
2 (5 ounce) packages
   grated parmesan
   cheese, divided   2 (145 g)
1 (8 ounce) package
   vermicelli (thin
   spaghetti) pasta,
   cooked   230 g

- Preheat oven to 400° (205° C).

- Place cutlets and top each with about ¼ cup (60 ml) spaghetti sauce and heaping tablespoon (15 ml) parmesan in sprayed 9 x 13-inch (23 x 33 cm) baking dish. Bake for 15 minutes.

- Place cooked spaghetti on serving platter and top with cutlets. Sprinkle remaining cheese over cutlets. Heat remaining spaghetti sauce and serve with chicken and spaghetti. Serves 8.

Quick Meal Fix

1 (7 ounce) box macaroni
   and cheese dinner   200 g
¼ cup (½ stick) butter   60 g
½ cup milk   125 ml
1 (10 ounce) package frozen
   broccoli florets, thawed 280 g
2 cups bite-size chunks
   rotisserie chicken   280 g
1 cup shredded sharp
   cheddar cheese   115 g
1 (4 ounce) jar chopped
   pimentos, drained   115 g

- Prepare macaroni and cheese in saucepan according to package directions, but increase butter to ¼ cup (60 g) and milk to ½ cup (125 ml). Add at end of cooking time.

- Add cheese sauce mix and broccoli; stir to blend well. Stir in chicken, cheese and pimentos; mix well.

- Place mixture in microwave-safe bowl and heat on full power, for about 2 minutes. Stir well for flavors to blend well. Serves 4 to 6.

Rich Chicken Florentine

1 teaspoon minced garlic	5 ml
4 boneless, skinless chicken breast halves, cut in strips	
3 tablespoons olive oil	45 ml
1 (16 ounce) package frozen spinach, thawed	455 g
1 (4.5 ounce) package dry alfredo sauce mix	130 g
2 tablespoons pesto	30 ml
1 (8 ounce) package capelli d'angelo (angel hair) pasta	230 g
¼ cup shredded mozzarella cheese	30 g

- Cook garlic and chicken strips with oil in large skillet over medium-high heat for about 8 minutes on each side. When chicken is no longer pink, add spinach and saute all together for about 4 minutes.

- Prepare alfredo sauce in saucepan according to package directions, stir in pesto and set aside.

- Cook pasta in large saucepan until al dente. Rinse in cold water and drain. Add chicken-spinach mixture to pasta and toss with pesto-alfredo sauce. Mix well and top with mozzarella cheese. Serves 8.

Capelli d'angelo literally means "angel hair" in Italian.

Robust Cajun Chicken

1 (8 ounce) package linguine
  (thin egg noodles) pasta 230 g
4 small boneless, skinless
  chicken breast halves
1 heaping tablespoon Cajun
  seasoning 15 ml
3 tablespoons butter 40 g
1 red bell pepper, seeded,
  sliced
1 green bell pepper, seeded,
  sliced
1 (8 ounce) carton fresh
  mushrooms, stems
  removed 230 g
1½ cups whipping cream 115 g
1 teaspoon dried basil 5 ml
1 teaspoon lemon pepper 5 ml
2 teaspoons minced garlic 10 ml
½ cup grated parmesan
  cheese 50 g

- Cook linguine until al dente according to package directions, drain and set aside. Keep warm.

- Place chicken on cutting board, cut each breast into about 4 strips and place in resealable plastic bag. Add Cajun seasoning and shake to coat.

- Melt butter in large skillet on medium-high heat and cook chicken until tender, about 8 minutes. Add bell peppers and mushrooms, cook and stir for an additional 3 minutes.

- Reduce heat to medium and stir in cream, basil, lemon pepper and garlic. Cook until mixture is thoroughly hot. Add cooked linguine, toss while mixture is still on medium heat. Heat just until mixture is thoroughly hot.

- Serve right from skillet or transfer to serving bowl and sprinkle with parmesan cheese. Serves 8.

Rotini Chicken

2 (14 ounce) cans chicken
   broth   2 (400 g)
1 teaspoon minced garlic   5 ml
1 (12 ounce) package
   rotini (spiral) pasta   340 g
1 (16 ounce) package
   frozen broccoli,
   cauliflower, carrots   455 g
1 pound chicken tenders,
   halved   455 g
1 - 2 teaspoons Italian
   seasoning   5 - 10 ml
2 tablespoons olive oil   30 ml
⅓ cup shredded
   mozzarella cheese   40 g

- Combine broth, garlic and ½ cup (125 ml) water in large saucepan and bring to a boil. Add pasta, reduce heat to medium-low heat and cook for about 10 minutes or until tender.

- Add vegetables and bring to a boil again. Reduce heat to medium and cook for 10 minutes or until vegetables are tender.

- Sprinkle chicken tenders with Italian seasoning and ½ teaspoon (2 ml) pepper. Cook chicken in skillet with oil for about 10 minutes and turn once.

- Add chicken to pasta-vegetable mixture and heat on low until thoroughly hot. Spoon mixture onto serving platter and sprinkle cheese over top. Serve immediately. Serves 8 to 10.

Savory Chicken Fettuccini

2 pounds boneless, skinless chicken thighs, cubed	910 g
½ teaspoon garlic powder	2 ml
1 red bell pepper, seeded, chopped	
2 ribs celery, chopped	
1 (10 ounce) can cream of celery soup	280 g
1 (10 ounce) can cream of chicken soup	280 g
1 (8 ounce) package cubed Velveeta® cheese	230 g
1 (4 ounce) jar diced pimentos	115 g
1 (16 ounce) package spinach fettuccini (medium egg noodles) pasta	455 g

- Place chicken in sprayed slow cooker. Sprinkle with garlic powder, ½ teaspoon (2 ml) pepper, bell pepper and celery. Mix soups (no water) in bowl and pour on chicken.

- Cover and cook on HIGH for 4 to 6 hours or until chicken juices are clear. Stir in cheese and pimentos. Cover and cook until cheese melts.

- Cook fettuccini in saucepan according to package directions and drain. Place fettuccini in serving bowl and spoon chicken over fettuccini. Serve hot. Serves 10.

Spicy Orange Chicken over Noodles

1 pound boneless, skinless chicken tenders	455 g
2 tablespoons olive oil	30 ml
2 tablespoons soy sauce	30 ml
1 (16 ounce) package frozen stir-fry vegetables, thawed	455 g

- Lightly brown chicken tenders in oil in large skillet over medium-high heat. Add soy sauce and cook for additional 3 minutes.

- Add stir-fry vegetables and cook for about 5 minutes or until vegetables are tender-crisp.

Sauce:

⅔ cup orange marmalade	210 g
1 tablespoon olive oil	15 ml
1 tablespoon soy sauce	15 ml
1½ teaspoons lime juice	7 ml
½ teaspoon minced ginger	2 ml
½ teaspoon cayenne pepper	2 ml
1 (6 ounce) package chow mein noodles	170 g

- Combine marmalade, oil, soy sauce, lime juice, ginger and cayenne pepper in saucepan and mix well.

- Heat and pour over stir-fry chicken and vegetables. Serve over chow mein noodles. Serves 8.

Warming plates before serving pasta helps the food remain warm while being eaten. Put plates or dishes in a 250° (120° C) oven for 10 or 15 minutes. Or pour hot water into dishes and let stand until ready to use; then dry the bowls and serve the pasta.

Stir-Fry Cashew Chicken

Olive oil
1 pound chicken tenders,
    cut into strips   455 g
1 (16 ounce) package
    frozen broccoli,
    cauliflower and carrots 455 g
1 (8 ounce) jar stir-fry sauce 230 g
⅓ cup cashew halves   45 g
1 (12 ounce) package chow
    mein noodles   340 g

- Place a little oil and stir-fry chicken strips in 12-inch (32 cm) wok or skillet over high heat for about 4 minutes.

- Add vegetables and stir-fry for additional 4 minutes or until vegetables are tender. Stir in stir-fry sauce and cashews and cook just until mixture is hot. Serve over chow mein noodles. Serves 6.

Stir-Fry Chicken

Olive oil
1 pound chicken tenders,
    cut into strips   455 g
1 (16 ounce) package frozen
    broccoli, cauliflower
    and carrots   455 g
1 (8 ounce) jar stir-fry sauce 230 g
1 (12 ounce) package chow
    mein noodles   340 g

- Place a little oil and stir-fry chicken strips in 12-inch (32 cm) wok over high heat for about 4 minutes.

- Add vegetables and stir-fry for additional 4 minutes or until vegetables are tender. Stir in stir-fry sauce and cook just until mixture is hot. Serve over chow mein noodles. Serves 6.

Stir-Fry Chicken Spaghetti

1 pound boneless, skinless chicken breast halves	455 g
Olive oil	
1½ cups sliced mushrooms	105 g
1½ cups bell pepper strips	135 g
1 cup sweet-and-sour stir-fry sauce	250 ml
1 (16 ounce) package spaghetti pasta, cooked	455 g
¼ cup (½ stick) butter	60 g

- Season chicken with salt and pepper and cut into thin slices. Brown chicken slices in large skillet with a little oil on medium-low heat and cook for 5 minutes. Transfer to plate and set aside.

- In same skillet with a little more oil, stir-fry mushrooms and bell pepper strips for 5 minutes. Add chicken strips and sweet-and-sour sauce and stir until ingredients are hot.

- While spaghetti is still hot, drain well, add butter and stir until butter melts. Place in large bowl and toss with chicken mixture. Serve hot. Serves 8.

Sweet-and-Sour Chicken-Veggies

1 (3 ounce) package chicken-flavored ramen noodles	10 g
1 (16 ounce) package frozen broccoli, cauliflower and carrots	455 g
⅔ cup sweet-and-sour sauce	150 ml
1 tablespoon soy sauce	15 ml
3 boneless, skinless, cooked chicken breast halves, cut in strips (can use deli turkey)	

- Cook noodles and vegetables in 2 cups (500 ml) water (set aside seasoning packet) in large saucepan for 3 minutes or until liquid is absorbed.

- Add seasoning packet, chicken (or turkey) sweet-and-sour sauce, soy sauce and a little salt and pepper. Heat on medium-low heat, stirring until all is thoroughly hot. Serves 6.

Tantalizing Chicken Alfredo

1 (12 ounce) package fettuccini (medium egg noodles) pasta	340 g
4 tablespoons extra-virgin olive oil, divided	60 ml
⅔ cup finely chopped green onions	110 g
½ cup finely chopped bell pepper	75 g
4 - 5 large boneless, skinless chicken breast halves	
1 tablespoon minced garlic	15 ml
1 quart whipping cream	1 L
¼ cup (½ stick) butter	60 g
1 tablespoon Italian seasoning	15 ml
½ cup grated romano cheese	50 g

- Cook fettuccini in saucepan according to package directions. Rinse, drain and place in large bowl. Drizzle 2 tablespoons (30 ml) olive oil over pasta and stir to coat every strand. Set aside.

- Heat remaining oil in large skillet or soup pot and quickly saute onions and bell pepper just until they are slightly softened. Remove from pot and set aside.

- Cut chicken into thin slices and place chicken and garlic in pot and saute for about 5 minutes. (Add more oil if needed.) Spoon onion-bell pepper mixture back into pot and stir until mixture blends well.

- Turn heat to high, pour in cream and cook, stirring constantly, until mixture thickens. Add butter and Italian seasoning and continue stirring until mixture is semi-thick paste.

- Reduce heat to medium-low and simmer for 10 minutes. Fold fettuccini into chicken-cream mixture and heat on medium just until mixture is thoroughly hot. Sprinkle with cheese and serve immediately. Serves 8 to 10.

Thank Goodness Chicken

4 boneless, skinless chicken breast halves	
2 tablespoons butter	30 g
2 tablespoons flour	15 g
2 tablespoons dry ranch salad dressing mix	30 ml
1¼ cups nonfat half-and-half cream	390 g
1 (16 ounce) package fettuccini (medium egg noodles) pasta	455 g
¼ cup finely shredded parmesan cheese	15 g

- Cut chicken breasts into bite-size pieces. Melt butter in skillet and cook chicken until juices run clear and outside browns evenly.

- Sprinkle flour and salad dressing mix over chicken and stir well. Stir in half-and-half cream and cook, stirring constantly, until it thickens and bubbles.

- Cook noodles in saucepan according to package directions. Drain and place on serving platter. Spoon creamy chicken mixture over noodles; sprinkle with cheese and serve immediately. Serves 8.

Rule-the-Roost Casserole

1 (7 ounce) box chicken-flavored rice and macaroni pasta	200 g
1 (10 ounce) can cream of mushroom soup	280 g
1 (10 ounce) can cream of celery soup	280 g
3 cups cooked, chopped chicken or turkey	420 g
1 (10 ounce) package frozen peas, thawed	280 g
1 cup shredded cheddar cheese	115 g

- Preheat oven to 350° (175° C).

- Cook rice and macaroni in saucepan according to package directions.

- Mix both soups with ½ cup (125 ml) water in bowl.

- Combine chicken, cooked rice and macaroni, soups, peas and cheese and mix well.

- Pour into sprayed 3-quart (3 L) baking dish. Cover and bake for 40 minutes. Serves 8.

Three-Cheese Chicken Marinara

1 cup fine breadcrumbs	60 g
6 boneless, skinless chicken breast halves	
2 eggs, beaten	
¼ cup (½ stick) butter	60 g
1 (15 ounce) carton marinara sauce	425 g
½ cup evaporated milk	125 ml
3 slices mozzarella cheese, halved crosswise	
6 slices Swiss cheese	
2 tablespoons grated parmesan cheese	15 g
1 (12 ounce) package fettuccini (medium egg noodles) pasta	340 g

- Preheat oven to 350° (175° C).

- Combine breadcrumbs and ½ teaspoon (2 ml) salt in shallow bowl and set aside.

- In separate shallow bowl, place beaten eggs and dip each chicken breast in eggs and breadcrumbs. Melt butter in large skillet over medium heat.

- Add chicken breasts, one at a time, and cook for about 2 minutes on each side or until golden brown. Remove chicken and drain.

- Combine marinara sauce and evaporated milk in small bowl and mix well. Reserve ¼ cup (60 ml) plus 2 tablespoons (30 ml) and set aside. Pour remaining sauce mixture into sprayed 9 x 13-inch (23 x 33 cm) baking pan. Place each chicken breast in baking pan, cover and bake for 25 minutes.

- Remove from oven and place slices of mozzarella and Swiss cheese on each chicken breast half. Top with 1 tablespoon (15 ml) reserved sauce and sprinkle with parmesan cheese. Cover and bake for an additional 5 minutes.

- Cook egg noodles in saucepan according to package directions, drain and place on hot serving platter. Top with chicken breasts and remaining sauce. Serves 6.

Tortellini-Chicken Supper

1 (9 ounce) package refrigerated cheese tortellini pasta	255 g
1 (10 ounce) package frozen green peas, thawed	280 g
1 (8 ounce) carton cream cheese with chives and onion	230 g
½ cup sour cream	120 g
1 (9 ounce) package frozen, cooked chicken breast strips	255 g

- Cook tortellini in saucepan according to package directions. Place peas in colander and pour hot pasta water over peas. Return tortellini and peas to saucepan.

- In separate small saucepan, combine cream cheese and sour cream, heat on low and stir well until cream cheese melts. Spoon mixture over tortellini and peas, toss and keep heat on low.

- Heat cooked chicken in microwave according to package directions. Spoon tortellini and peas in serving bowl and place chicken on top. Serve hot. Serves 6.

Vermicelli Toss

1 (10 ounce) package vermicelli (thin spaghetti) pasta	280 g
1 (10 ounce) package frozen sugar snap peas	280 g
2 tablespoons butter	30 g
3 cups rotisserie-cooked chicken strips	420 g
1 (11 ounce) can mandarin oranges, drained	310 g
⅔ cup stir-fry sauce	150 ml

- Cook vermicelli in saucepan according to package directions. Stir in sugar snap peas and cook for additional 1 minute. Drain and stir in butter until butter melts. Spoon into bowl.

- Add chicken strips, oranges and stir-fry sauce. Toss to coat. Serves 6.

Winner's Circle Pasta

1 (12 ounce) package whole
   wheat rotini (spiral)
   pasta   340 g
4 boneless, skinless
   chicken breast halves
Lemon pepper
1 teaspoon minced garlic   5 ml
2 tablespoons olive oil   30 ml
1 (10 ounce) can chicken
   broth   280 g
1 (10 ounce) package
   frozen green peas,
   thawed   280 g
½ (16 ounce) package
   shredded carrots   ½ (455 g)
1 (3 ounce) package
   cream cheese   85 g
2 teaspoons lemon juice   10 ml
½ cup grated parmesan
   cheese   50 g

- Cook pasta in saucepan according to package directions, drain and keep warm.

- Cut chicken into strips, sprinkle liberally with lemon pepper and place in large skillet. Add garlic and oil; cook on medium-high heat until chicken juices are clear. Remove from skillet and keep warm.

- In same skillet, add broth, peas, carrots, cream cheese and lemon juice, cook and stir until cheese melts. Stir pasta and chicken into vegetable mixture and heat thoroughly. Sprinkle with parmesan cheese. Serve right from the skillet. Serves 4 to 6.

Spaghetti Tango

2 tablespoons olive oil	30 ml
1 (10 ounce) package chopped onions and bell peppers	280 g
2 teaspoons minced garlic	10 ml
1 pound hot Italian turkey sausage	455 g
2 (15 ounce) cans Italian stewed tomatoes	2 (425 g)
1 (10 ounce) can tomatoes and green chilies	280 g
1 teaspoon dried basil	5 ml
1 (8 ounce) package vermicelli (thin spaghetti) pasta, cooked, drained	230 g
½ cup grated parmesan cheese	120 ml

- Heat oil in large skillet on medium-high heat and cook onions and bell peppers, and garlic for about 6 minutes. Remove casing on sausage and add to skillet. Break up sausage with fork and cook for 5 minutes.

- Stir in tomatoes, tomatoes and green chilies, basil, and a little salt and pepper. Bring to a boil, reduce heat to medium-low, stirring often, and simmer for 30 minutes. While sauce cooks, break up tomatoes with back of spoon.

- Place hot spaghetti on serving platter and spoon sausage-tomato mixture over spaghetti. Sprinkle parmesan cheese over top; serve immediately. Serves 6 to 8.

The availability of electricity in the early 20th century made the labor-intensive process of manufacturing pasta easier and more economical.

3-Cheese Turkey Casserole

1 (8 ounce) package fettuccini (medium egg noodles) pasta	230 g
1 teaspoon olive oil	5 ml
3 tablespoons butter	90 g
¾ cup chopped green bell pepper	110 g
½ cup chopped celery	50 g
½ cup chopped onion	80 g
1 (10 ounce) can cream of chicken soup	280 g
½ cup milk	125 ml
1 (6 ounce) jar whole mushrooms	170 g
1 (16 ounce) carton small curd cottage cheese	455 g
4 cups diced turkey or chicken	560 g
1 (12 ounce) package shredded cheddar cheese	340 g
¾ cup freshly grated parmesan cheese	75 g

- Preheat oven to 350° (175° C).

- Combine noodles in 3 quarts (3 L) hot water, add 1 tablespoon (15 ml) salt and oil in large soup pot and cook according to package directions.

- Melt butter in skillet and saute bell pepper, celery and onion.

- Combine noodles, bell pepper-onion mixture, chicken soup, milk, mushrooms, ½ teaspoon (2 ml) pepper, cottage cheese, turkey and cheddar cheese in large bowl.

- Pour into sprayed 9 x 13-inch (23 x 33 cm) baking dish and top with parmesan cheese. Bake for 40 minutes. Serves 8.

Stuffed Turkey Shells

28 (2 inch) gigantoni (extra large tubes) pasta	28 (5 cm)
1 pound ground turkey	455 g
½ cup finely minced onion	80 g
½ cup breadcrumbs	30 g
½ cup grated parmesan cheese	50 g
3 eggs, beaten	
1 (10 ounce) package frozen chopped spinach, thawed, drained*	280 g
1 (15 ounce) carton marinara sauce	425 g
1 (8 ounce) can tomato sauce	230 g
1 (8 ounce) package shredded mozzarella cheese	230 g

- Preheat oven at 350° (175° C).

- Cook pasta shells in saucepan according to package directions, drain and place on strip of wax paper where shells will not touch.

- Brown ground turkey and onion in large skillet; drain fat. Add breadcrumbs, parmesan cheese, eggs, spinach and a little salt and pepper; mix well. Carefully stuff mixture into shells and set aside.

- Mix marinara sauce and tomato sauce in bowl and spoon 1 cup (250 ml) sauce into sprayed 2 to 3-quart (2 to 3 L) baking dish. Arrange stuffed shells over sauce and pour remaining sauce over shells.

- Top with mozzarella, cover and bake for 40 minutes or until mixture is hot and bubbly. Uncover for last 5 minutes of cooking time. Serves 6 to 8.

TIP: Squeeze spinach between paper towels to completely remove excess moisture.

Tempting Turkey over Fettuccini

1 tablespoon olive oil	15 ml
2 teaspoons minced garlic	10 ml
2 (15 ounce) cans Italian stewed tomatoes	2 (425 g)
1 (4 ounce) can green chilies	115 g
½ teaspoon sugar	2 ml
⅔ cup whipping cream	50 g
1 pound deli smoked turkey breast, cut into thin strips	455 g
2 tablespoons chopped fresh parsley	10 g
1 (8 ounce) package whole wheat fettuccini (medium egg noodles) pasta	230 g
¼ cup grated parmesan cheese	25 g

- Heat oil in large skillet and saute garlic 1 minute. Add stewed tomatoes and green chilies and break tomatoes up by hand as you put them in skillet.

- Stir in sugar and a little salt and pepper. Bring mixture to a boil, reduce heat to medium and cook for 15 minutes, stirring often, until mixture thickens. Stir constantly over medium heat and gradually add cream, turkey and parsley. Remove from heat.

- Cook fettuccini in saucepan according to package directions, drain and place on serving platter. To serve, spoon tomato-turkey mixture over pasta and sprinkle with parmesan cheese. Serves 6.

Tri-Color Pasta with Turkey Supper

1 (12 ounce) package tri-color fusilli (spiral) pasta	340 g
1 (4 ounce) can sliced ripe olives, drained	115 g
1 cup fresh broccoli florets	70 g
1 cup cauliflower florets	100 g
2 small yellow squash, sliced	
1 cup halved cherry tomatoes	150 g
1 (8 ounce) bottle cheddar-parmesan ranch dressing	230 g
Slices from 1½ pound hickory smoked cracked pepper turkey breast	680 g

- Cook pasta in saucepan according to package directions. Drain and rinse in cold water. Place in large salad bowl and add olives, broccoli, cauliflower, squash and tomatoes. Toss with dressing.

- Place thin slices of turkey breast, arranged in a row over salad. Serve immediately. Serves 6.

Turkey and Noodles

1 (8 ounce) package fettuccini (medium egg noodles) pasta	230 g
2½ cups diced, cooked turkey	350 g
1 (1 ounce) package chicken gravy, prepared	30 g
2 cups round, buttery cracker crumbs	120 g

- Preheat oven to 350° (175° C).

- Boil noodles in saucepan according to package directions and drain.

- Arrange alternate layers of noodles, turkey and gravy in sprayed 2-quart (2 L) baking dish. Cover with cracker crumbs.

- Bake for 35 minutes. Serves 6.

Turkey and Noodles Plus

1 (12 ounce) package
   fettuccini (medium egg
   noodles) pasta   340 g
3 cups cooked, diced
   turkey   420 g
1 (16 ounce) package
   frozen peas and
   carrots, thawed   455 g
2 (12 ounce) jars turkey
   gravy   2 (340 g)
2 cups slightly crushed
   potato chips   110 g

- Preheat oven to 350° (175° C).

- Cook noodles in saucepan
  according to package directions
  and drain.

- Arrange alternate layers of noodles,
  turkey, peas and carrots, and gravy
  in sprayed 9 x 13-inch (23 x 33 cm)
  baking dish. Cover and bake for
  20 minutes.

- Remove from oven, sprinkle potato
  chips over casserole and return to
  oven for 15 minutes or until chips
  are light brown. Serves 12.

Turkey Spaghetti

2 pounds ground turkey   910 g
2 (10 ounce) cans tomato
   bisque soup   2 (280 g)
1 (14 ounce) can chicken
   broth   400 g
2 (7 ounce) boxes ready-
   cut spaghetti, cooked,
   drained   2 (200 g)
1 (15 ounce) can whole
   kernel corn, drained   425 g
1 (4 ounce) can sliced
   mushrooms, drained   115 g
¼ cup ketchup   70 g

- Cook ground turkey and season
  with a little salt and pepper in
  non-stick skillet. Place cooked
  turkey in 5 to 6-quart (5 to 6 L)
  slow cooker. Add in soups, broth,
  spaghetti, corn, mushrooms and
  ketchup and stir to blend.

- Cover and cook on LOW for
  5 to 7 hours or on HIGH for
  3 hours. Serves 4 to 6.

Turkey Stuffed Peppers

2 red bell peppers
2 yellow bell peppers
1½ pounds ground turkey   680 g
½ onion, finely chopped
1 (15 ounce) can Italian
   stewed tomatoes   425 g
½ cup orzo (tiny) pasta   90 g
½ teaspoon dried oregano   2 ml
½ teaspoon dried basil   2 ml
½ teaspoon ground allspice   2 ml
¾ cup grated parmesan
   cheese, divided   75 g

- Preheat oven to 375° (190° C).

- Halve bell peppers lengthwise and remove stem ends, seeds and membranes. Immerse in large pot of boiling water for 3 minutes.

- Remove peppers with slotted spoon, sprinkle insides with a little salt and invert on paper towels to drain.

- Saute turkey and onion in skillet over medium heat for about 5 minutes. Drain fat and stir in tomatoes, orzo, oregano, basil, allspice, a little salt and ½ cup (125 ml) water.

- Cover and cook on medium-low heat for 10 minutes.

- Stir in half parmesan cheese and mix until all ingredients mix well.

- Fill pepper halves with turkey mixture and place in sprayed 3-quart (3 L) baking dish. Place any remaining meat mixture around peppers. Bake for 15 minutes and sprinkle with remaining cheese. Serves 6 to 8

Turkey Tetrazzini

¼ cup (½ stick) butter	60 g
½ cup chopped onion	80 g
1 rib celery, chopped	
¼ cup flour	30 g
1 cup milk	250 ml
1 (10 ounce) can chicken broth	280 g
½ teaspoon dried tarragon	2 ml
1 teaspoon dried parsley	5 ml
1 (8 ounce) package spaghetti pasta	230 g
2 cups cooked, chopped turkey	480 ml
¾ cup shredded Swiss cheese, divided	80 g

- Preheat oven at 350° (175° C).

- Melt butter in large skillet and saute onion and celery for 2 minutes. On medium heat, add flour and stir well.

- Gradually add milk and chicken broth and stir constantly until mixture thickens and bubbles. Stir in tarragon, parsley and a little salt and pepper.

- Break spaghetti in half and cook in saucepan according to package directions and drain. Add spaghetti, turkey and ½ cup (55 g) cheese to onion-broth mixture and mix well.

- Spoon into sprayed 2-quart (2 L) baking dish, cover and bake for 25 minutes. Uncover and sprinkle remaining cheese over top and return to oven for 5 minutes. Serves 4 to 5.

Pasta
with Pork

From tenderloins to bacon, pork is perfect with pasta! Savory recipes will make your family say "yummy"!

Pasta with Pork

A Different Macaroni

1 (8 ounce) package macaroni (tube) pasta	230 g
½ cup whipping cream	40 g
1 (8 ounce) carton shredded gorgonzola cheese	230 g
1 (10 ounce) package frozen green peas, thawed	280 g
2 cups cooked, cubed ham	280 g

- Cook macaroni in saucepan according to package directions and drain. Add cream and gorgonzola cheese and stir until cheese melts.

- Fold in peas and ham and cook on low heat, stirring constantly, for 5 minutes or until mixture is thoroughly hot. Spoon into serving bowl and serve hot. Serves 10.

Absolute Alfredo Ham

1 (9 ounce) package refrigerated tortellini pasta	255 g
2 tablespoons butter	30 g
1½ cups cooked ham, cut in thin slices	210 g
1 (10 ounce) package frozen green peas, thawed	280 g
1 (8 ounce) carton mushrooms, sliced	230 g
1 (4 ounce) jar chopped pimentos	115 g
1 (16 ounce) jar alfredo pasta sauce	455 g

- Cook tortellini in saucepan according to package directions; drain and set aside. Melt butter in large skillet over medium heat and stir in ham, peas, mushrooms, pimentos and a little salt and pepper.

- Add alfredo sauce and tortellini and stir to mix well. Cover and let mixture simmer on low heat for about 5 to 6 minutes; serve immediately. Serves 4 to 6.

Bow-Tie Ham Supper

1 (8 ounce) package farfalle (bow-tie) pasta	230 g
1 (8 ounce) carton chive and onion cream cheese	230 g
¾ cup half-and-half cream	235 g
1 cup baby carrots, cut in half lengthwise	135 g
½ yellow bell pepper, seeded, julienned	
1 (8 ounce) can cut green beans, drained	230 g
2 cups cooked ham strips	280 g
¼ teaspoon dried basil	1 ml
⅓ cup grated parmesan cheese	35 g

- Cook pasta according to package directions and drain.

- Place cream cheese and half-and-half cream in large sprayed skillet and cook over medium heat for 2 or 3 minutes, stirring constantly until mixture is smooth.

- Stir in carrots and bell pepper and cook for about 5 minutes, stirring occasionally. Stir in green beans, ham and basil. Cook, stirring occasionally just until dish is thoroughly hot.

- Spoon into serving bowl and sprinkle top with parmesan cheese. Serves 8.

Farfalle pasta is commonly called bow-tie because of its shape. Farfalle actually means "butterfly" in Italian. It's called farfalle tonde when the corners are rounded. It's very attractive in salads.

Bow-Tie Pasta, Ham and Veggies

1 (8 ounce) package farfalle
   (bow-tie) pasta   230 g
1 (10 ounce) package each
   frozen broccoli florets
   and green peas, thawed 280 g
1 (16 ounce) jar alfredo
   sauce   455 g
1 pound cooked, cubed ham 455 g

- Cook pasta in large saucepan according to package directions. Add broccoli and peas during last 3 minutes of cooking time. Drain well.

- Add alfredo sauce and ham. (This is a good time to use that leftover ham.) Cook and stir gently over very low heat to keep ingredients from sticking to pan. Spoon into serving bowl. Serves 6.

TIP: *To substitute with deli*
      ham, have the butcher cut
      a thick slice and you cut
      ham into chunks.

Creamed Ham with Spaghetti

2 (10 ounce) cans cream of
   mushroom soup with
   roasted garlic   2 (280 g)
1 cup sliced fresh
   mushrooms   70 g
2 - 2½ cups cooked,
   cubed ham   420 - 475 g
1 (5 ounce) can
   evaporated milk   145 g
1 (7 ounce) box ready-cut
   spaghetti pasta   200 g

- Combine soups, mushrooms, ham, evaporated milk and a little salt and pepper in slow cooker.

- Cover and cook on LOW for 2 hours and mix well after cooking.

- Cook spaghetti in saucepan and drain. Add spaghetti to slow cooker and toss to coat. Serves 4 to 6.

Ham and Pasta Bake

1 (10 ounce) can broccoli-cheese soup	280 g
½ cup grated parmesan cheese	50 g
1 cup milk	250 ml
1 tablespoon spicy brown mustard	15 ml
1 (16 ounce) package frozen broccoli florets, thawed	455 g
2 cups macaroni (tube) pasta, cooked	210 g
8 ounces (deli) cooked ham, cut in bite-size chunks	230 g
Thin strips red bell pepper for garnish	

- Combine soup, parmesan cheese, milk and mustard in large skillet and mix well. Add broccoli and stir over medium heat.

- Reduce heat to low, cover and cook for 5 minutes or until broccoli is tender-crisp.

- Stir in macaroni and ham and heat thoroughly. Transfer to sprayed 2-quart (2 L) baking dish.

- Garnish with very thin strips of bell pepper. Serves 8 to 10.

Peppery Pasta and Peas

2 tablespoons olive oil	30 ml
1 onion, chopped	
1 (15 ounce) can Mexican stewed tomatoes	425 g
1 (5 ounce) can evaporated milk	145 g
2 teaspoons dried basil	10 ml
A scant ¼ teaspoon crushed red pepper flakes	1 ml
1 (8 ounce) package farfalle (bow-tie) pasta, cooked, drained	230 g
1 (8 ounce) can green peas, drained	230 g
1 cup cooked, cubed ham	140 g
¼ cup grated parmesan cheese	25 g

- Heat oil in large skillet and saute onion for about 8 minutes. Add tomatoes, evaporated milk, basil, red pepper and a little salt. Bring to a boil, reduce heat to low and simmer for about 10 minutes or until it thickens slightly. Stir often.

- Stir in pasta, peas and ham and toss well. Place in serving bowl and sprinkle with parmesan cheese. Serves 4.

Ham, Noodles and the Works

1 (8 ounce) package
   linguine (thin egg
   noodles) pasta   230 g
2 (10 ounce) cans cream
   of broccoli soup   2 (280 g)
1 (8 ounce) carton
   whipping cream   230 g
1 (8 ounce) can whole
   kernel corn, drained 230 g
1 (16 ounce) package
   frozen broccoli,
   cauliflower and
   carrots, thawed   455 g
3 cups cooked, cubed ham 420 g
1 (8 ounce) package
   shredded cheddar-
   Jack cheese, divided 230 g

- Preheat oven to 325° (160° C).

- Cook noodles in saucepan according to package directions.

- Combine broccoli soup, cream, corn, broccoli-carrot mixture, ham and a little salt and pepper in large bowl. Fold in noodles and half of cheese.

- Spoon into sprayed 9 x 13-inch (23 x 33 cm) baking dish. Cover and bake for 45 minutes. Remove from oven, sprinkle remaining cheese over top and return to oven for 5 minutes. Serves 8.

When boiling pasta for a baked dish, reduce the cooking time because the pasta will finish cooking when the dish is baked. The pasta should be flexible but still firm; usually one-third to one-half the usual cooking time will be sufficient.

Ham-Linguine Special

2 teaspoons minced garlic	10 ml
¾ cup coarsely chopped walnuts	100 g
2 red bell peppers, seeded, julienned	
1 green bell pepper, seeded, julienned	
¼ cup olive oil	60 ml
1 pound cooked ham, cut in strips	455 g
1 (16 ounce) jar creamy alfredo sauce	455 g
1 (8 ounce) carton sour cream	230 g
1 (5 ounce) package grated parmesan cheese	145 g
1 (12 ounce) package shredded mozzarella cheese	340 g
1 (12 ounce) package linguine (thin egg noodles) pasta, cooked	340 g
1½ cups seasoned breadcrumbs	180 g
¼ cup (½ stick) butter, melted	60 g

- Preheat oven to 325° (160° C).

- Saute garlic, walnuts and bell peppers with oil in large skillet for 1 to 2 minutes.

- Combine garlic-bell pepper mixture, ham, alfredo sauce, sour cream, parmesan cheese and mozzarella cheese in large bowl; mix well.

- Gently fold in cooked linguine and spoon into sprayed 10 x 15-inch (25 x 38 cm) baking dish.

- Combine breadcrumbs and melted butter in bowl and sprinkle over top of casserole.

- Bake for 40 to 45 minutes or until breadcrumbs are light brown. Serves 20.

Linguine and Ham

1 (8 ounce) package whole wheat linguine (thin egg noodles) pasta	230 g
2 tablespoons butter	30 g
½ cup chopped onion	80 g
1 - 2 cups cooked, chopped ham	140 - 280 g
1 (14 ounce) can chicken broth	400 g
2 tablespoons chopped fresh sage leaves	10 g
1 (9 ounce) package baby spinach	255 g
¼ cup grated parmesan cheese	25 g

- Cook linguine in saucepan according to package directions, drain and keep warm.

- Melt butter in skillet and saute onion for 5 minutes. Stir in ham, chicken broth and sage leaves; cook on medium-low heat for 2 minutes.

- Add spinach and cook just until spinach wilts. Add a little salt and pepper, toss ham-spinach mixture with linguine and serve sprinkled with parmesan cheese. Serves 8.

Mac 'n Cheese Casserole

4 eggs	
1½ cups milk	375 ml
1 (12 ounce) package macaroni (tube) pasta, cooked	340 g
1 (8 ounce) package shredded cheddar cheese	230 g
2 cups cooked, cubed ham	280 g
¾ cup seasoned breadcrumbs	90 g
¼ cup (½ stick) butter, cubed	60 g

- Preheat oven to 350º (175° C).

- Lightly beat eggs and milk with a little salt and pepper in large bowl. Stir in macaroni, cheese and ham.

- Spoon into sprayed 7 x 11-inch (18 x 28 cm) baking dish and bake for 20 minutes. Remove from oven, sprinkle with breadcrumbs and dot with butter. Continue baking for additional 15 minutes. Serves 8.

Noodles-Ham Veggie Mix

1 (8 ounce) package fettuccini (medium egg noodles) pasta	230 g
1 (10 ounce) can cream of celery soup	280 g
1 (10 ounce) can cream of broccoli soup	280 g
1 teaspoon chicken bouillon granules	5 ml
1½ cups half-and-half cream	465 g
1 (8 ounce) can whole kernel corn, drained	230 g
1 (16 ounce) package frozen broccoli, cauliflower and carrots, thawed	455 g
3 cups cooked cubed ham	420 g
1 (8 ounce) package shredded cheddar-Jack cheese, divided	230 g

- Preheat oven to 350° (175° C).

- Cook noodles in saucepan according to package directions and drain.

- Combine soups, chicken bouillon, half-and-half cream, corn, broccoli-carrot mixture, ham, ½ teaspoon (2 ml) each of salt and pepper in large bowl and mix well.

- Fold in egg noodles and half of cheese.

- Spoon into sprayed 9 x 13-inch (23 x 33 cm) baking dish. Cover and bake for 45 minutes.

- Uncover and sprinkle remaining cheese over top of casserole. Return to oven and bake for additional 10 minutes or until cheese bubbles. Serves 8.

Picky Eater's Paradise Pie

1 (8 ounce) package capelli d'angelo (angel hair) pasta	230 g
1 tablespoon olive oil	15 ml
1 cup cooked, shredded ham	140 g
¾ cup fresh sliced mushrooms	55 g
1 (2 ounce) can chopped pimentos, drained	60 g
2 tablespoons flour	30 ml
1 (12 ounce) can evaporated milk	340 g
1 cup shredded Swiss cheese, divided	110 g

- Preheat oven at 400° (205° C).

- Cook spaghetti in saucepan according to package directions, drain and set aside.

- Heat oil in large skillet over medium heat and cook ham and mushrooms for 4 minutes or until mushrooms are tender. Stir in pimentos and flour and cook 1 minute.

- Gradually add evaporated milk and a little salt and pepper; cook over medium heat, stirring constantly, until it thickens. Stir in ham-mushroom mixture, spaghetti and ½ cup (55 g) cheese.

- Spoon evenly into sprayed 9-inch (23 cm) pie pan and sprinkle with remaining cheese.

- Bake for 15 minutes. Let stand for 5 minutes before cutting into wedges to serve. Serves 6.

Prime Time Mac 'n Ham

1 (12 ounce) package rotelle
   (wagon wheels) pasta   340 g
1 (10 ounce) package
   frozen green peas,
   thawed   280 g
1 cup milk   250 ml
2 (8 ounce) cartons garden
   vegetable cream cheese 2 (230 g)
¾ cup shredded cheddar
   cheese   30 g
2 cups cooked, cubed ham   280 g
1 (8 ounce) can whole
   kernel corn, drained   230 g

- Cook pasta in large saucepan
  according to package directions and
  stir in peas last minute of cooking
  time. Drain pasta and peas and
  return to saucepan.

- Place milk, cream cheese and
  cheddar cheese in medium
  saucepan on medium heat. Heat
  and stir until cheese melts and
  mixture is smooth.

- Add ham and corn, mix well and
  heat until mixture is thoroughly
  hot. Fold into cooked pasta and
  place in serving bowl. Serves 8.

Ravioli-Ham Supper

2 (9 ounce) packages
   refrigerated cheese-
   filled ravioli pasta   2 (255 g)
1 (26 ounce) jar tomato
   pasta sauce   740 g
1 (4 ounce) can sliced
   mushrooms   115 g
1 tablespoon dried onion
   flakes   15 ml
1 cup cooked, chopped
   ham   140 g
1½ cups shredded
   mozzarella cheese   175 g

- Cook ravioli according to package
  directions; drain and cover to
  keep warm.

- Combine pasta sauce, mushrooms,
  onion flakes and ham in saucepan
  and mix well. Bring mixture to a
  boil, reduce heat and simmer for
  10 minutes or until sauce is slightly
  thick, stirring frequently.

- Stir in ravioli and stir gently
  to coat. Spoon into serving
  platter and sprinkle with cheese.
  Serves 6 to 8.

Rich Fettuccini

¼ cup (½ stick) butter	60 g
2 teaspoons minced garlic	10 ml
1 (8 ounce) carton fresh mushrooms, sliced	230 g
1 small red bell pepper, seeded, chopped	
2 teaspoons dried basil	10 ml
2 teaspoons dried oregano	10 ml
½ teaspoon cayenne pepper	2 ml
2 cups cooked, chopped ham	280 g
1 (1 pint) carton whipping cream	500 ml
1 cup spaghetti sauce	250 g
1 (16 ounce) package fettuccini (medium egg noodles) pasta	455 g
Parmesan cheese	

- Melt butter in large saucepan on medium heat and cook garlic, mushrooms and bell pepper for about 5 minutes, stirring often. Add in basil, oregano, cayenne pepper, ham and a little salt and cook for additional 5 minutes.

- Pour in cream and bring to a boil and slowly stir in spaghetti sauce, stirring often. Reduce heat to medium and stir until sauce reduces by one-third and begins to thicken.

- Cook fettuccini in saucepan according to package directions, drain and transfer to serving bowl. Ladle sauce over fettuccini and serve hot. Sprinkle parmesan cheese over top. Serves 8.

Rotelle pasta is shaped like a wagon wheel and it means "little wheels" in Italian.

Spinach with Pasta

1 (9 ounce) package fresh spinach	255 g
1 (10 ounce) package frozen, sliced yellow squash	280 g
1 (8 ounce) package refrigerated whole grain fettuccini (medium egg noodles) pasta	230 g
2 tablespoons olive oil	30 ml
1 small onion, finely chopped	
1 tablespoon flour	15 ml
1 tablespoon sugar	15 ml
1 cup chicken broth	250 ml
2 tablespoons red wine vinegar	30 ml
¾ pound deli ham, cut into strips	340 g

- Bring 1 cup (250 ml) water to a boil in large saucepan and cook spinach and squash for about 5 minutes; drain and keep warm.

- Cook fettuccini in saucepan according to package directions and drain. Transfer to serving platter and keep warm.

- Heat oil in large skillet and saute onion until tender. Stir in flour, sugar and a little salt and pepper. Quickly stir in broth and vinegar, cook on medium heat and stir until mixture thickens.

- Stir in ham and spinach-squash mixture and mix well. Spoon over pasta and serve immediately. Serves 8.

Carbonara sauce is a relatively modern invention dating from World War II when American soldiers in Italy asked for bacon and eggs. The sauce is made with bacon, eggs and cream.

Tortellini-Ham Supper

2 (9 ounce) packages fresh
  tortellini pasta   2 (255 g)
1 (10 ounce) package
  frozen green peas,
  thawed   280 g
1 (16 ounce) jar alfredo
  sauce   455 g
2 - 3 cups cooked, cubed
  ham   280 - 420 g

- Cook tortellini in saucepan
  according to package directions.
  Add green peas for about 5 minutes
  before tortellini is done. Drain.

- Heat alfredo sauce and ham in
  saucepan until thoroughly hot.
  Toss with tortellini and peas.
  Serves 8 to 10.

Carbonara Skillet Pie

1 (8 ounce) package
  spaghetti pasta   230 g
8 slices bacon, chopped
3 eggs
1 (16 ounce) jar alfredo
  sauce, divided   455 g
½ cup grated parmesan
  cheese   50 g
1 (8 ounce) can green peas,
  drained   230 g

- Cook spaghetti in saucepan
  according to package directions
  and drain. Cook bacon in skillet on
  medium-high heat until crisp and
  drain; discard bacon drippings.

- Whisk eggs, 1 cup (250 ml) alfredo
  sauce and cheese in large bowl.
  Stir in spaghetti, peas and chopped
  bacon and place in same skillet
  used to cook bacon. Cook over
  medium heat for about 5 minutes or
  until bottom is slightly crisp.

- Spoon remaining sauce over
  top, cover and cook for
  7 to 8 minutes. Cut in wedges
  to serve. Serves 5 to 6.

Cheesy Fettuccini and Bacon

1 (16 ounce) package
    fettuccini (medium egg
    noodles) pasta   455 g
1 (8 ounce) package
    precooked bacon   230 g
3 large eggs
⅔ cup grated parmesan
    cheese   70 g
1½ cups half-and-half
    cream   470 g
1 (8 ounce) can baby green
    peas, drained   230 g

- Cook fettuccini in saucepan according to package directions and drain. Cut bacon into ½-inch (1.2 cm) pieces with scissors.

- Beat eggs, cheese, half-and-half cream, peas and a little salt and pepper in bowl. Pour egg mixture and bacon pieces over pasta and gently toss with tongs.

- Return pasta mixture to pan on low heat and cook, stirring constantly for about 2 to 3 minutes or until it thickens slightly. (Do not overcook or eggs will scramble.) Serves 8.

Pork 'n Pasta

1 (1 pound) pork tenderloin,
    cut into ½-inch
    pieces   455 g/1.2 cm
1 (10 ounce) package
    frozen mixed vegetables 280 g
½ cup rotini (spiral) pasta,
    cooked
¼ teaspoon cayenne pepper 1 ml
1 (15 ounce) can great
    northern beans, drained 425 g
3 Italian plum tomatoes,
    seeded, chopped
1 cup alfredo sauce   250 ml
⅓ cup grated parmesan
    cheese   35 g

- Cook pork in large skillet on medium-high for 10 minutes, stirring frequently.

- Stir in vegetables, pasta and cayenne pepper; mix well. Reduce heat to medium; cover and cook for 7 to 8 minutes or until vegetables are tender-crisp, stirring occasionally.

- Stir in beans, tomatoes and alfredo sauce and cook until mixture is thoroughly hot. Place in serving bowl and sprinkle with parmesan cheese. Serves 8.

Sensational Spaghetti

Forget the tomato sauce.
This is spaghetti to love!

½ cup (1 stick) butter	115 g
1½ teaspoons minced garlic	7 ml
1 (12 ounce) package vermicelli (thin spaghetti) pasta	340 g
1 cup grated parmesan cheese	100 g
1 (1 pint) carton whipping cream	455 g
1 teaspoon dried parsley flakes	5 ml
10 - 12 strips bacon, fried crisp, crumbled	

- Preheat oven to 325° (160° C).

- Melt butter in large skillet and saute garlic until slightly brown. Cook spaghetti in saucepan according to package directions and drain.

- Combine garlic mixture, spaghetti, parmesan cheese, cream, parsley flakes, and ½ teaspoon (2 ml) each of salt and pepper in bowl and mix well.

- Spoon into sprayed 2-quart (2 L) baking dish. Cover and bake just until warm, for about 15 minutes.

- Uncover and sprinkle crumbled bacon over casserole. Serves 6 to 8.

The word macaroni (maccheroni in Italian) which is used generically for all forms of pasta except pasta made with eggs (noodles) is thought to come from a Sicilian word " maccarruni" which means made into a dough by force.

Oodles of Noodles

1½ - 2 pounds pork tenderloin	680 - 910 g
3 tablespoons olive oil	45 ml
2 cups celery, chopped	200 g
1 green and 1 red bell pepper, seeded, chopped	
1 onion, chopped	
1 (4 ounce) can sliced mushrooms	115 g
1 (10 ounce) can tomatoes and green chilies	280 g
1 (10 ounce) can cream of mushroom soup with garlic	280 g
1 (10 ounce) can cream of celery soup	280 g
¼ cup soy sauce	60 ml
1 (7 ounce) package elbow macaroni (tube) pasta, cooked, drained	200 g
2 cups chow mein noodles	110 g

- Preheat oven to 350° (175° C).

- Cut pork into 1-inch (2.5 cm) cubes. Brown pork in oil in skillet and cook on low heat for about 15 minutes. Remove pork with slotted spoon to side dish.

- Saute celery, bell peppers and onion in same skillet in remaining oil. Combine pork, celery-onion mixture, mushrooms, tomatoes and green chilies, soups, soy sauce and macaroni in large bowl.

- Spoon casserole into 1 sprayed 9 x 13-inch (23 x 33 cm) baking dish or 2 smaller baking dishes. Top with chow mein noodles.

- Bake for 50 minutes. Serves 10.

TIP: *If you make 2 smaller casseroles, you may freeze one. Wait to sprinkle the chow mein noodles over casserole until just before you place it in the oven to cook.*

Pork-Noodles Supreme

Olive oil
2 pounds pork
    tenderloin, cut
    into 1-inch cubes   **910 g/2.5 cm**
2 ribs celery, chopped
1 red and 1 green bell pepper,
    seeded, chopped
1 onion, chopped
1 (12 ounce) package
    fettuccini (medium
    egg noodles) pasta,
    cooked, drained   **340 g**
1 (10 ounce) can cream
    of celery soup   **280 g**
1 (10 ounce) can cream
    of chicken soup   **280 g**
1 (15 ounce) can cream-
    style corn   **425 g**
¾ cup half-and-half cream   **235 g**
1½ cups corn flakes, crushed **45 g**
3 tablespoons butter, melted **45 g**

- Preheat oven to 350° (175° C).

- Heat a little oil in skillet, brown and cook pork for about 15 minutes. Spoon pork into large bowl.

- With a little oil in skillet, saute celery, bell pepper and onion. Spoon into bowl with pork. Add noodles, soups, creamed corn, half-and-half cream, and a little salt and pepper to pork.

- Mix well and pour into sprayed 9 x 13-inch (23 x 33 cm) baking dish.

- Combine crushed corn flakes and butter in bowl and sprinkle over casserole. Cover and bake for about 30 minutes. Serves 8.

Supper Ready Stir-Fry

2 tablespoons olive oil	30 ml
1 (16 ounce) package frozen bell peppers and onion stir-fry vegetables	455 g
1 (1 pound) pork tenderloin, cut in strips	455 g
2½ teaspoons Jamaican jerk seasoning	12 ml
½ cup prepared peanut sauce	125 ml
1 teaspoon light soy sauce	5 ml
1 (12 ounce) package vermicelli (thin spaghetti) pasta	340 g
2 tablespoons butter	30 g
½ cup chopped peanuts	85 g

- Heat oil in wok (or skillet) over medium-high heat and add stir-fry vegetables. Cook and stir for 6 to 8 minutes or until vegetables are tender-crisp. Remove from wok.

- In same wok, toss pork with jerk seasoning. Add more oil if needed. Cook and stir for about 5 minutes or until pork is no longer pink. Add peanut sauce and soy sauce and return vegetables and cook just until thoroughly hot.

- Cook spaghetti in saucepan according to package directions and drain. Place in hot serving bowl, add butter and stir until butter melts. Spoon pork-vegetable mixture over spaghetti and top with peanuts. Serves 8.

Tasty Noodles and Pork

1½ pounds pork
    tenderloin, cubed   680 g
Olive oil
2 cups chopped celery   200 g
2 cups chopped onion   320 g
1 green bell pepper,
    seeded, chopped
1 red bell pepper,
    seeded, chopped
1 (15 ounce) can Mexican
    stewed tomatoes   425 g
2 (10 ounce) cans golden
    mushroom soup   2 (280 g)
¼ cup soy sauce   60 ml
1½ cups elbow macaroni
    (tube) pasta, cooked,
    drained   160 g
2 cups chow mein noodles 110 g

- Preheat oven to 350° (175° C).

- Brown pork in skillet with a little oil and cook on low heat for 15 minutes. Transfer pork with slotted spoon to side dish.

- In same skillet, saute celery, onion and bell peppers.

- Combine pork, celery-pepper mixture, stewed tomatoes, mushroom soup, soy sauce and macaroni in large bowl.

- Spoon into sprayed 9 x 13-inch (23 x 33 cm) baking dish. Sprinkle chow mein noodles on top of casserole and bake for 40 minutes. Serves 8.

Tenderloin, Noodles and Peas

1½ pounds pork tenderloin, cubed	680 g
Olive oil	
1 cup chopped onion	160 g
1 cup chopped celery	100 g
2 red bell peppers, seeded, chopped	
1 (8 ounce) package linguine (thin egg noodles) pasta, cooked	230 g
1 (10 ounce) can cream of chicken soup	280 g
½ cup whipping cream	40 g
1 (10 ounce) package frozen green peas, thawed	280 g
1½ cups seasoned breadcrumbs	180 g
½ cup chopped walnuts	65 g

- Preheat oven to 350° (175° C).

- Brown pork tenderloin in large skillet with little oil. Reduce heat and cook for 20 minutes. Remove pork to separate plate.

- In same skillet, saute onions, celery and bell peppers. Add pork, noodles, soup, cream, peas and a little salt and pepper.

- Spoon into sprayed 4-quart (4 L) baking dish and sprinkle with breadcrumbs and walnuts. Bake for 30 minutes or until casserole bubbles around edges. Serves 8.

Best Bubbling Pasta

1 (16 ounce) package fusilli
    (spiral) pasta   455 g
1 pound Italian sausage   455 g
2 (15 ounce) cartons
    marinara sauce   2 (425 g)
1 teaspoons dried basil   5 ml
1 (15 ounce) carton
    ricotta cheese   425 g
2 teaspoons Italian
    seasoning, divided 10 ml
1 (16 ounce) package
    shredded mozzarella
    cheese   455 g

- Preheat oven to 350° (175° C).

- Cook pasta in saucepan according to package directions and drain. Remove casing on sausage and cook in large skillet over medium-high heat until evenly brown; drain and crumble. Set aside. In separate saucepan, place marinara sauce and heat with basil.

- Combine ricotta with 1 teaspoon (5 ml) Italian seasoning and a little salt and pepper in medium bowl.

- Spread about 1 cup (250 ml) marinara sauce in sprayed 9 x 13-inch (23 x 33 cm) baking dish. Layer half pasta, half sausage, half ricotta and half mozzarella cheese.

- Spoon half remaining sauce over top and repeat layers. Sprinkle top with remaining Italian seasoning. Bake for 35 to 40 minutes or until bubbly around edges. Serves 6 to 8.

Colorful Sausage Supper

**1 pound cooked Polish
    sausage, cut into
    ¼-inch slices   455 g/6 mm**
**1 red bell pepper,
    seeded, julienned**
3 small zucchini, sliced
**3 small yellow squash,
    sliced**
¼ cup olive oil, divided   60 ml
**1 (16 ounce) package penne
    (tube) pasta   455 g**
**1 (26 ounce) jar spaghetti
    sauce, heated   740 g**

- Saute sausage, bell pepper, zucchini and squash with 2 tablespoons (30 ml) oil in large skillet until vegetables are tender-crisp. Keep warm.

- Cook pasta in saucepan according to package directions, drain and stir in remaining oil. Add a little salt and pepper.

- Spoon into large serving bowl and spread hot spaghetti sauce over pasta.

- Use slotted spoon to top with sausage-vegetable mixture and serve immediately. Serve with hot, buttered garlic bread. Serves 8.

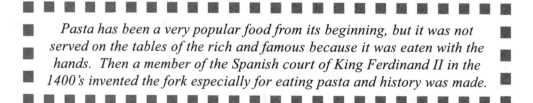

Pasta has been a very popular food from its beginning, but it was not served on the tables of the rich and famous because it was eaten with the hands. Then a member of the Spanish court of King Ferdinand II in the 1400's invented the fork especially for eating pasta and history was made.

Creamy Fettuccini

1 (8 ounce) package fettuccini (medium egg noodles) pasta	230 g
1 pound Italian sausage	455 g
1 (10 ounce) can cream of mushroom soup	280 g
1 (16 ounce) carton sour cream	455 g

- Preheat oven to 325° (160° C).

- Cook fettuccini in saucepan and drain.

- Cut sausage into 1-inch (2.5 cm) pieces, brown in skillet over medium heat and cook for about 8 minutes. Drain.

- Mix all ingredients in bowl and place in sprayed 2-quart (2 L) baking dish.

- Bake for 30 minutes. Serves 4.

Ideal Linguine and Sausage

2 tablespoons olive oil	30 ml
1 pound Polish sausage, cut in ½-inch pieces	455 g/1.2 cm
1 red bell pepper, seeded, chopped	
1 (4 ounce) can sliced mushrooms, drained	115 g
1 (4 ounce) can sliced ripe olives	115 g
½ teaspoon dried oregano	2 ml
1 (12 ounce) package linguine (thin egg noodles) pasta	340 g
½ cup prepared pesto sauce	125 g
½ cup grated parmesan cheese	50 g
4 green onions, sliced	

- Heat oil in large skillet on medium-high and cook sausage and bell pepper for about 8 minutes. Stir in mushrooms, olives and oregano and mix well.

- Cook linguine in saucepan according to package directions, drain and stir in pesto sauce and parmesan cheese. Toss until they blend well. Garnish with sliced green onions. Serves 6.

Italian Sausage-Tortellini

½ pound ground round steak	230 g
1 (1 pound) package bulk Italian sausage	455 g
1 (15 ounce) carton refrigerated marinara sauce	425 g
1 (15 ounce) can Italian stewed tomatoes with liquid	425 g
1½ cups sliced fresh mushrooms	105 g
1 (9 ounce) package refrigerated cheese tortellini pasta	255 g
1½ cups shredded mozzarella cheese	175 g

- Brown and cook ground beef and sausage in large skillet for about 10 minutes on medium-low heat and drain.

- Combine meat mixture, marinara sauce, tomatoes and mushrooms in 4 to 5-quart (4 to 5 L) slow cooker.

- Cover and cook on LOW for 6 to 8 hours.

- Stir in tortellini and sprinkle with mozzarella cheese.

- Turn cooker to HIGH and continue cooking for additional 10 to 15 minutes or until tortellini is tender. Serves 4 to 6.

Marinara sauce is a tomato-based sauce used in many pasta dishes. Its name relates to the Italian word for sailor. Because of this, some purists believe that the sauce must contain something from the sea such as anchovies, but most marinara sauces do not contain an ingredient of this nature.

Knock Out Hot Sausage Pasta

3 tablespoons olive oil	45 ml
1 pound hot Italian sausage	455 g
1 tablespoon minced garlic	15 ml
1 red and 1 green bell pepper, seeded, cut in strips	
1 (8 ounce) carton mushrooms, sliced	227 g
2 eggs at room temperature, separated	
⅓ cup whipping cream, whipped	80 ml
¾ cup grated romano cheese	180 ml
1 (16 ounce) package vermicelli (thin spaghetti) pasta	455 g
1 teaspoon dried parsley	5 ml

- Heat oil in skillet and saute sausage, garlic, bell peppers and mushrooms for about 10 minutes or until sausage is cooked.

- Beat egg yolks and egg whites separately. Gently stir beaten eggs and whipped cream, season with salt and pepper and fold in cheese.

- Cook spaghetti in saucepan according to package directions, drain and rinse in hot water. Drain again. Transfer spaghetti to large, hot serving bowl and pour egg-cheese mixture over spaghetti. Toss until sausage mixture coats spaghetti well.

- Stir in sausage-mushroom mixture and parsley and toss again. Serve immediately. Serves 6 to 8.

Layered Sausage and Rotini

1 (9 ounce) package refrigerated rigatoni (large tubes) pasta	255 g
1 pound bulk Italian pork sausage	455 g
1 (28 ounce) can diced tomatoes with liquid	795 g
2 teaspoons dried basil leaves	10 ml
2 teaspoons minced garlic	10 ml
1 (5 ounce) package grated parmesan cheese	145 g
1 (7 ounce) jar roasted red bell peppers, drained, chopped	200 g
1 (8 ounce) package shredded mozzarella cheese	230 g

- Preheat oven to 375° (190° C).

- Cook pasta according to package directions; drain but keep warm

- Cook sausage in large skillet over medium heat for about 10 minutes, stirring often and until no longer pink; drain.

- Combine tomatoes, basil and garlic in bowl. Layer half each of pasta, sausage, tomato-garlic mixture, parmesan cheese, bell peppers and mozzarella cheese in sprayed 9 x 13-inch (23 x 33 cm) baking dish. Repeat layers.

- Bake for 35 to 45 minutes or until bubbly hot and cheese is golden brown. Serves 8.

The more complex the shape of a pasta, the better a sauce or seasoning will cling to its ridges and grooves, nooks and crannies.

Outstanding Sausage and Broccoli

1 (12 ounce) package farfalle
    (bow-tie) pasta   340 g
1 (10 ounce) package frozen
    broccoli florets   280 g
2 tablespoons olive oil   30 ml
1 pound Polish sausage,
    cut into ¼-inch
    slices   455 g/6 mm
2 teaspoons minced garlic 10 ml
1 red bell pepper, seeded,
    julienned
1 tablespoon flour   15 ml
¼ teaspoon red pepper
    flakes   1 ml
1 (10 ounce) can chicken
    broth   280 g
2 tablespoons balsamic
    vinegar   30 ml

- Cook pasta in large saucepan according to package directions, but add broccoli for last 5 minutes of cooking time. Drain immediately and return pasta and broccoli to warm pan.

- Heat oil in large skillet and cook sausage, garlic and bell pepper for 5 to 6 minutes. Stir in flour, red pepper and a little salt. Add broth and vinegar. Cook, stirring often, for 2 minutes.

- On medium-low heat, pour sausage-broth mixture over pasta and toss. Heat thoroughly and serve immediately. Serves 8 to 10.

Pepperoni Twirls

2 cups tomato-spinach macaroni (twirls) pasta	210 g
1 pound bulk Italian sausage	455 g
1 onion, chopped	
1 green bell pepper, seeded, chopped	
1 (15 ounce) can pizza sauce	425 g
1 (8 ounce) can tomato sauce	230 g
⅓ cup milk	75 ml
1 (3 ounce) package sliced pepperoni, halved	85 g
1 (4 ounce) jar sliced mushrooms, drained	115 g
1 (2 ounce) can sliced ripe olives, drained	60 g
1 (8 ounce) package shredded mozzarella cheese, divided	230 g

- Preheat oven to 350° (175° C).

- Cook macaroni twirls in saucepan according to package directions and drain.

- Cook sausage, onion and bell pepper in skillet over medium heat until sausage is no longer pink and drain.

- Combine pizza sauce, tomato sauce and milk in large bowl. Stir in sausage mixture, macaroni twirls, pepperoni, mushrooms, olives and half cheese and mix well.

- Spoon into sprayed 9 x 13-inch (23 x 33 cm) baking dish. Cover and bake for 30 minutes.

- Remove from oven and sprinkle remaining cheese over top of casserole and return to oven for 5 to 10 minutes or just until cheese is melted. Serves 8.

Proud Italian Spaghetti

1 pound Italian sausage	455 g
1 green bell pepper, seeded, coarsely chopped	
1 onion, chopped	
1 (26 ounce) can spaghetti sauce with mushrooms	740 g
1 (10 ounce) can tomatoes and green chilies	280 g
1 (12 ounce) package spaghetti pasta	340 g
1 (8 ounce) package shredded mozzarella cheese	230 g

- Lightly brown sausage in large skillet on medium heat. Add bell pepper and onion and cook until soft, but not brown. Stir in spaghetti sauce and tomatoes and green chilies. Reduce heat to medium-low and simmer for about 15 minutes.

- Cook spaghetti in saucepan according to package directions, drain and place on serving platter. Spoon sausage-tomato sauce mixture over spaghetti and sprinkle cheese over top. Serves 4 to 5.

Ravioli and Tomatoes

1 (9 ounce) package refrigerated sausage-filled ravioli pasta	255 g
1 (15 ounce) can Italian-stewed tomatoes	425 g
2 (4 ounce) cans sliced mushrooms	2 (115 g)
1 (5 ounce) package grated parmesan cheese	145 g

- Cook ravioli in saucepan according to package directions and drain well. Stir in stewed tomatoes and mushrooms and bring to a boil. Reduce heat to low and simmer for about 5 minutes.

- Transfer to serving dish and sprinkle cheese on each serving. Serves 6.

Zesty Ziti

1 pound Italian sausage
    links, cut into
    ½-inch pieces   455 g/1.2 cm
1 onion, coarsely
    chopped
1 green bell pepper,
    seeded, sliced
Olive oil
1 (15 ounce) can diced
    tomatoes   425 g
1 (15 ounce) can Italian
    stewed tomatoes   425 g
2 tablespoons ketchup   35 g
1 (16 ounce) package ziti
    (thin tubes) pasta   455 g
1 cup shredded mozzarella
    cheese   115 g

- Preheat oven to 350° (175° C).

- Cook sausage, onion and bell pepper in a little oil in large skillet over medium heat and drain.

- Add diced tomatoes, stewed tomatoes and ketchup and mix well.

- Cook ziti in saucepan according to package directions and drain.

- Combine sausage-tomato mixture in large bowl and toss with pasta and cheese.

- Spoon into sprayed 3-quart (3 L) baking dish. Cover and bake for 20 minutes. Serves 8.

Pasta
with Seafood

Gifts from the sea are enhanced with pasta in these delectable recipes. The texture and variety makes menu selection easy.

Pasta with Seafood Contents

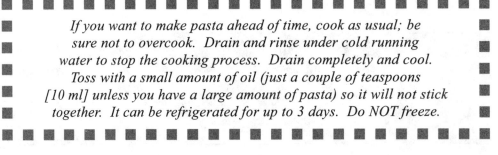

*If you want to make pasta ahead of time, cook as usual; be
sure not to overcook. Drain and rinse under cold running
water to stop the cooking process. Drain completely and cool.
Toss with a small amount of oil (just a couple of teaspoons
[10 ml] unless you have a large amount of pasta) so it will not stick
together. It can be refrigerated for up to 3 days. Do NOT freeze.*

Fettuccini of the Sea

¼ cup (½ stick) butter	60 g
¼ cup flour	30 g
1 teaspoon Creole seasoning	5 ml
1 tablespoon minced garlic	15 ml
1 (16 ounce) carton half-and-half cream	455 g
½ cup milk	125 ml
½ cup red bell pepper, seeded, finely chopped	75 g
2 (6 ounce) cans tiny shrimp, picked, veined	2 (170 g)
2 (6 ounce) cans crabmeat, drained, flaked	2 (170 g)
1 (6 ounce) can chopped clams, drained	170 g
½ cup grated parmesan cheese	50 g
1 (12 ounce) package fettuccini (medium egg noodles) pasta, cooked al dente	340 g

- Preheat oven to 325° (160° C).

- Melt butter in saucepan and add flour, Creole seasoning, ¾ teaspoon (4 ml) pepper and garlic and mix well. Gradually add half-and-half cream and milk and mix well. Cook on medium heat, stirring constantly, until it thickens.

- Add bell pepper, shrimp, crabmeat, clams and parmesan cheese and heat thoroughly.

- Spoon half fettuccini and half seafood sauce in sprayed 9 x 13-inch (23 x 33 cm) baking dish. Repeat layers.

- Cover and bake for 25 minutes or just until casserole bubbles. Serves 8.

Flavors that Thai

1 (8 ounce) package vermicelli (thin spaghetti) pasta	230 g
1 cup fresh snow peas	100 g
1 tablespoon olive oil	15 ml
1 (8 ounce) package sliced mushrooms	230 g
1 rib celery, finely sliced	
1 (16 ounce) package shredded carrots	455 g
1 (8 ounce) package frozen salad shrimp, thawed	230 g
1 (8 ounce) jar Thai peanut sauce	230 g
½ teaspoon hot pepper sauce	2 ml
2 teaspoons toasted sesame seeds	10 ml

- Cook spaghetti in saucepan according to package directions and add snow peas last 2 minutes of cooking time. Set aside and keep warm.

- Heat oil in large skillet over medium-high heat and add mushrooms, celery and carrots. Cook and stir for 3 minutes or until celery and carrots are tender.

- Add shrimp, cook and stir until mixture is thoroughly hot. Add peanut sauce and hot pepper sauce. Cook and stir until mixture is thoroughly hot.

- Drain spaghetti and snow peas well and place into serving bowl. Spoon shrimp-peanut sauce mixture over spaghetti mixture and top with sesame seeds. Serves 4.

Florentine Shrimp and Pasta

2 (9 ounce) frozen boil-in-
    bag creamed spinach   2 (255 g)
1 (12 ounce) package
    penne (tube) pasta   340 g
¼ cup whipping cream   20 g
1 teaspoon Cajun
    seasoning   5 ml
1 pound peeled, medium
    shrimp   455 g
2 tablespoons olive oil   30 ml

- Bring large pot of water to boil and add spinach pouches. Cook according to package directions.

- In separate large saucepan, cook pasta according to package directions. Drain, add cream and Cajun seasoning and mix until they blend well.

- Cook shrimp in skillet with olive oil for about 3 minutes or until thoroughly cooked (but not over-cooked.)

- Cut spinach pouches and add to pasta. Stir in shrimp and transfer to serving dish. Serves 6.

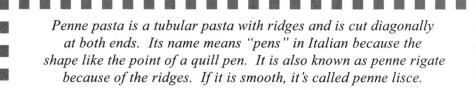

Penne pasta is a tubular pasta with ridges and is cut diagonally at both ends. Its name means "pens" in Italian because the shape like the point of a quill pen. It is also known as penne rigate because of the ridges. If it is smooth, it's called penne lisce.

Marinara Shrimp and Veggies

1 (8 ounce) package vermicelli (thin spaghetti) pasta	230 g
2 tablespoons olive oil	30 ml
1 teaspoon minced garlic	5 ml
½ cup chopped onion	80 g
1 medium zucchini, sliced	
2 small yellow summer squash, sliced	
1 (16 ounce) package salad shrimp	455 g
1 (8 ounce) carton marinara sauce, heated	230 g
2 tablespoons fresh chopped parsley	10 g

- Cook vermicelli according to package directions and drain.

- Heat oil in large skillet and cook garlic and onion for about 3 minutes or until onion is tender-crisp.

- Stir in zucchini, squash and a little salt and pepper. Cook for 2 to 3 minutes or until squash is tender; remove squash from skillet.

- Place shrimp in skillet and cook on medium heat for 2 minutes, stirring often.

- Spoon vermicelli into serving bowl; spoon half marinara sauce and top with vegetables and shrimp. Drizzle with remaining marinara sauce and sprinkle with parsley. Serves 8.

Lasagna-Tomato Toss

1 (16 ounce) package lasagna
   noodles   455 g
1 onion, chopped
1 tablespoon olive oil   15 ml
1 (28 ounce) can diced
   tomatoes   795 g
¼ teaspoon cayenne pepper   1 ml
¾ teaspoon dried oregano   4 ml
1 (16 ounce) package frozen
   salad shrimp, thawed   455 g
2 teaspoons dried parsley   10 ml
¾ cup crumbled feta cheese,
   divided   100 g

- Break lasagna noodles in half and cook in saucepan according to package directions, but add 2 minutes to cooking time. Drain later.

- Cook onion with oil in skillet for about 6 minutes and stir in tomatoes, cayenne pepper and oregano. Heat to boiling and break up tomatoes with side of spoon.

- Reduce heat to medium and cook for about 8 minutes to thicken slightly. Stir in shrimp and cook until thoroughly hot.

- Drain pasta and return to saucepan. Add shrimp mixture, parsley and ½ cup (70 g) feta cheese to pasta in saucepan and toss to coat well. Sprinkle with remaining feta cheese. Serves 4 to 6.

Drain cooked pasta but do not rinse it unless the recipe calls for this process. Usually, pasta is rinsed for use in salads. It's also a good idea to rinse lasagna so the noodles do not stick together.

Seafood Lasagna

8 lasagna noodles
2 tablespoons butter   30 g
1 onion, chopped
1 (8 ounce) package
    cream cheese, softened   230 g
1 (15 ounce) carton
    ricotta cheese   425 g
1 (4 ounce) jar chopped
    pimentos, drained   115 g
1 egg, beaten
2 teaspoons dried basil   10 ml
1 (10 ounce) can cream
    of shrimp soup   280 g
1 (10 ounce) can fiesta
    nacho cheese soup   280 g
¼ cup milk   60 ml
⅓ cup white wine   75 ml
1 pound small, cooked
    shrimp, peeled, veined   455 g
2 (6 ounce) cans crabmeat,
    drained, flaked   2 (170 g)
¼ cup grated parmesan
    cheese   25 g
1 cup shredded cheddar
    cheese   115 g

- Preheat oven to 350° (175° C).

- Cook noodles in saucepan according to package directions and set aside.

- Melt butter in skillet and saute onion until tender, but do not brown. Stir in cream cheese, ricotta cheese, pimentos, egg, basil, ½ teaspoon (2 ml) each of salt and pepper.

- Combine soups, milk and wine in saucepan and heat just to mix well. Add shrimp and crabmeat.

- Layer four noodles in sprayed 9 x 13-inch (23 x 33 cm) baking dish.

- Spread half of cream cheese-pimento mixture over noodles and top with half seafood mixture. Repeat layers with remaining four noodles, cream cheese-pimento mixture, then seafood mixture.

- Sprinkle with parmesan cheese and bake for 45 minutes.

- Remove from oven, top with cheddar cheese and return to oven for 3 to 4 minutes or just until cheese melts. Serves 8 to 10.

Shrimp and Pasta Alfredo

1 (8 ounce) package farfalle
   (bow-tie) pasta   230 g
2 slices bacon, cut into
   ½-inch (1.2 cm) pieces
2 ribs celery, sliced
1 (10 ounce) package frozen
   green peas
1 (16 ounce) package salad
   shrimp   455 g
1 cup refrigerated alfredo
   sauce   245 g
2 tablespoons chopped
   fresh chives   6 g

- Cook pasta according to package directions, drain and set aside.

- Cook bacon in large skillet on medium heat for about 5 minutes or until crisp. Stir in celery, green peas and add ¼ cup water; cover and cook for 2 minutes, stirring often, until water has evaporated.

- Add shrimp and cook for 3 minutes until shrimp are pink. Stir in alfredo sauce and pasta and cook over medium-low heat, stirring gently until thoroughly hot. Sprinkle with chives. Serves 8.

Alfredo sauce is made with cheese and butter. It is named for the Roman chef who created it.

Shrimp Florentine

1 tablespoon olive oil	15 ml
1½ cups orzo (tiny) pasta	155 g
1 red bell pepper, seeded, chopped	
3 green onions, chopped	
1 teaspoon minced garlic	5 ml
½ teaspoon dried dill weed	2 ml
1 (14 ounce) can chicken broth	400 g
1 teaspoon lemon juice	5 ml
2 cups shredded spinach	60 g
1 (16 ounce) package salad shrimp	455 g
⅓ cup grated parmesan cheese	35 g

- Heat oil in large skillet on medium-high heat and cook orzo, bell pepper, onions and garlic for 3 to 4 minutes or until vegetables are tender-crisp.

- Stir in dill weed, broth, lemon juice and 1 cup (250 ml) water. Heat to boiling; reduce heat. Cover and simmer for about 10 minutes or until pasta is tender.

- Stir in spinach and shrimp and cook for 2 to 3 minutes or until shrimp are tender. Spoon into serving bowl and sprinkle parmesan cheese over top. Serves 8.

The name of the tiny, rice-shaped pasta known as "orzo" means "barley".

Shrimply Delicious

¼ cup olive oil	60 ml
1 tablespoons minced garlic	15 ml
1 yellow bell pepper, seeded, cut into thin strips	
3 (15 ounce) cans Italian stewed tomatoes with liquid	3 (425 g)
1½ teaspoons Italian seasoning	7 ml
¾ cup whipping cream	55 g
1 (16 ounce) package frozen salad shrimp, thawed, drained	455 g
½ teaspoon red pepper flakes	2 ml
1 (16 ounce) package spinach linguine (thin egg noodles) pasta	455 g
1½ cups fresh broccoli florets	105 g
½ cup grated parmesan cheese	50 g

- Heat oil in large, deep skillet and saute garlic and bell pepper for 5 minutes.

- Drain stewed tomatoes and save liquid. Add Italian seasoning and puree in blender or food processor. Add pureed mixture and liquid to skillet and bring to a boil. Reduce heat to medium and cook for 25 minutes or until mixture thickens.

- Stir cream, shrimp and red pepper into skillet with tomato mixture and heat thoroughly over medium heat, stirring occasionally.

- Cook linguine in saucepan according to package directions, except add broccoli last 4 minutes of cooking time. Drain and place onto hot serving platter. Spoon shrimp sauce over linguine-broccoli mixture and top with parmesan cheese to serve. Serves 6 to 8.

Simple Shrimp and Asparagus

1 (16 ounce) package frozen salad shrimp	455 g
1 bunch fresh asparagus spears	
1 (8 ounce) package fusilli (spiral) pasta	230 g
2 tablespoons flour	15 g
½ cup sour cream	120 g
1 (10 ounce) can chicken broth	280 g
1 tablespoon lemon juice	15 ml
¼ teaspoon white pepper	1 ml

- Thaw shrimp and cut asparagus spears into 1½-inch (3 cm) pieces. Cook asparagus in ¾ cup (175 ml) boiling water in saucepan for about 8 minutes or until tender-crisp. Drain and reserve ¼ cup (60 ml) liquid.

- Set aside 1 cup (135 g) asparagus pieces, especially tips and keep warm. Puree remaining asparagus with reserved liquid in food processor until nearly smooth.

- Cook pasta in saucepan according to package directions, but add shrimp last 3 minutes of cooking time. Drain immediately and return pasta and shrimp to pan and add remaining asparagus pieces.

- Combine flour and sour cream in medium saucepan and mix well. Over medium heat, add broth, lemon juice, white pepper and a little salt. Stir and cook until mixture thickens; cook and stir for additional 1 minute. Pour broth mixture over pasta mixture, toss and serve immediately. Serves 6 to 8.

Spiced Shrimp Over Pasta

1 (8 ounce) package ziti (thin tubes) pasta	230 g
1 (16 ounce) package frozen broccoli florets, thawed, drained	455 g
1 (10 ounce) can chicken broth	280 g
2 tablespoons cornstarch	15 g
1 tablespoon dijon-style mustard	15 ml
2 tablespoon lemon juice	30 ml
1 teaspoon red pepper flakes	5 ml
2 tablespoons olive oil	30 ml
1 pound peeled, veined shrimp	455 g

- Cook ziti in saucepan according to package directions and add broccoli last 5 minutes of cooking time. Drain.

- Stir broth, cornstarch, mustard, lemon juice and red pepper in small bowl; set aside.

- Heat oil in large skillet over medium-high heat and add shrimp; saute for 1 minute, stirring constantly. Stir broth-cornstarch mixture again and stir into skillet with shrimp.

- Cook and stir for about 2 minutes or until sauce thickens and bubbles and shrimp turn pink. Toss sauce with pasta-broccoli mixture and serve immediately. Serves 4 to 6.

Winner's Circle Shrimp

1 (16 ounce) package frozen salad shrimp, thawed	455 g
1 tablespoon olive oil	15 ml
1 tablespoon Cajun seasoning	15 ml
1 (8 ounce) package fettuccini (medium egg noodles) pasta	230 g
2 tablespoons butter	30 g
2 (8 ounce) packages mushrooms, sliced	2 (230 g)
¼ cup finely diced onion	30 g
1 (14 ounce) can chicken broth, divided	400 g
½ cup sour cream	120 g
1 tablespoon cornstarch	15 ml
1 cup roasted red bell peppers, drained, chopped	135 g
1 tablespoon capers, drained	15 ml

- Place thawed, drained shrimp in bowl and add oil and Cajun seasoning; toss to coat.

- Cook fettuccini in saucepan according to package directions, drain and keep warm.

- Melt butter in large skillet over medium heat, cook mushrooms and onion for about 5 minutes. Remove from pan and stir in shrimp; set aside.

- In same skillet add ⅔ cup (150 ml) broth and bring to a boil. Cook until reduced to about ¼ cup (60 ml).

- Stir sour cream and cornstarch in small bowl. Mix into remaining broth and cook until thick and bubbly.

- Stir in shrimp, mushroom mixture, roasted bell peppers and capers. Heat just until thoroughly hot. Spoon fettuccini into serving bowl and spoon shrimp mixture over pasta. Serves 4 to 6.

Neptune Lasagna

3 tablespoons butter	45 g
1 red bell pepper, seeded, chopped	
1 onion, chopped	
1 (8 ounce) package cream cheese, softened	230 g
1 (16 ounce) carton small curd cottage cheese	455 g
1 egg, beaten	
2 teaspoons dried basil	10 ml
2 teaspoons Creole seasoning	10 ml
1 (10 ounce) can cream of shrimp soup	280 g
1 (10 ounce) can cream of celery soup	280 g
2 teaspoons dried basil	10 ml
½ cup white wine	125 ml
¾ cup milk	175 ml
2 (8 ounce) packages imitation crabmeat	2 (230 g)
2 (6 ounce) packages small shrimp, rinsed, drained	2 (170 g)
9 lasagna noodles, cooked, drained	
1 (3 ounce) package grated parmesan cheese	85 g
1 cup shredded white cheddar cheese	115 g

- Preheat oven to 350° (175° C).

- Heat butter in skillet and saute bell pepper and onion. Reduce heat and add cream cheese and stir until cream cheese melts.

- Remove from heat and add cottage cheese, egg, basil, ½ teaspoon (2 ml) pepper and Creole seasoning and set aside.

- Combine both soups, basil, white wine, milk, crabmeat and shrimp in bowl and mix well.

- Arrange 3 noodles in sprayed 9 x 13-inch (23 x 33 cm) baking dish. Spread with one-third of cottage cheese mixture and one-third seafood mixture. Repeat layers twice.

- Sprinkle with parmesan cheese. Cover and bake for about 40 minutes.

- Uncover and sprinkle with white cheddar cheese and bake for additional 10 minutes or until casserole bubbles. Let stand for at least 15 minutes before serving. Serves 9.

Angel Hair and Crab Bake

1 onion, chopped
1 bell pepper, seeded,
   chopped
2 ribs celery, chopped
6 tablespoons (¾ stick)
   butter   90 g
1 teaspoon dried basil   5 ml
1 teaspoon parsley flakes   5 ml
2 (15 ounce) cans Italian
   stewed tomatoes   2 (425 g)
½ cup dry white wine   125 ml
1 pound crabmeat,
   picked, flaked   455 g
1 (10 ounce) package
   capelli d'angelo (angel
   hair) pasta, cooked   280 g
⅓ cup parmesan cheese   35 g

- Saute onion, bell pepper and celery in large saucepan with melted butter in large saucepan. Stir in basil, parsley flakes and a little salt and pepper. Add stewed tomatoes and wine. Bring to boil, reduce heat and simmer for 5 minutes.

- Add crabmeat and simmer for 10 minutes. Spread angel hair pasta on serving platter and top with crab-mixture. Sprinkle parmesan over crab-mixture. Serves 6.

Before tomatoes were brought to Europe from the Americas, pasta was generally eaten with seasoning or with cheese. Tomatoes revolutionized pasta. Italy had an ideal growing climate for tomatoes. Tomato sauces were popular with pasta by the early 1800's.

Complete Crab Casserole

2 (6 ounce) cans crabmeat, drained	2 (170 g)
1 (10 ounce) can cream of shrimp soup	280 g
1 (4 ounce) can chopped pimentos	115 g
¾ cup milk	175 ml
⅔ cup mayonnaise	150 g
¾ cup shredded cheddar cheese	85 g
2 cups tagliatelle (thin egg noodles) pasta	210 g
½ cup seasoned breadcrumbs	60 g

- Preheat oven to 350° (175° C).

- Combine all ingredients except breadcrumbs in large bowl and pour into sprayed 3-quart (3 L) baking dish. Sprinkle breadcrumbs over top of casserole. Cover and bake for 45 minutes. Serves 6 to 8.

Thai Peanuts and Noodles

1 (5.5 ounce) box Thai stir-fry rice noodles	155 g
1 pound peeled, veined shrimp	455 g
1 (10 ounce) package frozen broccoli florets, thawed	280 g
Olive oil	
½ cup chopped peanuts	85 g

- Bring 3 cups (750 ml) water in saucepan on high heat to a boil and stir in noodles. Turn heat off and let noodles soak for about 5 minutes. Drain and rinse in cold water.

- Saute shrimp and broccoli in skillet with a little oil for about 8 minutes or just until shrimp is pink. Add softened noodles, seasoning packet and peanuts. Serves 6.

TIP: *If noodles are still to firm, add 1 tablespoon (15 ml) water and stir-fry until tender. There are chopped peanuts in seasoning, but this is better if you add more peanuts.*

Halibut with Orzo

½ cup extra-virgin olive oil, divided	125 ml
¼ cup fresh lemon juice	60 ml
4 (6 ounce) halibut fillets	4 (170 g)
1 (16 ounce) package orzo (tiny) pasta	455 g
2 teaspoons minced garlic	10 ml
1 (9 ounce) package baby spinach	255 g
1½ cups halved cherry tomatoes	225 g

- Preheat oven to 400° (205° C).

- Whisk 4 tablespoons (60 ml) olive oil and lemon juice in bowl. Place halibut on sprayed baking pan and sprinkle with a little salt and pepper. Drizzle with dressing and bake for about 12 minutes or just until opaque in center.

- Cook orzo in saucepan according to package directions and drain. Add remaining olive oil and garlic to same saucepan and saute over medium heat for 1 minute.

- Stir in drained pasta, spinach and tomatoes and stir to coat. Season with a little salt and pepper.

- Remove from heat, cover and let stand for 1 to 2 minutes (spinach will wilt.) Place orzo mixture on serving platter, top with halibut fillets and remaining dressing. Serves 4.

Celebration Clams and Linguine

1 (12 ounce) package
    linguine (thin egg
    noodles) pasta   340 g
1½ cups chicken broth,
    divided   375 ml
½ onion, finely chopped
2 teaspoons minced garlic 10 ml
2 (6 ounce) cans chopped
    clams with liquid   2 (170 g)
1 tablespoon dried parsley 15 ml
2 teaspoons lemon juice   10 ml

- Cook linguine in saucepan according to package directions.

- While pasta cooks, place ½ cup (125 ml) chicken broth, onion and garlic in large saucepan on high heat and bring to a boil. Reduce heat to medium-low and cook for about 5 minutes or until onion is soft.

- Add clam liquid and remaining broth and bring to a boil. Reduce heat to medium and simmer for 4 minutes for flavors to blend. Stir in clams and cook until mixture is thoroughly hot.

- Drain pasta and return to pot; add clam sauce, parsley, lemon juice and a little salt and pepper. Toss to mix well and pour into warmed serving bowl. Serves 6 to 8.

There are at least 350 different shapes and sizes of pasta.

Red Clam Sauce over Vermicelli

1 tablespoon olive oil	15 ml
1 teaspoon minced garlic	5 ml
2 (7 ounce) cans chopped clams with liquid	2 (200 g)
1 (8 ounce) can tomato sauce	230 g
1 teaspoon dried parsley	5 ml
3 tablespoons grated parmesan cheese, divided	20 g
½ teaspoon dried basil	2 ml
½ teaspoon dried oregano	2 ml
Dash of cayenne pepper	
1 (8 ounce) package vermicelli (thin spaghetti) pasta	230 g
1 cup bean sprouts	35 g

- Place oil in skillet over medium-high heat and saute garlic for 1 minute. Drain clams and save liquid from 1 can. Set clams aside.

- Add saved liquid, tomato sauce, parsley, 1 tablespoon (15 ml) cheese, basil, oregano and cayenne pepper to skillet. Cover and simmer on low heat for 30 minutes. Stir in clams and cook until clam sauce is thoroughly hot.

- Cook vermicelli in saucepan according to package directions, drain and place in serving bowl. Add bean sprouts and toss. Pour clam sauce over pasta and sprouts and sprinkle with remaining cheese. Serves 3 to 4.

Spaghetti with Clam Sauce

1 (8 ounce) package vermicelli (thin spaghetti) pasta	230 g
1 (14 ounce) can minced clams	400 g
About 2 cups milk	500 ml
¼ cup (½ stick) butter	60 g
1 tablespoon instant chopped onion flakes	15 ml
1 teaspoon minced garlic	5 ml
¼ cup flour	30 g
½ teaspoon dried basil	2 ml
¼ cup white wine	60 ml
¼ cup grated parmesan cheese	25 g

- Cook pasta in saucepan according to package directions, drain and keep warm in serving bowl.

- Drain clams and save liquid. To liquid, add enough milk to equal 1¾ cups (425 ml).

- To make clam sauce, melt butter in saucepan over medium heat. Saute onion and garlic for 1 minute and stir in flour, basil and a little salt and pepper.

- Add milk mixture and cook, while stirring, until it thickens and bubbles, for about 5 minutes. Stir in wine and clams.

- Spoon sauce over spaghetti, sprinkle with cheese and serve immediately. Serves 4.

Don't read this if you're eating lunch! Vermicelli is the Italian word for "little worms".

Crawfish Alfredo

4 tablespoons extra-virgin olive oil	60 ml
½ cup finely chopped fresh green onions	50 g
½ cup finely chopped green bell pepper	75 g
2 ribs celery, finely chopped	
1 tablespoon minced garlic	15 ml
1 quart whipping cream	1 L
¼ cup (½ stick) butter	60 g
1 tablespoon Italian seasoning	15 ml
¼ teaspoon cayenne pepper	1 ml
2 pounds processed crawfish tails and fat (if frozen, thaw)	910 g
1 (8 ounce) package fettuccini (medium egg noodles) pasta, cooked	230 g
⅔ cup grated romano cheese	65 g
1 teaspoon dried parsley	5 ml

- Heat oil in large, heavy soup pot and saute onions, bell pepper, celery and garlic for 3 to 4 minutes. Stir often to keep garlic from burning.

- With heat on high, gradually add in cream, stirring constantly and cook until mixture thickens. Add butter and continue cooking and stirring until sauce thickens to texture of semi-thick paste.

- Add Italian seasoning, cayenne pepper, crawfish tails and fat; cook for 3 minutes or until tails curl up slightly and fat blends into cream sauce.

- Add cooked fettuccini to crawfish-cream mixture in soup pot and gently fold all ingredients. Stir in cheese, parsley and a little salt. With soup pot on low, heat just until mixture is thoroughly hot. Serve piping hot. Serves 8 to 10.

Fettuccini a la Crawfish

1 (12 ounce) package
  fettuccini (medium
  egg noodles) pasta   340 g
3 bell peppers, seeded,
  chopped
3 onions, chopped
6 ribs celery, chopped
1½ cups (3 sticks) butter   345 g
1 (14 ounce) package
  frozen crawfish tails
  thawed, drained   400 g
2 tablespoons snipped
  parsley   30 ml
4 - 5 cloves garlic, minced
1 (1 pint) carton half-and-
  half cream   500 ml
½ cup flour   60 g
1 (16 ounce) package cubed
  Mexican Velveeta®
  cheese   455 g

- Preheat oven to 300° (150° C).

- Cook noodles in saucepan according to package directions. Drain and set aside.

- Saute bell pepper, onion and celery with butter in skillet

- Add crawfish tails, simmer for 8 to 10 minutes and stir occasionally.

- Add parsley, garlic and half-and-half cream and mix well. Gradually stir in flour and mix well. Simmer for 30 minutes and stir occasionally.

- Add cheese and continue to stir until it melts and blends. Mix fettuccini with sauce.

- Pour all into sprayed 6-quart (6 L) baking dish. Bake for 15 to 20 minutes or until it is hot. Serves 8.

Alfredo Salmon and Noodles

3 cups fettuccini (medium egg noodles) pasta	315 g
1 (16 ounce) package frozen broccoli florets, thawed	455 g
1 cup prepared alfredo sauce	250 ml
1 (15 ounce) can salmon, drained, boned, flaked	425 g

- Cook noodles in large saucepan according to package directions and add broccoli last 5 minutes of cooking. (Discard some of broccoli stems.) Drain.

- Stir in alfredo sauce and salmon and cook on low heat, stirring occasionally, until mixture heats thoroughly. Spoon into serving bowl. Serves 6.

Cashew Tuna

1 (10 ounce) can cream of mushroom soup	280 g
1 (6 ounce) can tuna, drained	170 g
2 ribs celery, chopped	
¼ cup finely chopped onion	40 g
1 (4 ounce) can chopped pimentos	115 g
1 (3 ounce) package cashew pieces	85 g
¾ cup chow mein noodles, divided	40 g

- Preheat oven to 350° (175° C).

- Combine soup with ¼ cup (60 ml) water in large bowl and mix well. Stir in tuna, celery, onion, pimentos, cashews, ¼ cup (60 ml) chow mein noodles and a little black pepper.

- Pour into sprayed 2-quart (2 L) baking dish, sprinkle remaining noodles over top and bake for 30 minutes. Serves 4.

Tuna Casserole

1 (8 ounce) package elbow
   macaroni (tube) pasta 230 g
1 (8 ounce) package
   shredded Velveeta®
   cheese   230 g
2 (6 ounce) cans tuna,
   drained   2 (170 g)
1 (10 ounce) can cream
   of celery soup   280 g
1 cup milk   250 ml

- Preheat oven to 350° (175° C).

- Cook macaroni in saucepan according to package directions. Drain well, add cheese and stir until cheese melts.

- Add tuna, celery soup and milk and continue stirring. Spoon into sprayed 7 x 11-inch (18 x 28 cm) baking dish. Cover and bake for 35 minutes or until bubbly. Serves 6.

Tuna Linguine

1 (8 ounce) package linguine
   (thin egg noodles)
   pasta   230 g
1 (10 ounce) package
   frozen cut green beans 280 g
1 (8 ounce) package baby
   carrots, cut in half
   lengthwise   230 g
½ cup pesto   125 g
⅓ cup whipping cream 25 g
2 (6 ounce) cans albacore
   tuna, drained, flaked 2 (170 g)
½ cup grated fresh
   parmesan cheese   50 g

- Cook linguine in large saucepan according to package directions. Drain and return to saucepan. Cover to keep warm.

- Cook green beans and carrots in microwave according to green bean package directions, drain.

- Add warm vegetables, pesto, whipping cream and a little salt and pepper to linguine and toss to mix. Gently stir in tuna and spoon into serving bowl and sprinkle with parmesan cheese. Serves 8

Tuna Noodles

1 (8 ounce) package
    pappardelle (wide egg
    noodles) pasta, cooked,
    drained   230 g
2 (6 ounce) cans white
    tuna, drained   2 (170 g)
1 (10 ounce) can cream
    of chicken soup   280 g
¾ cup milk   175 ml
¾ cup chopped black
    olives   95 g

- Preheat oven to 300° (150° C).

- Place half noodles in sprayed
  2-quart (2 L) baking dish.

- Combine tuna, soup, milk and
  olives in saucepan. Heat just
  enough to mix well.

- Pour half soup mixture over
  noodles and repeat layers.

- Cover and bake for 20 minutes.
  Serves 6.

Tuna-Tomato Bowl

2 tablespoons olive oil   30 ml
1 teaspoon minced garlic   5 ml
¼ teaspoon cayenne pepper 1 ml
2 teaspoons dried basil   10 ml
1 (15 ounce) can stewed
    tomatoes   425 g
1 (12 ounce) can water-
    packed tuna, drained 340 g
¾ cup pitted green olives,
    sliced   95 g
¼ cup drained capers   30 g
1 cup favorite pasta, cooked 105 g

- Heat olive oil in saucepan and add
  garlic, cayenne pepper and basil;
  cook on low heat for 2 minutes.
  Add tomatoes and bring to a boil,
  reduce heat and simmer for
  20 minutes.

- Combine tuna, olives, capers, pasta
  and a little salt in bowl. Stir in
  oil-tomato sauce and toss. Serve
  immediately. Serves 6.

Simple Pasta

These recipes have great appeal.
Use as side dishes or add
your favorite choice of meat
to turn into main dishes.

Simple Pasta Contents

Creamy Pasta

1 (8 ounce) jar roasted red peppers, drained	230 g
1 (14 ounce) can chicken broth	400 g
1 (3 ounce) package cream cheese	85 g
8 ounces pasta, cooked	230 g

- Combine red peppers and broth in blender and mix well.

- Pour into saucepan and heat to boiling.

- Turn heat down and whisk in cream cheese. Serve over your favorite pasta. Serves 4.

Ranch Spaghetti

1 (12 ounce) package spaghetti pasta	340 g
¼ cup (½ stick) butter, cut in 3 pieces	60 g
¾ cup sour cream	180 g
¾ cup bottled ranch dressing	175 ml
½ cup grated parmesan cheese	50 g

- Cook spaghetti in saucepan according to package directions, drain and return to saucepan. Stir in butter, sour cream and ranch dressing and toss. Spoon into serving bowl and sprinkle with grated parmesan cheese. Serves 8.

TIP: You can make a main dish with this recipe just by adding 1 to 2 cups (140 to 420 g) cubed ham or turkey.

Cheese-Spaghetti and Spinach

1 (7 ounce) box ready-cut spaghetti pasta	200 g
2 tablespoons butter	30 g
1 (8 ounce) carton sour cream	230 g
1 cup shredded cheddar cheese	115 g
1 (8 ounce) package Monterey Jack cheese, divided	230 g
1 (12 ounce) package frozen, chopped spinach, thawed, very well drained	340 g
1 (6 ounce) can cheddar french-fried onions	170 g

- Cook spaghetti according to package directions, drain and stir in butter until it melts.

- Combine sour cream, cheddar cheese, half Monterey Jack cheese, spinach and half can onions in large bowl.

- Fold into spaghetti and spoon into sprayed slow cooker.

- Cover and cook on LOW for 2 to 4 hours.

- When ready to serve, sprinkle remaining Jack cheese and fried onion rings over top. Serves 4.

The word spaghetti is derived from the Italian word "spago" meaning "twine". "Spaghetto" means "little twine" and "spaghetti" is the plural form.

Ready Spaghetti and Veggies

1 (16 ounce) package frozen Italian style vegetables	455 g
2 tablespoons cornstarch	15 g
1 (14 ounce) can chicken broth, divided	400 g
1 teaspoon Italian seasoning	5 ml
1 (16 ounce) package spaghetti pasta, cooked, drained	455 g
1 cup shredded mozzarella cheese	115 g
¼ cup grated parmesan cheese	30 g

- Microwave vegetables according to package directions, cover and set aside.

- Combine cornstarch with ¼ cup (60 ml) broth in large saucepan and stir until cornstarch dissolves. Add remaining broth and bring to a boil on medium-high heat, reduce heat, stirring constantly, until it thickens.

- Combine vegetables, sauce, Italian seasoning, spaghetti and mozzarella cheese in large bowl. Toss and mix thoroughly. Sprinkle parmesan cheese over top and serve immediately. Serves 6 to 8.

Vermicelli with Mushroom Sauce

1½ cups sliced mushrooms	110 g
½ cup chopped onion	80 g
1 rib celery, sliced	
¼ cup (½ stick) butter	60 g
1 (10 ounce) can beef broth	280 g
1 (10 ounce) can cream of mushroom soup	280 g
¼ cup white wine	60 ml
1 teaspoon Italian seasoning	5 ml
1 (8 ounce) package vermicelli (thin spaghetti) pasta	230 g

- Saute mushrooms, onions, celery and butter in skillet over medium heat. Stir in broth, mushroom soup, wine and Italian seasoning; mix well.

- Cook vermicelli in saucepan according to package directions, drain and return to saucepan. Spoon mushroom mixture over vermicelli and toss until mushroom sauce coats each ingredient. Serves 4 to 6.

Pasta Frittata

1 onion, chopped
1 green bell pepper, seeded,
    chopped
1 red bell pepper, seeded,
    chopped
2 tablespoons butter   30 g
1 (7 ounce) box vermicelli
    (thin spaghetti) pasta,
    slightly broken, cooked   200 g
1 (8 ounce) package
    shredded mozzarella
    cheese   230 g
5 eggs
1 cup milk   250 ml
⅓ cup shredded parmesan
    cheese   35 g
1 tablespoon dried basil   15 ml
1 teaspoon oregano   5 ml

- Preheat oven to 375° (190° C).

- Saute onion and bell peppers with butter in skillet over medium heat for about 5 minutes, but do not brown.

- Combine onion-pepper mixture and spaghetti in large bowl and toss. Add mozzarella cheese and toss.

- In separate bowl, beat eggs, milk, parmesan cheese, basil, oregano, ½ teaspoon (2 ml) each of salt and pepper. Add spaghetti mixture and pour into sprayed 9 x 13-inch (23 x 33 cm) baking dish.

- Cover and bake for about 15 to 20 minutes. Uncover and make sure eggs are set. If not, bake for additional 2 to 3 minutes. Serves 8.

TIP: *This can be put together, refrigerated and baked later. Let it get to room temperature before placing in oven. Cut into squares to serve. It is a great dish for a luncheon or late night supper.*

Favorite Pasta

4 ounces spinach linguine (thin egg noodles) pasta	115 g
1 cup whipping cream	75 g
1 cup chicken broth	250 ml
½ cup freshly grated parmesan cheese	50 g
½ cup frozen English peas	50 g

• Cook linguine in saucepan according to package directions, drain and keep warm. Combine whipping cream and chicken broth in saucepan and bring to a boil.

• Reduce heat and simmer mixture for 25 minutes or until it thickens and reduces to 1 cup (250 ml). Remove from heat, add cheese and peas and stir until cheese melts.

• Toss with linguine and serve immediately. Serves 4.

Love This Linguine

2 tablespoons olive oil	30 ml
2 teaspoons minced garlic	10 ml
2 red bell peppers, seeded, chopped	
½ teaspoon cayenne pepper	2 ml
1 cup roasted red peppers, drained diced	150 g
1 (12 ounce) package linguine (thin egg noodles) pasta, cooked, drained	340 g
¾ cup grated parmesan cheese, divided	75 g

• Heat oil in heavy skillet over medium-high and saute garlic, bell peppers, cayenne pepper and a little salt for about 5 minutes. Remove from heat and add roasted peppers, linguine and ½ cup (50 g) parmesan cheese and mix well.

• Transfer to serving bowl and sprinkle remaining parmesan cheese over top. Serves 4.

Artichoke Fettuccini

1 (12 ounce) package
    fettuccini (medium
    egg noodles) pasta   340 g
1 (14 ounce) can water-
    packed artichoke hearts,
    drained, chopped   400 g
1 (10 ounce) box frozen
    green peas, thawed   280 g
1 (16 ounce) jar alfredo
    sauce   455 g
2 heaping tablespoons
    crumbled blue cheese   30 g

- Cook fettuccini in saucepan according to package directions. Drain and place in serving bowl to keep warm.

- Heat artichoke hearts, peas and alfredo sauce in large saucepan. Stir well, spoon into bowl with fettuccini and toss. Sprinkle with blue cheese and serve hot. Serves 10.

Cheesy Noodle Casserole

1 (8 ounce) package fettuccini
    (medium egg noodles)
    pasta   230 g
1 (16 ounce) package frozen
    broccoli florets, thawed   455 g
1 red bell pepper, seeded,
    chopped
1 (8 ounce) package
    shredded Velveeta®
    cheese   230 g
1 cup milk   250 ml
¾ cup coarsely crushed
    bite-size cheese crackers 45 g

- Preheat oven to 350° (175° C).

- Cook noodles in large saucepan according to package directions. Add broccoli and bell pepper for last 2 minutes of cooking time. Drain in colander.

- In same saucepan, combine cheese and milk over low heat and stir until cheese melts. Stir in noodle-broccoli mixture and spoon into sprayed 3-quart (3 L) baking dish.

- Sprinkle with crushed crackers and bake for 25 to 30 minutes or until top is golden brown. Serves 10.

Buttered Noodle Casserole

2 (12 ounce) packages fettuccini (medium egg noodles) pasta	2 (340 g)
1¼ cups (2½ sticks) butter, divided	285 g
¼ cup grated parmesan cheese	25 g
½ cup grated romano cheese	50 g
1 (16 ounce) package frozen green peas, thawed	455 g
1 cup fresh breadcrumbs	60 g
½ teaspoon cayenne pepper	2 ml

- Preheat oven at 375° (190° C).

- Cook noodles in large saucepan according to package directions and drain; return to saucepan.

- In separate saucepan, melt 1 cup (230 g) butter and stir into noodles. Add parmesan and romano cheese, peas and a little salt. Stir until mixture combines well and spoon into sprayed 4-quart (4 L) baking dish.

- Melt remaining butter and toss with breadcrumbs and cayenne pepper. Sprinkle over noodles and bake for 15 minutes or until edges are bubbly. Serves 10 to 12.

Noodles are mentioned in the Jerusalem Talmud, a Jewish text from around 200 A.D. Wheat has been grown in the Middle East for 8,000 to 10,000 years. It is thought that some ancient form of pasta would have been made because of the evidence of the use of wheat flour.

Dreamy Baked Fettuccini

1 (16 ounce) package
   fettuccini (medium
   egg noodles) pasta   455 g
½ cup (1 stick) butter, cut
   into chunks   115 g
1 cup nonfat half-and-half
   cream   250 ml
3 large eggs, beaten
1½ cups grated parmesan
   cheese, divided   150 g
⅓ cup seasoned
   breadcrumbs   40 g

- Preheat oven to 350° (175° C).

- Cook fettuccini in saucepan according to package directions, drain and return to saucepan. Add butter and stir until butter melts.

- Stir in half-and-half cream, eggs and 1 cup (100 g) parmesan cheese and spoon into sprayed 3-quart (3 L) baking dish.

- Combine remaining cheese and breadcrumbs in bowl and sprinkle over noodles. Bake for 25 minutes. Serves 8.

Favorite Fettuccini

1 (16 ounce) package
   fettuccini (medium
   egg noodles) pasta   455 g
2 tablespoons butter   30 g
¾ cup grated fresh
   parmesan cheese   75 g
1¼ cups whipping cream   95 g

- Cook fettuccini in saucepan according to package directions.

- Melt butter in large saucepan over medium and stir in parmesan cheese, cream and a little black pepper.

- Cook for 1 minute and stir constantly. Reduce heat, pour in fettuccini and toss gently to coat. Serves 6.

Faithful Fettuccini Fiesta

3 tablespoons olive oil	45 ml
1 yellow bell pepper, seeded, chopped	
1 onion, chopped	
2 teaspoons minced garlic	10 ml
2 tablespoons real bacon bits	30 ml
1 (7 ounce) jar roasted red bell peppers, drained, sliced	200 g
1 (10 ounce) package frozen baby green peas, thawed	280 g
⅓ cup canned chicken broth	75 ml
1 (8 ounce) package fettuccini (medium egg noodles) pasta, cooked, drained	230 g
½ cup shredded mozzarella cheese	60 g

- Heat oil in large skillet on medium-high and cook yellow bell pepper, onion and garlic for about 4 minutes.

- Stir in bacon bits, roasted bell peppers, peas and broth; reduce heat to low and simmer for 10 minutes.

- Transfer to large bowl and toss with cooked fettuccini, cheese and a little salt and pepper. (You might want to garnish with more mozzarella cheese.) Serves 4 to 6.

Not Your Ordinary Noodles

1 (16 ounce) package fettuccini (medium egg noodles) pasta	455 g
½ cup (1 stick) butter, melted	115 g
1 (16 ounce) package cottage cheese, drained	455 g
1 (8 ounce) package cream cheese, softened	230 g
1 (16 ounce) carton sour cream	455 g
1 teaspoon vanilla	5 ml
1 cup sugar	200 g
¾ cup packed brown sugar	165 g
6 large eggs, beaten	

- Preheat oven to 375° (190° C).

- Cook noodles in large saucepan according to package directions and drain. Place in large bowl and stir in ½ cup (115 g) melted butter. Cover and keep warm.

- Beat cottage cheese and cream cheese in mixing bowl until smooth. Stir in sour cream, vanilla, sugar, brown sugar and eggs; mix until they blend well.

- Fold mixture into buttered noodles, mix well and spoon into sprayed 9 x 13-inch (23 x 33 cm) baking pan.

Topping:

2 cups graham cracker crumbs	210 g
½ cup (1 stick) butter, melted	115 g
⅔ cup sugar	135 g
½ cup chopped pecans	55 g

- Combine graham cracker crumbs, butter, sugar and pecans in bowl, mix well and sprinkle evenly over top of noodle mixture. Bake for 15 minutes.

- Reduce heat to 325° (160° C) and bake for additional 40 minutes. Cool to room temperature before cutting into squares to serve. Serves 18.

Speedy Zucchini and Fettuccini

1 (9 ounce) package refrigerated fresh fettuccini (medium egg noodles) pasta	255 g
⅓ cup extra-virgin olive oil, divided	75 ml
1 tablespoon minced garlic	15 ml
4 small zucchini, grated	
1 tablespoon lemon juice	15 ml
½ cup pine nuts, toasted	65 g
⅓ cup grated parmesan cheese	30 g

- Cook fettuccini in saucepan according to package directions, drain and place in serving bowl.

- Heat large skillet over high heat and add 2 tablespoons (30 ml) oil, garlic and zucchini. Saute for 1 minute.

- Add zucchini mixture to pasta with lemon juice, pine nuts and a little salt and pepper.

- Stir in remaining olive oil and toss to combine. Sprinkle parmesan cheese over top of dish to serve. Serves 8 to 10.

St. Pat's Noodles

1 (12 ounce) package fettuccini (medium egg noodles) pasta	340 g
1 cup half-and-half cream	310 g
1 (10 ounce) package frozen chopped spinach, thawed	280 g
6 tablespoons (¾ stick) butter, melted	90 g
2 teaspoons seasoned salt	10 ml
1½ cups shredded cheddar-Monterey Jack cheese	175 g

- Cook noodles in saucepan according to package directions and drain.

- Place in 5 to 6-quart (5 to 6 L) slow cooker. Add half-and-half cream, spinach, butter and seasoned salt and stir until they blend well.

- Cover and cook on LOW for 2 to 3 hours.

- When ready to serve, fold in cheese. Serves 4.

Wonderful Alfredo Fettuccini

2 (16 ounce) packages
    fettuccini (medium
    egg noodles) pasta   2 (455 g)
¼ cup (½ stick) butter   60 g
1½ cups grated fresh
    parmesan cheese   150 g
2½ cups whipping cream   190 g

- Cook fettuccini in saucepan according to package directions.

- Melt butter in large saucepan over medium heat and stir in parmesan cheese, cream and a little salt. Cook for 2 minutes and stir constantly. Reduce heat, stir into fettuccini and toss gently to coat fettuccini. Serves 10 to 12.

Creamy Seasoned Noodles

1 (8 ounce) package
    pappardelle (wide
    egg noodles) pasta   230 g
1 (1 ounce) packet Italian
    salad dressing mix   30 g
½ cup whipping cream   40 g
¼ cup (½ stick) butter   60 g
¼ cup grated parmesan
    cheese   30 g

- Cook noodles in saucepan according to package directions and drain.

- (Cut butter in chunks so it will melt easier.) Add remaining ingredients and toss lightly to blend thoroughly.

- Serve hot. Serves 6.

Creamy Macaroni and Cheese

Yes, this is more trouble than opening that "blue box", but it is well worth the time to make this macaroni and cheese.

1 (12 ounce) package macaroni (tube) pasta	340 g
6 tablespoons (¾ stick) butter	90 g
¼ cup flour	30 g
2 cups milk	500 ml
1 (1 pound) package cubed Velveeta® cheese	455 g

- Preheat oven to 350° (175° C).

- Cook macaroni in saucepan according to package directions and drain.

- Melt butter in saucepan and stir in flour, ½ teaspoon (2 ml) each of salt and pepper until they blend well.

- Slowly add milk, stirring constantly, and heat until it begins to thicken. Add cheese and stir until cheese melts.

- Pour cheese sauce over macaroni and mix well.

- Pour into sprayed 2½-quart (2.5 L) baking dish. Cover and bake for 30 minutes or until bubbly. Serves 8.

Tube pastas like macaroni and penne and shapes like shells work very well for casseroles and salads. Fresh pasta and egg noodle pasta are suitable for salads.

Double Pleasure Pasta

¼ cup olive oil	60 ml
1 onion, chopped	
3 teaspoons minced garlic	15 ml
1½ tablespoons dried oregano	22 ml
¼ - ½ teaspoon crushed red pepper	1 ml
2 (15 ounce) can diced tomatoes	2 (425 g)
1 cup sliced green olives	130 g
1 cup sliced black olives	130 g
1 (12 ounce) package whole wheat elbow macaroni (tube) pasta	340 g
1 (8 ounce) package shredded mozzarella cheese, divided	230 g

- With oil in soup pot over medium-high heat, saute onion, garlic and oregano for 5 minutes. Stir in red pepper, tomatoes, green and black olives and bring to a boil. Reduce heat to medium, stir often and simmer for about 6 minutes or until sauce begins to thicken.

- Cook macaroni in saucepan according to package directions, drain and stir in ½ teaspoon (2 ml) salt.

- Add pasta and 1½ cups (170 g) cheese to onion-tomato mixture and toss. Transfer to serving bowl and sprinkle with remaining cheese. Serves 8.

Whole wheat pasta has more nutrition than plain pasta. The whole wheat flour makes it darker which adds interesting color.

Good Stuff Macaroni

1 (16 ounce) package macaroni (tube) pasta	455 g
2 eggs, well beaten	
½ cup (1 stick) butter	115 g
1 cup finely chopped onion	160 g
1 cup finely chopped green bell pepper	150 g
1 (8 ounce) carton whipping cream	230 g
1 (8 ounce) package shredded sharp cheddar cheese, divided	230 g
½ cup shredded Swiss cheese	60 g
½ cup shredded Velveeta® cheese	60 g

- Preheat oven to 350° (175° C).

- Cook macaroni in saucepan according to package directions. Rinse in cold water, drain and return shells to saucepan. Add beaten eggs, mix well and spoon into sprayed 9 x 13-inch (23 x 33 cm) baking dish.

- Melt butter in large saucepan over medium heat and saute onion and bell pepper just until they wilt. Stir in cream and a little salt and pepper. Reduce heat to low and gradually add half cheddar cheese, Swiss cheese and finally Velveeta®. Stir constantly as you add cheeses so they do no stick to saucepan and burn.

- Pour cheese sauce evenly over shells and stir just a little to incorporate sauce into shells.

- Sprinkle remaining cheddar cheese over top and bake for 40 to 45 minutes or until cheese on top melts and starts to brown. Serves 8.

Cheesy Mac Florentine

1 (16 ounce) package elbow macaroni (tube) pasta	455 g
1 (12 ounce) box frozen spinach souffle	340 g
¼ cup milk	60 ml
1 (8 ounce) package shredded Velveeta® cheese	230 g
¼ cup grated parmesan cheese	25 g
½ cup seasoned breadcrumbs	60 g

● Preheat oven to 350° (175° C).

● Bring large pot of salted water to a boil. Add pasta, cook until al dente and drain.

● Cut spinach souffle into 1-inch (2.5 cm) pieces and stir into pasta. Add milk and both cheeses; mix well.

● Spoon into sprayed 9 x 13-inch (23 x 33 cm) baking dish and sprinkle breadcrumbs over top. Bake for 15 minutes. Serves 6.

Macaroni and Cheese

1 cup macaroni (tube) pasta	105 g
1½ cups small curd cottage cheese	340 g
1½ cups shredded cheddar or American cheese	175 g
4 tablespoon grated parmesan cheese	50 g

● Preheat oven to 350° (175° C).

● Cook macaroni in saucepan according to package directions and drain. Combine cottage cheese and both cheeses. Combine macaroni with cheese mixture.

● Spoon into sprayed 2-quart (2 L) baking dish.

● Cover and bake for 35 minutes. Serves 4.

Macaroni and Cheese Deluxe

1 (8 ounce) package	
macaroni (tube) pasta	230 g
3 tablespoons butter, melted	45 g
1 (15 ounce) can stewed	
tomatoes	425 g
1 (8 ounce) package	
shredded Velveeta®	
cheese	230 g
1 cup crushed potato chips,	
optional	55 g

- Preheat oven to 350° (175° C).

- Cook macaroni in saucepan according to package directions, drain and place in bowl. While macaroni is still hot, stir in butter, tomatoes, cheese and a little salt and pepper and mix well.

- Pour into sprayed 2-quart (2 L) baking dish, cover and bake for 25 minutes. Uncover and sprinkle with crushed potato chips. Bake for additional 10 minutes or until potato chips are light brown. Serves 8.

Macaroni and Cheese Reward

2 cups macaroni (tube)	
pasta	210 g
2 cups milk	500 ml
¼ cup flour	30 g
1 (16 ounce) package	
shredded sharp	
cheddar cheese	455 g
¼ cup (½ stick) melted	
butter	60 g
1 cup soft breadcrumbs	60 g

- Preheat oven to 350° (175° C).

- Cook macaroni in saucepan according to package directions, drain and set aside. Combine milk, flour and ample amount of seasoned salt in jar with lid. Shake to mix well.

- Combine macaroni, flour-milk mixture and cheese in large bowl and mix well. Pour into sprayed 9 x 13-inch (23 x 33 cm) baking dish. Stir melted butter over breadcrumbs in bowl and toss. Sprinkle breadcrumbs over top.

- Cover and bake for 35 minutes; remove cover and return to oven for 10 minutes. Serves 6.

Macaroni, Cheese and Tomatoes

2 cups elbow macaroni (tube)
  pasta   210 g
1 (14 ounce) can stewed
  tomatoes with liquid   400 g
1 (8 ounce) package
  shredded cheddar
  cheese   230 g
2 tablespoons sugar   25 g
1 (6 ounce) package
  cheese slices   170 g

- Preheat oven to 350° (175° C).

- Cook macaroni in saucepan according to package directions and drain. Combine macaroni, tomatoes, shredded cheese, sugar, ¼ cup (60 ml) water and a little salt in large mixing bowl and mix well.

- Pour into 9 x 13-inch (23 x 33 cm) baking dish and place cheese slices on top.

- Bake for 30 minutes or until bubbly. Serves 6.

Magic Macaroni and Veggies

1 (8 ounce) package
  macaroni (tube) pasta   230 g
3 eggs, beaten
1¼ cups milk   310 g
1 cup soft breadcrumbs   60 g
1½ teaspoons seasoned salt   7 ml
1 (15 ounce) can diced
  tomatoes   425 g
1 (8 ounce) package
  shredded cheddar cheese   230 g
1 (10 ounce) package frozen
  chopped onions and
  bell pepper, thawed   280 g
1 (10 ounce) package frozen
  chopped carrots and
  green peas, thawed   280 g

- Preheat oven at 350° (175° C).

- Cook macaroni in saucepan according to package directions, drain and place in large bowl.

- Stir in eggs, milk, breadcrumbs, seasoned salt, tomatoes, cheese, onions and bell peppers, and carrot and peas. Bake for 1 hour 5 minutes. Serves 8.

Minute Mac and Cheese

1 (12 ounce) package elbow
   macaroni (tube) pasta   **340 g**
1 (8 ounce) package
   shredded Velveeta®
   cheese   **230 g**
¾ cup shredded mozzarella
   cheese   **85 g**
1¼ cups milk   **310 ml**
1 teaspoon mustard   **5 ml**

- Preheat oven to 325° (160° C).

- Cook macaroni in saucepan according to package directions and drain. Stir in Velveeta® cheese, mozzarella cheese, milk and mustard and mix until they blend well.

- Transfer to sprayed 3-quart (3 L) baking dish, cover and bake for 10 minutes or just until thoroughly hot. Serves 8.

Pasta with Basil

2½ cups macaroni (tube)
   pasta   **260 g**
1 small onion, chopped
2 tablespoons olive oil   **30 ml**
2½ tablespoons dried basil   **35 ml**
1 cup shredded mozzarella
   cheese   **115 g**

- Cook pasta in saucepan according to package directions. Saute onion in oil in skillet.

- Stir in basil, 1 teaspoon salt (5 ml) and ¼ teaspoon (1 ml) pepper. Cook and stir for 1 minute. Drain pasta leaving about ½ cup (125 ml) so pasta won't be too dry and add to basil mixture.

- Remove from heat and stir in cheese just until it begins to melt. Serve immediately. Serves 6.

So-Easy Macaroni Bake

1 (8 ounce) package elbow
    macaroni (tube) pasta   230 g
2 tablespoons olive oil   30 ml
4 large eggs
2¼ cups milk   560 ml
1 cup crumbled feta cheese   135 g
1 cup low-fat, small curd
    cottage cheese   225 g
1 (4 ounce) jar chopped
    pimentos   115 g

- Preheat oven to 375° (190° C).

- Cook macaroni in saucepan
  according to package directions,
  drain and stir in olive oil. Transfer
  to sprayed 9 x 13-inch (23 x 33 cm)
  baking dish.

- Beat eggs in medium bowl with
  fork and stir in milk, feta cheese,
  cottage cheese, pimentos and
  ½ teaspoon (2 ml) salt.

- Pour cheese mixture over macaroni
  in baking dish, cover and bake
  for 40 minutes. Uncover dish and
  return to oven for 10 minutes.

- Let macaroni stand for 10 minutes
  before serving. Serves 8.

Special Macaroni and Cheese

1 (8 ounce) package gnocchi
    (small shells) pasta   230 g
1 (15 ounce) can stewed
    tomatoes   425 g
1 (8 ounce) package cubed
    Velveeta® cheese   230 g
3 tablespoons butter, melted 45 g

- Preheat oven to 350° (175° C).

- Cook shells in saucepan according
  to package directions and drain.

- Combine shells, tomatoes, cheese
  cubes and butter in large bowl.

- Pour into sprayed 2-quart (2 L)
  baking dish.

- Cover and bake for 35 minutes.
  Serves 6.

Southern Macaroni and Cheese

1 (16 ounce) package
    macaroni (tube) pasta   455 g
2 tablespoons butter   30 g
3 eggs, beaten
1 (16 ounce) carton half-
    and-half cream   455 g
1 (12 ounce) package
    cheddar cheese, divided   340 g
⅛ teaspoon cayenne pepper   .5 ml

- Preheat oven to 350° (175° C).

- Combine pasta and 2 teaspoons (10 ml) salt in large saucepan and cook for 6 minutes. (Pasta should not cook completely.)

- Drain pasta and stir in butter to keep it from sticking. Transfer to sprayed 2½-quart (2.5 L) baking dish.

- Combine eggs, half-and-half cream, three-fourths cheese and cayenne pepper in bowl and mix well. Pour mixture over pasta and sprinkle remaining cheese over top.

- Cover and bake for 35 minutes. Uncover and broil just enough to lightly brown top. Serves 8.

Maccheroni in Italy refers to a specific style of tube pasta while the word macaroni is used for all forms of tubular pasta in the United States.

Creamy King Macaroni

1 (16 ounce) package
   cavatappi (corkscrew)
   pasta   455 g
2 tablespoons olive oil   30 ml
3 tablespoons butter   40 g
1 onion, finely chopped
2 ribs celery, thinly sliced
1 (8 ounce) carton
   whipping cream   230 g
¼ cup sliced ripe olives   30 g
1 (12 ounce) package
   shredded Velveeta®
   cheese   340 g
2 teaspoons dried parsley 10 ml

- Preheat oven to 350° (175° C).

- Cook pasta in saucepan according to package directions, rinse in cold water and drain in colander. Drizzle in olive oil and stir. Make sure each piece of pasta has oil on it. Transfer to sprayed 9 x 13-inch (23 x 33 cm) baking dish.

- Melt butter in large skillet and saute onion and celery until they are soft. Turn heat to high and add whipping cream, stirring constantly. Cook until mixture begins to thicken. (Mixture needs to be reduced to half original volume.)

- Slowly add olives, cheese, parsley and a little salt and pepper; stir until sauce blends well.

- Pour cheese sauce evenly over pasta in baking dish. With large spoon work cheese sauce until sauce absorbs into pasta.

- Bake for about 15 minutes or until casserole is piping hot. Serves 8 to 10.

Wild About Macaroni

1 (8 ounce) package elbow macaroni (tube) pasta	230 g
½ cup mayonnaise	110 g
½ cup finely chopped green bell pepper	75 g
1 small onion, finely chopped	
1 (4 ounce) can pimento, drained	115 g
1 (10 ounce) can cream of celery soup	280 g
2 tablespoons butter, melted	30 g
1 cup shredded cheddar cheese, divided	115 g
1 cup milk	250 ml

- Preheat oven to 375° (190° C).

- Cook macaroni in saucepan according to package directions, drain and place in large bowl.

- Add mayonnaise, bell pepper, onion, pimento, celery soup, butter, half cheese and a little salt and pepper.

- Spoon mixture into sprayed 2-quart (2 L) baking dish. Top with remaining cheese and add milk. Bake for 20 to 25 minutes. Serves 8.

Pasta Alarm!

1 (8 ounce) package tri-color cavatappi (corkscrew) pasta	230 g
2 tablespoons olive oil	30 ml
1 green bell pepper, seeded, chopped	
1 onion, chopped	
2 teaspoons minced garlic	10 ml
1 teaspoon chili powder	5 ml
1 teaspoon ground cumin	5 ml
½ teaspoon crushed red pepper flakes	2 ml
1 (8 ounce) can tomato sauce	230 g
1 (15 ounce) can black beans, rinsed, drained	425 g
1 cup shredded Mexican 4-cheese blend	115 g

- Cook pasta in saucepan according to package directions and drain. Heat oil in large skillet on medium and cook bell pepper, onion, garlic, chili powder, cumin and red pepper for about 5 minutes.

- Stir in tomato sauce, black beans and a little salt. Bring to a boil, reduce heat and simmer for 5 minutes or until thoroughly hot. Gently stir in pasta and mix well. Sprinkle with cheese. Serves 6 to 8.

Penne and Vegetables

1 (8 ounce) package penne
(tube) pasta   230 g
2 tablespoons olive oil   30 ml
½ cup chopped onion   80 g
½ cup chopped green bell
pepper   75 g
1 carrot, peeled, chopped
1 teaspoon minced garlic   5 ml
1 (15 ounce) can cannellini
beans, drained   425 g
1 (15 ounce) can stewed
tomatoes   425 g
½ cup grated parmesan
cheese   50 g

- Cook pasta according to package directions and drain. Place in serving bowl, cover and keep warm.

- Heat oil in large saucepan over medium-high heat and cook onion, bell pepper, carrot and garlic for 6 minutes or until vegetables are tender-crisp, stirring frequently.

- Stir in beans and tomatoes; bring to a boil. Reduce heat to medium-low and simmer for 6 minutes or until mixture is thoroughly hot. Serve over penne pasta and sprinkle with parmesan cheese. Serves 8.

Tomatoes met pasta in the 17th century when tomatoes were first imported from the Americas. Eight species of tomato still grow in the wild in Peru.

Ready to Please Pasta

1 (8 ounce) package penne (tube) pasta	230 g
1 onion, chopped	
1 cup chopped celery	100 g
2 teaspoons minced garlic	10 ml
1 tablespoon olive oil	15 ml
1 (15 ounce) can Italian stewed tomatoes	425 g
1 (15 ounce) can navy beans, rinsed, drained	425 g
1 (10 ounce) can low-sodium chicken broth	280 g
¾ cup shredded mozzarella cheese, divided	85 g
1 (10 ounce) package frozen chopped spinach, thawed, drained*	280 g

- Preheat oven to 375° (190° C).

- Cook pasta in large saucepan according to package directions, drain and return pasta to saucepan.

- Saute onion, celery and garlic with oil in skillet on medium-high heat until tender. Stir in tomatoes, beans, broth, ¼ cup (30 g) cheese and ½ teaspoon (2 ml) pepper. Bring to a boil and stir in spinach.

- Spoon onion-bean mixture into saucepan with pasta and toss until they mix well.

- Transfer to sprayed 3-quart (3 L) baking dish and sprinkle remaining cheese on top. Bake for 15 minutes or until center is hot and top is golden. Serves 8.

TIP: Squeeze spinach between paper towels to completely remove excess moisture.

Zucchini and Creamy Penne

6 - 8 medium zucchini,
   sliced
2 tablespoons olive oil   30 ml
2 (16 ounce) packages
   penne (tube) pasta   2 (455 g)
2 (8 ounce) cartons
   whipping cream   2 (230 g)
12 ounces crumbled goat
   cheese   340 g

- Cook zucchini in saucepan with a little salted water, drain and add olive oil.

- In separate saucepan, cook penne according to package directions. Drain and add remaining olive oil.

- While zucchini and pasta are still hot, combine ingredients in bowl, stir in whipping cream and goat cheese and toss. Serve hot. Serves 8.

Creamy Tomato Pasta

1 (8 ounce) package penne
   (tube) pasta   230 g
1 (26 ounce) jar pasta sauce 740 g
½ cup shredded mozzarella
   cheese   60 g
½ cup half-and-half cream   155 g
½ cup grated parmesan
   cheese   50 g

- Cook penne pasta in saucepan according to package directions, drain and keep warm.

- Combine pasta sauce, mozzarella cheese and half-and-half cream in saucepan and cook over medium heat, stirring often, until mixture is thoroughly hot and slightly thick. Pour over penne and toss to mix.

- Transfer to serving bowl and sprinkle parmesan cheese over mixture. Serves 8.

A Different Spaghetti Sauce

2 tablespoons olive oil	30 ml
2 teaspoons minced garlic	10 ml
1 rib celery, finely sliced	
1 red bell pepper, seeded, finely chopped	
2 (15 ounce) cans Italian stewed tomatoes	2 (425 g)
8 anchovies, chopped	
12 ripe olives, sliced	
1 teaspoon capers	5 ml
1 teaspoon dried basil	5 ml
¼ teaspoon red pepper flakes	1 ml
1 (8 ounce) package ziti (thin tubes) pasta	230 g
2 tablespoons butter	30 g

- Heat oil in large skillet and saute garlic, celery and bell pepper for about 5 minutes.

- Press tomatoes through sieve or food mill and add to skillet along with anchovies. Bring to a boil, reduce heat to medium heat and cook for 10 minutes. Stir in olives, capers, basil, red pepper and a little salt and simmer for an additional 15 minutes.

- Cook ziti pasta in saucepan according to package directions, drain and return pasta to saucepan. Stir in butter until butter melts. Pour onto heated serving bowl and pour sauce over pasta. Serve immediately. Serves 6 to 8.

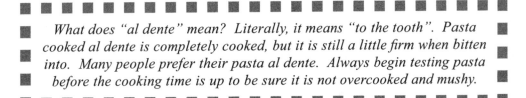

What does "al dente" mean? Literally, it means "to the tooth". Pasta cooked al dente is completely cooked, but it is still a little firm when bitten into. Many people prefer their pasta al dente. Always begin testing pasta before the cooking time is up to be sure it is not overcooked and mushy.

A Summertime Deal

1 (12 ounce) package ziti
   (thin tubes) pasta   340 g
¼ cup olive oil   60 ml
1 bunch green onions,
   chopped
1 teaspoon minced garlic   5 ml
1 cup halved cherry
   tomatoes   75 g
1 (10 ounce) box frozen
   green peas, thawed,
   drained   280 g
1 (8 ounce) package cubed
   cheddar cheese   230 g
4 ounces fresh basil, torn
   in thirds   115 g
1 (4 ounce) can chopped
   ripe olives, drained   115 g
½ cup Italian salad dressing 125 ml
½ cup grated parmesan
   cheese   50 g

- Cook ziti in saucepan according to package directions, drain and set aside.

- Heat oil in large skillet and saute green onions, garlic, tomatoes and a little salt and pepper for about 3 minutes.

- Stir in pasta, green peas, cheese, basil, olives and salad dressing.

- Toss well and sprinkle parmesan cheese over top. Serve immediately. Serves 6.

Florentine Manicotti

1 (16 ounce) package manicotti (large tubes) pasta	455 g
1 (12 ounce) package frozen spinach souffle	340 g
2 tablespoons finely chopped red bell pepper	30 ml
1 (15 ounce) carton ricotta cheese	425 g
1 cup Italian breadcrumbs	120 g
1 (15 ounce) can Italian stewed tomatoes	425 g

- Preheat oven to 325° (160° C).

- Cook pasta in saucepan according to package directions. Drain and place each shell on wax paper. Cook spinach souffle in microwave according to package directions.

- Combine cooked spinach souffle, bell pepper, ricotta cheese and breadcrumbs in large bowl. Carefully stuff mixture into shells and place in sprayed baking pan.

- Cover manicotti with stewed tomatoes and bake for 15 minutes or until thoroughly hot. Serves 8.

Red Peppered Rotini

1 (8 ounce) package refrigerated whole wheat rotini (spiral) pasta	230 g
2 tablespoons olive oil, divided	30 ml
1 onion, finely chopped	
1 rib celery, finely chopped	
2 teaspoons minced garlic	10 ml
1½ cups roasted red bell peppers, drained	200 g
½ cup evaporated milk	125 ml
⅛ teaspoon cayenne pepper	.5 ml

- Cook rotini in saucepan according to package directions, drain and return pasta to saucepan. Toss with 1 tablespoon (15 ml) oil, cover and keep warm.

- Heat remaining oil in skillet, cook and stir onion, celery and garlic on medium heat for about 3 minutes.

- Place onion-celery mixture, roasted peppers, evaporated milk and cayenne pepper in food processor and puree until smooth. Spoon sauce over rotini and stir to coat well. Serve immediately. Serves 4.

Merry Manicotti

1 (15 ounce) carton ricotta
    cheese   425 g
2 eggs
1 (10 ounce) package frozen
    chopped spinach,
    thawed, drained*   280 g
1½ cups shredded
    mozzarella cheese   170 g
1 tablespoon sugar   15 ml
12 manicotti (large tubes)
    pasta
1 (28 ounce) jar spaghetti
    sauce, divided   795 g
⅓ cup grated parmesan
    cheese   35 g

- Beat ricotta cheese and eggs in bowl. Stir in spinach, mozzarella cheese, sugar and ½ teaspoon (2 ml) each of salt and pepper; mix well. Stuff cheese-spinach mixture into uncooked shells.

- Pour ½ cup (125 ml) spaghetti sauce and ¼ cup (60 ml) water in sprayed 9 x 13-inch (23 x 33 cm) baking pan. Arrange stuffed shells in single layer over sauce and pour remaining sauce over shells. Cover and refrigerate for 8 hours.

- When ready to bake, preheat oven to 375° (190° C).

- Let manicotti sit at room temperature for 10 to 15 minutes. Cover and bake for 45 minutes. Uncover, sprinkle parmesan cheese over top of manicotti and bake for additional 10 minutes. Serves 8.

*TIP: *Squeeze spinach between paper towels to completely remove excess moisture.*

Spinach-Cheese Manicotti

This does take a little extra time to fill the shells, but it is really a special dish and well worth the time it takes!

1 onion, minced
2 teaspoons minced garlic   10 ml
Olive oil
1 (15 ounce) carton ricotta
    cheese   425 g
1 (3 ounce) package cream
    cheese, softened   85 g
1 (8 ounce) package
    shredded mozzarella
    cheese, divided   230 g
1 (3 ounce) package grated
    parmesan cheese,
    divided   85 g
2 teaspoons Italian
    seasoning   10 ml
1 (10 ounce) box frozen
    chopped spinach,
    thawed, drained   280 g
9 manicotti (wide shells)
    pasta, cooked
1 (26 ounce) jar spaghetti
    sauce   740 g

- Preheat oven to 350° (175° C).

- Saute onion and garlic in a little oil in skillet and set aside.

- Combine ricotta, cream cheese, half mozzarella, half parmesan cheese, Italian seasoning, ½ teaspoon (2 ml) each of salt and pepper in mixing bowl and beat until blended well.

- Squeeze spinach between paper towels to completely remove excess moisture.

- Add spinach and onion to cheese mixture and mix well.

- Spoon this mixture into manicotti shells 1 teaspoon (5 ml) at a time. (Be careful not to tear shells.)

- Pour half of spaghetti sauce in sprayed 9 x 13-inch (23 x 33 cm) baking dish. Arrange shells over sauce and top with remaining sauce.

- Cover and bake for 30 minutes. Remove from oven, uncover and sprinkle remaining cheeses over top. Return to oven just until cheese melts. Serves 9.

Tonight Is Fresh and Fast

2 red onions
2 ribs celery
2 tablespoon olive oil   30 ml
1 red bell pepper, seeded,
    sliced
1 green bell pepper, seeded,
    sliced
1 (8 ounce) package fresh
    mushrooms, sliced   230 g
1 (16 ounce) package
    rigatoni (large tubes)
    pasta   455 g
1 teaspoon dries basil   5 ml
1½ cups cubed provolone
    cheese, divided   200 g

- Cut onions crosswise and slice. Cut celery in 1-inch (2.5 cm) slices. Cook onions and celery with oil in large, heavy skillet over high heat for about 8 minutes and stir often.

- Reduce heat to medium-high, add bell peppers and mushrooms and saute for about 8 minutes or until they are soft.

- Cook pasta in saucepan according to package directions and stir occasionally. Drain, but reserve ½ cup (125 ml) cooking liquid.

- Add reserved pasta liquid to onion-mushroom mixture, basil and ½ teaspoon (2 ml) salt; stir over medium-high heat. Add 1 cup (130 g) cheese and stir until cheese melts. Transfer pasta to serving bowl, pour sauce over pasta and toss. Sprinkle with remaining cheese. Serves 6.

Stuffed Jumbo Shells

12 jumbo pasta shells
1 (14 ounce) can chicken
   (or vegetable) broth   **400 g**
1 potato, peeled, finely
   chopped
1 carrot, peeled, finely
   chopped
1 zucchini, cut into ½-inch
   pieces   **1.2 cm**
½ cup finely chopped onion   **160 g**
1 teaspoon dried basil leaves **5 ml**
⅓ cup grated parmesan
   cheese   **35 g**
3 tablespoons seasoned
   breadcrumbs   **20 g**

- Preheat oven to 375° (190° C).

- Cook pasta shells according to package directions, drain and place on sheet of wax paper.

- Heat broth to boiling in large saucepan and stir in potato and carrot and cook for about 6 minutes. Stir in zucchini and onion and cook for additional 3 minutes. Drain vegetables and set aside broth.

- Combine vegetables, basil, 3 tablespoons (30 g) cheese and 1 tablespoon (15 ml) breadcrumbs. Carefully fill cooked jumbo shells with mixture and place sides up in sprayed 8-inch (20 cm) square baking dish. Pour set aside broth into dish with shells.

- Mix remaining cheese and breadcrumbs and sprinkle over shells. Bake for 12 minutes or until breadcrumbs are golden brown. When serving, spoon broth from dish over shells. Serves 4 to 6.

Fusilli with Garden Sauce

2 onions, chopped
½ cup minced parsley leaves   30 g
8 slices prosciutto, minced
2 carrots, shredded
1 large leek, minced
1 teaspoon dried basil   5 ml
2 teaspoons minced garlic   10 ml
½ cup (1 stick) butter,
    divided   75 g
3 tablespoons olive oil   45 ml
1 cup finely chopped
    cabbage   70 g
3 tomatoes, peeled, diced,
    drained
3 small zucchini, diced
1 (10 ounce) can chicken
    broth   280 g
1 (12 ounce) package fusilli
    (spiral) pasta   340 g
⅓ cup grated parmesan
    cheese   35 g

- Combine onions, parsley, prosciutto, carrots, leek, basil and garlic in bowl and mix well.

- Heat ¼ cup (60 g) butter and oil in large pot and stir in onion-carrot mixture. Cook on medium heat until onions and carrots are tender. Stir in cabbage, tomatoes, zucchini, broth and a little salt and pepper. Cover and simmer for 25 to 30 minutes.

- Cook pasta in saucepan according to package directions and drain. Place back into saucepan and stir in remaining butter. Toss until butter melts. Place pasta on heated serving platter and pour vegetable sauce over pasta. Sprinkle with parmesan cheese and serve hot. Serves 8 to 10.

Spice Up the Macaroni

Macaroni:

1 (8 ounce) package rotini (spiral) pasta	230 g
⅓ cup (5½ tablespoons) butter	75 g

* Cook rotini in saucepan according to package directions, drain and add butter, stir until butter melts. Cover, set aside and keep warm.

Spicy Tomatoes:

1 (8 ounce) package shredded Mexican Velveeta® cheese	230 g
1 (10 ounce) can tomatoes and green chilies with liquid	280 g
½ yellow onion, finely diced	
1 (8 ounce) carton sour cream	230 g

* Preheat oven to 325° (160° C).

* Combine cheese, tomatoes and green chilies, and onion in large saucepan. Stir in macaroni, heat on low for 5 minutes and stir occasionally.

* Fold in sour cream and pour into 2-quart (2 L) baking dish. Cover and bake for 20 minutes. Serves 8.

Fried Parmesan Pasta

1 (16 ounce) package farfalle (bow-tie) pasta	455 g
⅓ cup olive oil	75 ml
3 tablespoons grated parmesan cheese	45 ml
1 teaspoon onion powder	5 ml
1 teaspoon garlic powder	5 ml
1 teaspoon chili powder	5 ml

- Cook pasta in saucepan according to package directions, drain and rinse under cold water thoroughly.

- Heat oil in large skillet and fry individual pieces of pasta (about 1 cup/250 ml) at a time until golden. Drain in paper towels.

- Combine parmesan cheese, onion powder, garlic powder, chili powder and ½ teaspoon salt in large bowl. Place fried pasta in bowl and toss until pasta coats with mixture. Serves 10 to 12.

Southwest Veggie Bake

1 (8 ounce) package rotelle (wagon wheels) pasta	230 g
2 (16 ounce) jars hot, chunky salsa	2 (455 g)
1 (8 ounce) package shredded 4-cheese blend	230 g
1 (15 ounce) can chili beans with liquid	425 g
1 (15 ounce) can kidney beans, rinsed, drained	425 g
1 (11 ounce) can Mexicorn®, drained	310 g
1 cup shredded mozzarella cheese	115 g

- Preheat oven to 350° (175° C).

- Cook pasta in saucepan according to package directions and drain.

- Combine pasta, salsa, cheese, chili beans, kidney beans and corn in large bowl; mix well.

- Transfer to sprayed 9 x 13-inch (23 x 33 cm) baking dish. Cover and bake for 30 minutes. Uncover, top with mozzarella cheese and return to oven for 5 minutes. Serves 8 to 10.

Southwest Lasagna Rolls

1 (15 ounce) carton ricotta
   cheese   425 g
1 cup shredded mozzarella
   cheese   115 g
1 (4 ounce) can chopped
   green chilies, drained   115 g
8 lasagna noodles
1 (15 ounce) can black beans
   with jalapenos, drained   425 g
1 (16 ounce) jar salsa   455 g

- Preheat oven at 350° (175° C).

- Combine ricotta cheese, mozzarella cheese and green chilies in bowl and mix well.

- Cook lasagna noodles in saucepan according to package directions, drain and place on strip of wax paper. Spread cheese mixture on one side of each noodle. Carefully spoon black beans evenly over cheese mixture.

- Roll noodles in jellyroll fashion and place, seam-side down on sprayed 7 x 11-inch (18 x 28 cm) baking dish. Spoon salsa over rolls, cover and bake for 25 minutes or until thoroughly hot. Serves 8.

A Fast Italian Fix

1 (9 ounce) package
   refrigerated whole wheat
   4-cheese ravioli pasta   255 g
2 tablespoons olive oil   30 ml
2 teaspoons minced garlic   10 ml
½ pound fresh green beans,
   ends snapped   230 g
2 yellow summer squash,
   quartered, sliced
½ cup grated parmesan
   cheese   50 g

- Cook ravioli in saucepan according to package directions, drain and keep warm.

- Heat oil in large skillet over medium-high heat and cook garlic for 1 minute. Add green beans and a little salt and pepper and cook, stirring often for 5 minutes.

- Add squash and cook for additional 5 minutes. Toss in ravioli and cook on medium-low heat or until pasta is warm. Transfer to serving bowl and sprinkle cheese over top. Serve immediately. Serves 8.

Spinach Lover's Lasagna

1 (16 ounce) carton
low-fat, small curd
cottage cheese   455 g
3 eggs, beaten
2 (10 ounce) packages
frozen chopped
spinach, thawed,
drained*   2 (280 g)
1 teaspoon minced garlic 5 ml
1 (26 ounce) jar chunky
garden spaghetti
sauce, divided   740 g
9 cooked lasagna noodles,
divided
1 (8 ounce) package
shredded mozzarella
cheese, divided   230 g
¼ cup plus 3 tablespoons
grated parmesan
cheese   45 g

- Preheat oven at 350° (175° C).

- Combine cottage cheese, eggs, spinach and garlic in medium bowl; set aside.

- Spread ½ cup (125 ml) spaghetti sauce in sprayed 9 x 13-inch (23 x 33 cm) baking dish.

- Place 3 noodles over sauce; spoon one-third spinach mixture over noodles. Top with one-third remaining spaghetti sauce, ½ cup (60 g) mozzarella and 3 tablespoons (45 ml) parmesan.

- Repeat layers twice with remaining noodles, spinach mixture, spaghetti sauce, 1 cup (115 g) mozzarella and remaining parmesan cheese. Top with remaining mozzarella cheese.

- Bake for 35 minutes or until bubbly around edges of dish. Let stand for 10 minutes before serving. Serves 8.

*TIP: Squeeze spinach between paper towels to completely remove excess moisture.

Bell Pepper Topped Ravioli

2 (9 ounce) packages refrigerated cheese ravioli pasta	**2 (255 g)**
¼ cup olive oil	**60 ml**
1 onion, chopped	
1 large green bell pepper, seeded, julienned	
1 large red bell pepper, seeded, julienned	
2 cups chicken broth, divided	**500 ml**
⅛ teaspoon cayenne pepper	**.5 ml**

- Cook ravioli in saucepan according to package directions and drain. Transfer to serving bowl and keep warm.

- Heat oil in skillet over medium heat. Saute onion and bell peppers until tender, stirring often. Stir in 1 cup (250 ml) chicken broth and season with a little salt and cayenne pepper.

- Cook on medium heat for 5 to 6 minutes. Stir in remaining broth and continue cooking until most of liquid has evaporated. Spoon bell pepper mixture over ravioli and serve hot. Serves 3 to 4.

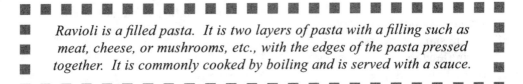

Ravioli is a filled pasta. It is two layers of pasta with a filling such as meat, cheese, or mushrooms, etc., with the edges of the pasta pressed together. It is commonly cooked by boiling and is served with a sauce.

Whole Wheat Ravioli Toss

2 (9 ounce) packages refrigerated 4-cheese ravioli pasta	2 (255 g)
2 tablespoons olive oil	30 ml
1 tablespoon minced garlic	15 ml
1 (10 ounce) package frozen cut green beans, thawed	280 g
2 yellow summer squash, quartered, sliced	
1 red bell pepper, seeded, chopped	
¾ cup shredded romano cheese	85 g

- Cook ravioli in saucepan according to package directions, drain and place in large serving bowl. Keep warm.

- Heat oil in large skillet and cook garlic, green beans, squash and bell pepper for 5 to 7 minutes or until vegetables are tender. Stir often.

- Transfer to bowl with ravioli, add a little salt and pepper and toss. Sprinkle with cheese and serve immediately. Serves 8 to 10.

Creamy Spinach Pasta

1 (7 ounce) package refrigerated cheese-filled spinach tortellini pasta	200 g
8 slices bacon, cooked, crumbled	
¼ cup chopped fresh parsley	15 g
1 (4 ounce) can chopped pimento, drained	115 g
½ cup grated parmesan cheese	50 g
Dash of cayenne pepper	
⅔ - ¾ cup sour cream	160 - 180 g
3 fresh green onions, thinly sliced	

- Cook tortellini in saucepan according to package directions, drain and place in bowl. Stir in crumbled bacon, parsley, pimento, cheese, cayenne pepper and a little salt; mix well.

- Add sour cream in small amounts until mixture is moist but not soggy. Top with green onions. Serves 4.

Nutty Stir-Fry Tortellini

1 (9 ounce) package refrigerated mixed cheese-filled tortellini pasta	255 g
1 (16 ounce) package frozen stir-fry vegetables, thawed	455 g
1 red bell pepper, seeded, julienned	
2 tablespoons olive oil	30 ml
¾ cup peanut stir-fry sauce	175 ml
⅓ cup chopped dry-roasted cashews	45 g

- Cook tortellini in saucepan according to package directions, drain and set aside. Stir-fry mixed vegetables and bell peppers in large skillet with oil over medium-high heat for 5 to 6 minutes or until tender-crisp.

- Add tortellini, stir-fry sauce and toss gently to coat well. Heat thoroughly and sprinkle with cashews. Serve immediately. Serves 4.

TIP: *Frozen stir-fry vegetables may vary so if bell peppers are included, choose a different second vegetable.*

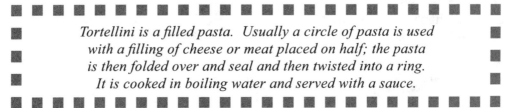

Tortellini is a filled pasta. Usually a circle of pasta is used with a filling of cheese or meat placed on half; the pasta is then folded over and seal and then twisted into a ring. It is cooked in boiling water and served with a sauce.

Italian Tortellini

2 (9 ounce) packages
   refrigerated cheese-filled
   tortellini pasta   (2 (255 g)
1 (16 ounce) package
   frozen broccoli florets,
   thawed   455 g
¾ cup drained, chopped
   sun-dried tomatoes
   in oil   40 g
2½ cups marinara sauce   630 g
3 tablespoons butter,
   melted   45 g
¾ cup Italian
   breadcrumbs   90 g

- Preheat oven to 350° (175° C).

- Cook tortellini in large saucepan according to package directions, drain and return to saucepan.

- Stir in broccoli, tomatoes, marinara sauce and spoon into 9 x 13-inch (23 x 33 cm) baking dish.

- Combine melted butter and breadcrumbs in small bowl and sprinkle over top.

- Bake for 30 minutes. Serves 8.

Savory Spinach Tortellini

2 tablespoons olive oil   30 ml
1 teaspoon minced garlic   5 ml
1 small onion, finely
   chopped
2 (15 ounce) cans Italian
   stewed tomatoes   2 (425 g)
1 tablespoon sugar   15 ml
2 (7 ounce) packages
   spinach tortellini pasta
   with cheese   2 (200 g)

- Heat oil in large skillet and saute garlic and onion; do not brown. Stir in stewed tomatoes and sugar. Bring to a boil, reduce heat and simmer on medium-low for about 30 minutes or until it thickens.

- Cook tortellini in saucepan according to package directions, drain and rinse. Transfer tortellini to serving bowl and spoon tomato sauce over top. Serve immediately. Serves 4 to 6.

Unforgettable Tortellini Bake

1 (18 ounce) package refrigerated cheese tortellini pasta, cooked, drained	510 g
1 (16 ounce) package frozen chopped broccoli, thawed, drained	455 g
1 (4 ounce) jar sliced pimentos	115 g
1 onion, chopped	
1 bell pepper, seeded, chopped	
2 (10 ounce) cans cream of chicken soup	2 (280 g)
1 teaspoon minced garlic	5 ml
1 teaspoon Italian seasoning	5 ml
1 (8 ounce) package shredded mozzarella cheese, divided	230 g

- Preheat oven to 350° (175° C).

- Combine tortellini, broccoli, pimentos, onion, bell pepper, soup, garlic and Italian seasoning in large bowl. Mix well. Fold in half cheese and pour into sprayed 3-quart (3 L) baking dish. Cover and bake for 45 minutes.

- Remove from oven, sprinkle remaining cheese over top and return to oven for 5 minutes. Serves 8.

Bubbling Butternut Squash and Orzo

1 (1½ pounds) butternut squash, peeled, seeded, cubed	680 g
1 (8 ounce) carton mushrooms, halved	230 g
1 yellow onion, cut in thin wedges	
1 teaspoon dried oregano	5 ml
2 tablespoons olive oil	30 ml
2 (14 ounce) cans chicken broth	2 (400 g)
1 (8 ounce) package orzo (tiny) pasta	230 g
1 teaspoon minced garlic	5 ml
½ cup chopped walnuts, toasted	65 g

- Preheat oven to 400° (205° C).

- Place squash pieces in sprayed 10 x 15-inch (25 x 38 cm) baking pan. Sprinkle with lots of black pepper, cover and bake for 10 minutes.

- Uncover and add mushrooms, onion, oregano and oil; toss. Return to oven and roast for 15 minutes or until vegetables are tender and light brown, stirring often.

- Bring broth in large saucepan to a boil, reduce heat and keep broth simmering. Spray skillet over medium heat and add orzo and garlic; cook, stirring often, for about 3 minutes or until orzo is light brown. Remove from heat.

- Stir in ½ cup (125 ml) hot broth and return to heat. Cook, stirring often, until liquid absorbs. Continue adding broth to orzo, ½ cup (125 ml) at a time and cook until liquid absorbs before adding more. Stir each time. Orzo will need about 15 minutes cooking time.

- Add roasted vegetables and walnuts to orzo mixture and stir well. Serves 4.

Confetti Orzo

¾ cup orzo (tiny) pasta	80 g
½ cup (1 stick) butter	115 g
1 (12 ounce) package frozen broccoli florets, thawed	340 g
1 bunch fresh green onions, chopped	
1 red bell pepper, seeded, chopped	
1 green bell pepper, seeded, chopped	
2 teaspoons minced garlic	10 ml
2 teaspoons chicken bouillon granules	10 ml
1 (16 ounce) jar creamy alfredo sauce	455 g

- Preheat oven to 325° (160° C).

- Cook orzo in saucepan according to package directions. Drain. Cook butter, broccoli, onions, bell peppers and garlic in large skillet on medium heat for 10 to 15 minutes, until tender-crisp.

- Spoon into large bowl, combine broccoli mixture, orzo, chicken bouillon and alfredo sauce and mix well. Cover and bake for 30 minutes. If you like, add 3 cups (420 g) cooked, cubed chicken to casserole. Serves 6.

While some consider couscous a pasta because it is made from semolina and water, purists tend to consider it a separate type of food. It is grain-shaped and is sometimes mistaken for a grain. Originally from North Africa, it is increasingly popular in the United States.

Mushroom Pasta

1 onion, chopped
1 cup celery, chopped   100 g
1 green bell pepper, seeded,
    chopped
1 red bell pepper, seeded,
    chopped
6 tablespoons (¾ stick)
    butter   90 g
1⅓ cups orzo (tiny) pasta   140 g
1 (14 ounce) can beef broth   400 g
1 (7 ounce) can sliced
    mushrooms, drained   200 g
1 tablespoon Worcestershire
    sauce   15 ml
¾ cup chopped walnuts   95 g
Chopped green onions

- Preheat oven to 325° (160° C).

- Saute onion, celery, bell pepper with butter in skillet.

- Cook orzo in beef broth and 1 cup (250 ml) water in saucepan for 10 to 11 minutes and drain.

- Combine onion-bell pepper mixture, orzo, mushrooms, Worcestershire, walnuts and ½ teaspoon (2 ml) each of salt and pepper in large bowl and mix well.

- Transfer to sprayed 2-quart (2 L) baking dish. Cover and bake for 30 minutes.

- When ready to serve, sprinkle chopped green onions over top of casserole. Serves 6.

The short tubes of ditali pasta give it its name which means "thimbles" and the name of the smaller ditalini means "little thimbles".

Orzo Bake

1 (12 ounce) package orzo (tiny) pasta	340 g
¼ cup (½ stick) butter, melted	60 g
1 pint cherry tomatoes, halved	300 g
½ cup diced green bell pepper	75 g
1¼ cups shredded mozzarella cheese, divided	145 g
½ cup white cooking wine	125 ml
1 teaspoon minced garlic	5 ml
1 tablespoon dried parsley	15 ml

- Preheat oven to 350° (175° C).

- Cook orzo in saucepan according to package directions and drain.

- Combine orzo, butter, cherry tomatoes, bell pepper, ¾ cup (85 g) cheese, wine, garlic, parsley and a little salt and pepper in bowl.

- Transfer to sprayed 2-quart (2 L) baking dish. Cover and bake for about 20 minutes. Uncover and sprinkle remaining cheese over top of casserole. Serves 8.

Spinach-Orzo Bake

1 (12 ounce) box frozen spinach souffle	340 g
1 (16 ounce) package orzo (tiny) pasta	455 g
2 tablespoons olive oil	30 ml
½ cup fire-roasted sweet red bell peppers, drained	70 g
½ cup shredded mozzarella cheese	60 g

- Cook spinach souffle in microwave according to package directions.

- Cook orzo in saucepan according to package directions, transfer to large bowl and stir in olive oil.

- Add spinach and roasted bell pepper; mix well. Transfer to sprayed 2-quart (2 L) baking dish. Cover with mozzarella cheese. Serve immediately or cover and heat for 10 minutes at 325° (160° C). Serves 4.

Fancy Green Beans

2 (16 ounce) package frozen French-style green beans, thawed	2 (455 g)
½ cup (1 stick) butter	115 g
1 (8 ounce) package fresh mushrooms, sliced	230 g
2 (10 ounce) cans cream of chicken soup	2 (280 g)
⅔ cup sliced roasted red bell peppers	90 g
2 teaspoons soy sauce	10 ml
1 cup shredded white cheddar cheese	115 g
⅔ cup chopped cashews	90 g
⅔ cup chow mein noodles	40 g

- Preheat oven to 325° (160° C).

- Cook green beans in saucepan according to package directions, drain and set aside. Melt butter in large saucepan and saute mushrooms for about 5 minutes, but do not brown.

- Stir in soups, ¼ cup (60 ml) water, roasted peppers, soy sauce and cheese and gently mix.

- Fold in drained green beans and spoon into sprayed 9 x 13-inch (23 x 33 cm) baking pan.

- Combine cashews and chow mein noodles in bowl, sprinkle over top of casserole and bake for 30 minutes or until edges are hot and bubbly. Serves 10 to 12.

Quick Glance Pasta Chart

Category	Italian Name	English Name/Description
Strands	spaghetti	different size strands
	vermicelli	thin spaghetti
	capelli d'angelo	angel hair
Ribbons	tagliatelle	thin egg noodles
	margherite	narrow egg noodles
	linguine	thin egg noodles (⅛ inch)
	fettuccini	medium egg noodles (¼ inch)
	pappardelle	wide egg noodles (⅝ inch)
Sheet	lasagna	very wide; sometimes fluted edges
Tubes	macaroni	different size tubes
	elbow macaroni	curved tubes
	ditali	short tubes
	penne	tubes cut diagonally
	mostaccioli	little moustaches
	ziti	thin tubes
	rigatoni	large tubes
	manicotti	large tubes
	gigantoni	extra large tubes

continued next page…

Quick Glance Pasta Chart – continued

Category	Italian Name	English Name/Description
Bow-ties	farfalle	butterfly pasta; bow-tie pasta
	tripolini	small bow-ties
Shells	cavatelli	short with ridges
	conchiglie	conch shells
	gnocchi	small shells
	maruzze	seashells
	lumache	large shell
Spirals	fusilli	spiral spaghetti (1½ inches long)
	rotini	short spirals (1 inch long)
	cavatappi	corkscrew pasta
Other Shapes	rotelle	wagon wheels
	stelline	stars
	orzo	small rice-shaped pasta
	riso	small rice-shaped pasta
	pastina	tiny dough balls

Index

T

U

V

Cookbooks Published by
Cookbook Resources, LLC
Bringing Family and Friends to the Table

*The Best of Cooking
with 3 Ingredients*

*The Ultimate Cooking
with 4 Ingredients*

*Easy Cooking
with 5 Ingredients*

*Healthy Cooking
with 4 Ingredients*

*Gourmet Cooking
with 5 Ingredients*

*4-Ingredient Recipes
for 30-Minute Meals*

*Essential 3-4-5
Ingredient Recipes*

The Best 1001 Short, Easy Recipes

1001 Fast Easy Recipes

1001 Community Recipes

*Busy Woman's
Quick & Easy Recipes*

*Busy Woman's
Slow Cooker Recipes*

Easy Slow Cooker Cookbook

Easy One-Dish Meals

Easy Potluck Recipes

Easy Casseroles

Easy Desserts

Sunday Night Suppers

Easy Church Suppers

365 Easy Meals

365 Easy Chicken Recipes

365 Easy Soups and Stews

365 Easy Vegetarian Recipes

Quick Fixes with Cake Mixes

Kitchen Keepsakes/
More Kitchen Keepsakes

Gifts for the Cookie Jar

All New Gifts
for the Cookie Jar

Muffins In A Jar

The Big Bake Sale Cookbook

Classic Tex-Mex
and Texas Cooking

Classic Southwest Cooking

Miss Sadie's Southern Cooking

Texas Longhorn Cookbook

Cookbook 25 Years

A Little Taste of Texas

A Little Taste of Texas II

Trophy Hunters'
Wild Game Cookbook

Recipe Keeper

Leaving Home Cookbook
and Survival Guide

Classic Pennsylvania
Dutch Cooking

Easy Diabetic Recipes

cookbook resources® LLC

www.cookbookresources.com

Your Ultimate Source for Easy Cookbooks

365 Easy Pasta Recipes

Pasta
Recipes

Delicious, Versatile
Recipes for Easy Meals

cookbook resources® LLC

www.cookbookresources.com